The German Print Portfolio 1890–1930

Serials for a Private Sphere

THE GERMAN PRINT PORTFOLIO 1890–1930

Serials for a Private Sphere

Robin Reisenfeld
Introduction by **Reinhold Heller**

Edited by
Richard A. Born and Stephanie D'Alessandro

Philip Wilson Publishers
in association with
The David and Alfred Smart Museum of Art
The University of Chicago

The German Print Portfolio 1890–1930   Serials for a Private Sphere

EXHIBITION SCHEDULE

The Detroit Institute of Arts   19 September – 8 November 1992

Tampa Museum of Art   20 December 1992 – 7 February 1993

Katonah Museum of Art   21 March – 9 May 1993

**The David and Alfred Smart
Museum of Art**   5 October – 12 December 1993

The exhibition and catalogue have been made possible in part by a grant from the National Endowment for the Arts, a federal agency.

Text © 1992 The Trustees of The University of Chicago.
Figs 3a–d and 4a–f © 1992 The Art Institute of Chicago,
All Rights Reserved; all other photography by
Jerry Kobylecky Museum Photography, Chicago.

Philip Wilson Publishers Limited
26 Litchfield Street, London WC2H 9NJ

Distributed in the USA by
Rizzoli International Publications, Inc.
300 Park Avenue South, New York, NY 10010

ISBN 0 85667 417 6

LC 92–080372

Designed by Andrew Shoolbred
Typeset by Tradeset Photosetting Ltd,
Welwyn Garden City, Herts
Printed and bound by Snoeck, Ducaju & Zoon,
NV, Ghent, Belgium

Contents

Preface

This innovative exhibition examines the print portfolio's central role in the modern graphic movement in Germany and Austria from 1890 to 1930. The rich examples in the Smart Museum's collection indicate how artists throughout this period employed the print portfolio both for its expressive potential and its ability to reach a broad-based, educated audience. Artists turned to the portfolio for its narrative possibilities, to communicate or confound ideas demanding a sequential reading. They experimented with it as a kind of *Gesamtkunstwerk* (total work of art), unifying various artistic principles, including literary and musical motifs. Many recognized its marketing advantages, and regarded the print portfolio as a way to assume control over the distribution of their artworks, a process traditionally determined by the Academy. Groups such as Brücke (Bridge) in Dresden, and later in Berlin, exploited the art form as an alternative means to promote themselves as artists, publicizing their works by producing annual portfolios for their subscribers.

It is the dream of every director of a university museum to mount exhibitions that relate to teaching, highlight the achievements of students, manifest the contributions of enlightened donors, and attract support by generous agencies—all of this executed by a superb staff. As Director of the David and Alfred Smart Museum of Art, it has been my pleasure and privilege to preside over such an exhibition.

The German Print Portfolio 1890–1930: Serials for a Private Sphere derives from the teaching and scholarship of Reinhold Heller, Professor of Art and Germanic Language and Literature at the University of Chicago. Professor Heller also helped in every material way with the exhibition, not least in contributing the introduction to the catalogue. We are all extremely grateful for this model of cooperation. Robin Reisenfeld, an advanced graduate student of Professor Heller, has done the considerable research and writing for this important catalogue. Her work is certain to be a vital contribution to the historiography of modern German printmaking.

In 1981, only seven years after the founding of the Smart Museum, Marcia and Granvil Specks began their donations to the collection. Two years later, they donated the first of the many portfolios they have contributed, Max Beckmann's *Carnival*. This exhibition is the direct result of their generosity as donors and lenders: it reflects their perspicacity and knowledge, and their unselfish desire to share their achievements with students, faculty, and a larger public. They have contributed to this project not only as donors, but as scholars. Knowing them and working with them has been another of the great joys of this project and we are exceedingly grateful for their continued philanthropy to this institution and its enterprises. We would also like to thank Perry Goldberg for his generous contribution of Ernst Barlach's *Schiller, Ode to Joy* and Mr. and Mrs. Berthold Regensteiner for their splendid gift of Rafaello Busoni's *Stock Market Frenzy.*

The Curator of the Smart Museum, Richard A. Born, not only suggested the exhibition, but also has made an enormous and vital contribution to this project as co-editor of the catalogue essays, co-compiler of the checklist, and coordinator of a myriad of details for the exhibition. His extensive knowledge of German prints, extraordinary dedication to this project, and attention to every detail could not be equalled, except perhaps by

Stephanie D'Alessandro, Assistant Curator of the Museum. Her scholarship and complete commitment to this project have been absolutely vital. Without Richard and Stephanie, this exhibition and its catalogue could not exist. Mention should also be made of the important input of Sue Taylor, the former Associate Curator, who made a central contribution to the genesis of the exhibition. Each of these individuals deserve our heartfelt thanks. Of course, everyone on the staff of the Smart Museum has helped in some vital way: thanks are due to Rudy Bernal, Preparator; Mary E. Braun, Registrar; Kathleen Gibbons, Education Coordinator; Felix Lambert, Security Supervisor; Rachel Lerner, Public Information Officer; Bruce Linn, Preparatorial Intern; Joelle Jacques-Rodriguez, Administrative Assistant; Britt Salvesen and Lilianna Sekula, Curatorial Interns; Priscilla Stratten, Operations Manager and Gavin Witt, Intern.

The production of this splendid catalogue is the result of the work of many at Philip Wilson Publishers Limited: Directors Philip Wilson and Anne Jackson; Joan A. Speers, Managing Editor; Sally Prideaux, Editor; Andrew Shoolbred, Designer; and Liz Jobling, Production. We are very grateful to them for their realization of our endeavors. Jerry Kobylecky has achieved his usual high level of accomplishment for the principal photographs. Supplementary photographs are due to the generosity of colleagues at the Art Institute of Chicago, most particularly Anselmo Carini, Department of Prints and Drawings; Alan Newman, Executive Director, Imaging and Technical Services; and Lieschen Potuznik, Photographic Rights Department. Robin Reisenfeld also wishes to thank Reinhold Heller for his assistance and suggestions in the research and Jeffrey for all his support and patience.

Making these extraordinary works of art and this superb scholarship available to a larger audience has been accomplished through our colleagues at the various venues of this exhibition. Many people certainly deserve our thanks but I hope I may be forgiven if I only mention Samuel Sachs, Director; Ellen Sharp and Chris Swenson, Curators; and Tara Robinson, Exhibition Coordinator at the Detroit Institute of Arts; Andrew Maas, Director; and Kay T. Morris, Registrar of the Tampa Museum of Art; and George King, Director; Virginia Gold, Exhibition Coordinator and Catherine Brawer, also a member of the Board of the Smart Museum, at the Katonah Museum of Art.

Thanks are due, finally, to the supporters of the exhibition. The National Endowment for the Arts has made a profound and significant contribution. Continued support from the Smart Family Foundation has likewise been vital to the project. Directors Joan and Robert Feitler and Raymond Smart deserve our particular thanks. As always, the Board of the Smart Museum, chaired by Richard Gray, has been of material assistance.

Just as these portfolios bring together diverse images to form a brilliant whole, we hope this exhibition, formed of many disparate parts, comes together to make a major contribution to the study of German art.

Teri J. Edelstein
Director, January 1990 – March 1992

REINHOLD HELLER

Observations, in the form of a survey, on the history of print cycles in German art from the fifteenth to the nineteenth century

Our society employs imagery primarily to communicate a simplified message or to accompany the narration of a written text. Through film (and also television, though the technique differs) we are accustomed to witnessing the action of an event, fictional or actual, by means of illusions of movement composed of numerous still images projected rapidly before us. Although the techniques involved are relatively recent inventions, the fundamental principle underlying our willingness to view multiple still images as movement dates back virtually to the beginnings of art—to the making of the first images. With but little exaggeration we can argue that the single, framed, and separate paintings, prints, or drawings we customarily admire, collect, and preserve as art in our museums or homes are self-contained perversions of that original artistic effort.

Today the most pervasive example of this practice of interrelating images is the comic strip. In it, single images—often accompanied by or incorporating explanatory or supplementary texts—are reproduced in a sequence that signifies causal, temporal, or plot interrelationship and that narrates an anecdote, concept, or extended story. Widely distributed in thousands of newspapers and comic books, in today's extended world consciousness, the comic strip provides us with an international visual vocabulary whose universality of communication and impact is unmatched by any single verbal language. The concept that individual drawings arranged in strips represent pregnant moments or significant situations, one following the other in consequential order, is understood and applied without ever being formally taught (unlike the ability to read a text, for example), thus permitting communication by means

of multiple visual images from infancy to old age and across the boundaries of culture and society. The linkage of images, rather than their isolation, forms an intrinsic part of our comprehension and appreciation of two-dimensional visual culture.

In its use of interactive imagery to communicate a preliterate or a-literate narrative, the comic strip and its broadsheet ancestors are linked conceptually to the multiple-imaged origins of art, but historically more directly and particularly to the cycles of frescoes seen on the walls of medieval and early Renaissance churches and other public buildings.[1] The interrelated events of the history of human salvation, the life of Christ or of a saint, or the scenes of a future apocalypse and Last Judgment were here presented, narrated, and communicated to a broad public that consisted of the churches' worshippers and visitors, irrespective of age, verbal literacy, or even religious faith. More than the written or spoken vocabulary of Latin, cycles of interactive visual images painted on walls, potentially for all to see, provided the unifying language of universal communication for Western Europe until the sixteenth century.

The comic strip is a direct descendant of these murals in its ability to convey a story visually to a broad public. That church mural and newspaper comic strip are to be distinguished from one another in numerous ways, however, is clearly apparent for we need only think of the difference, for example, in subject matter; form and material likewise contrast sharply. Thus while the mural is monumental in scale, the comic strip is small and intimate; while the

---

1. My perception of the nature of Christian murals and their public functions is dependent on the study by Hans Belting, *Bild und Kult: Eine Geschichte des Bild für dem Zeitalter der Kunst* (Munich: C.H. Beck, 1990).

mural exists only once in a specific place on a fixed and essentially immovable wall, the comic strip exists in innumerable examples printed on sheets of paper, usually newspaper or book pages intended for extensive distribution. The viewing or reading of a cycle of murals thus is a communal activity; comic strips, in contrast, usually are read and viewed by a lone individual. The mural acts as a communal link between individuals whereas the comic strip works within a personal realm.

Other than scale, the major factor inculpated in these distinctions is the comic strip's production by means of printing. The printing press makes possible its multiple appearance in newspapers, magazines, or books whose editions number into the millions. Ironically, however, historical links to wall painting remain here too. Among the first applications of the printing process, as it was developed in the fifteenth century was the translation onto paper of themes and motifs that dominated ecclesiastical mural and multi-paneled painting. By means of woodcut impressions that depicted the birth or crucifixion of Jesus, images of saints or allegories of a saintly life, the visual messages of conversion and conviction that wall paintings presented to their church congregations now became available to individuals wherever and whenever they wished to view them for private contemplation and devotion.[2] The image gained accessibility to a larger audience simultaneously with its accentuation of private, personal, preserved, and separate viewing and veneration. Broad popularity and restricted exclusivity thus ironically were simultaneous products of the printing process, the comic strip representing the continuation of the first, while the artist's print exemplifies the foregrounding of the latter characteristic today.

The distribution of an image to a large audience was among the printed woodcut's initial primary functions—the multiplication of the image to make it available for broadly popular consumption (a factor that also contributed to the intrusion of secular subject matter, as when prints functioned as playing cards or game boards)—the aesthetic value of the image also came to be recognized as a desirable quality potentially more significant even than content. In the formation of this accentuation of artistic quality the inclusion of woodcut illustrations in blockbooks emulating the composition and appearance of illuminated manuscripts was a significant contributing factor. Books, in the fifteenth and early sixteenth centuries, remained a relatively rare, expensive commodity even after the invention of movable type, and continued to be addressed largely to the educated elite dominated by clergy and aristocracy. For a text-oriented audience, however, print images did not need to function only as transmitters of information; instead, the viewer's attention could focus on, or at least place significant value on, the craft and art of print images, much as occurred simultaneously in painting as a new art audience emerged during the late Middle Ages and early Renaissance.

For artists, meantime, the duplication of an image afforded by the woodcut (as well as the developing techniques of engraving and etching) provided a means of reaching a more widespread audience relatively cheaply. Prints were a successful means of extending the artists' reach, of increasing their market beyond local limitations, and thus, of generating increased patronage and income for their work.[3] With prints functioning both as independent artworks and a form of advertisement for an artist's general skill and worth, particular care in their execution, especially in the exploitation of the unique qualities of the etching, engraving, or woodcut, and in the choice of attention-drawing images, benefitted both the artist establishing or maintaining a reputation and the patron desirous of owning aesthetically valued

2. Among the various histories of the print medium, the most generally valuable remains Arthur M. Hind, *An Introduction to the History of Woodcut, with a Detailed Survey of Work Done in the Fifteenth Century* (New York: Houghton Mifflin, 1935; New York: Dover, 1963).

3. An indication of the value prints could have for an artist is provided by Albrecht Dürer's law suit in 1506 against Marcantonio Raimondi for issuing engraved copies—complete with Dürer's monogram—of *The Life of the Virgin* woodcut series. Raimondi's copies represented a potential loss of income for Dürer.

images. The book remained as a means of promulgating a multiplicity of images, but with each sheet of paper devoted to a single image. Combined with appropriate texts (printed on the reverse side of the images and thus appearing opposite them) in German or Latin, Albrecht Dürer (1471–1528), for example, published his series of fifteen woodcuts devoted to the *Apocalypse* (1498), the twelve of *The Large Passion of Christ* (1511), and the twenty of the *Life of the Virgin* (see fig. 1) as separate books, but in 1511 also bound them together as a single volume which could serve as a compendium of his image-making skills and accomplishments. Dürer also published impressions of his blocks without the accompanying text and made them available for purchase. It was in this textless form that the images were also printed after Dürer's death, no longer bound into book form, using the original blocks, specifically for print collectors and connoisseurs seeking images unencumbered by the "interference" of rows of printed text. Although the prints of Dürer's *Apocalypse* may have originated conceptually to accompany a text, once the texts were dissociated from the prints, a print portfolio necessarily resulted: interrelated, separate print images began to function, not to augment, but rather to supplant a text.

Relieved of the need to correspond to a text, serial prints could be used by artists to explore single motifs or themes, but the production of an independent print portfolio, not physically linked to a book or any other text, remained relatively rare among artists in Germany after the time of Dürer and the early sixteenth century. When it was revived during the eighteenth century, the serially-conceived print images addressed a different audience. Following the example of William Hogarth in London, the Polish-Prussian artist Daniel Chodowiecki (1726–1801) in Berlin engraved small moralizing genre scenes of contemporary life and mores.[4] Beginning in 1778, when they were commissioned for annual pocket calendars or almanacs published in Göttingen by Georg Lichtenberg (who would publish extensive commentaries on Hogarth's print series between 1784 and

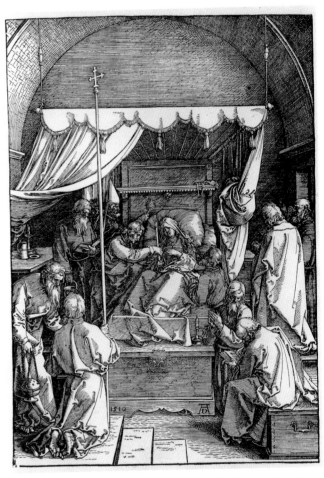

Fig. 1 Albrecht Dürer (German, 1471–1528), *The Death of the Virgin* from *The Life of the Virgin*, 1510, woodcut $12^{15}/_{16} \times 9^{9}/_{16}$ (32.6 × 24.3), The David and Alfred Smart Museum of Art, The University of Chicago, in memory of Mr. Hi Simons from his daughter, 1976.42

4. The standard catalogue of Chodowiecki's graphics is Jens-Heiner Bauer, *Daniel Nikolaus Chodowiecki: Das druckgraphische Werk* (Hannover: Verlag Galerie J.H. Bauer, 1982). Also see Klaus Gallwitz and Margret Stuffmann, *Bürgerliches Leben im 18. Jahrhundert: Daniel Chodowiecki 1726–1801 Zeichnungen and Druckgraphik* (exh. cat.) (Frankfurt a.M.: Städelsches Kunstinstitut und Städtische Galerie, 1978).

1796), Chodowiecki's print cycles were accompanied with explanatory texts, so that the former generation of illustrated texts was here reversed as images became the source of verbal commentary.[5] With their combination of essays, poetry, plays, and independent images in a format first made popular in France, the pocket almanacs were designed for wide circulation among the educated classes at a time when literacy in Prussia was being fostered by the introduction of universal education. As the elitism of the written word was undermined, so too was that of the print. Chodowiecki's series of naturalistic representations—*Marriage Proposals, Natural and Affected Scenes from Life,* and the *Centifolium Stultorum,* or *Follies*—humorously characterize or satirize the commonplace activities of contemporary life for an audience of shopkeepers, tradesmen, civil servants, lesser court officials, and women, all of them previously not specifically addressed except in the context of religious imagery. The power of the print series as an independent medium of narrative, amusement, commentary, and civic education for potentially the entire population, in accord with Enlightenment idealism, was highlighted while, unfortunately, in extensive editions and reprintings, the quality of the impressions was often completely neglected or at least of secondary importance.

The lure of the narrative power of serial images remained strong throughout the later eighteenth and nineteenth centuries, whether in cycles of prints or drawings, or in fresco cycles, both proposed and actual. Following the elevation of drawing and line over color in the aesthetics of neo-Classicism, and after the rediscovery of Albrecht Dürer as artistic prototype during the early manifestations of Romanticism, German artists as diverse as the anti-academic proto-Romantic, Asmus Jakob Carstens (1754–1798), or the officially recognized late-Romantic, Bonaventura Genelli (1800–1868), conceived of compositions to visualize texts by Homer and Dante, and had their line drawings translated into print portfolios by professional engravers. The practice was also employed by Philipp Otto Runge (1770–1810), one of the most prototypical of German Romantics. Even before he began to work out compositions for oil paintings, in 1803 Runge had four monumental engravings ($28^3/_8 \times 18^7/_8$ [72×48]) of his *The Times of the Day* carefully produced according to his own precise arabesque drawings (figs. 2a–d).[6] In an initial edition of twenty-five, he sent them to friends, other artists, and influential critics such as Johann Wolfgang von Goethe and Ludwig Tieck in order to gain support and recognition for his visualized perceptions of human life, humanity's salvation, and universal history—the interactions of divine spirit and material creation. Praising Runge as "one of the most inspired artists of our age", Goethe observed that ". . . the artist placed significance into the entire series, as well as meaning into each individual image, so that the prints are not only a pleasure for the eye, but also affect the inner senses; indeed their content reaches from the allegorical to the mystical."[7] Such enthusiastic reception led Runge to issue a larger edition (possibly 250 im-

Fig. 2a Philipp Otto Runge (German, 1777–1810), *Morning* from *The Times of the Day,* 1803–05, etching and engraving, 30 × 22⁷/₈ (76.2 × 58), Clarence Buckingham Collection, 1989.27.1, © 1992 The Art Institute of Chicago, All Rights Reserved

Fig. 2b *Afternoon,* 1989.27.2, © 1992 The Art Institute of Chicago, All Rights Reserved

Fig. 2c *Evening,* 1989.27.3, © 1992 The Art Institute of Chicago, All Rights Reserved

Fig. 2d *Night,* 1989.27.4, © 1992 The Art Institute of Chicago, All Rights Reserved

5. For Lichtenberg's commentaries, along with Chodowiecki's images, see Georg Christoph Lichtenberg, *Handlungen des Lebens: Erklärungen zu 72 Monatskupfern von Daniel Chodowiecki* (Stuttgart: Deutsche Verlags-Anstalt, 1971).

6. Jörg Traeger, *Philipp Otto Runge und sein Werk. Monographie und kritischer Katalog* (Munich: Prestel Verlag, 1975), nos. 280A–283A and 280B–283B. The engravers are Johann Adolph Darnstedt, Paulis Ephraim Gottlieb Krüger, and Johann Gottlieb Seyfert, all active in Dresden.

7. [Johann Wolfgang von Goethe], "Unterhaltungen über Gegenstände der bildenden Kunst," *Jenaische Allgemeine Literaturzeitung* (1807) as reproduced in Philipp Otto Runge, *Hinterlassene Schriften,* vol. II (Hamburg: Fredrich Perthes, 1841; Göttingen: Vandenhoeck & Ruprecht, 1965), 514.

pressions) in 1807, with the series and composition titles as well as his own name added to each massive sheet to facilitate comprehension and identification among a larger, less personal public without disrupting the images' independent suggestive power.

Consisting of a vocabulary conceived by Runge in pictorial terms, lacking a textual source, the four "verses" of this Romantic epic visual poem appeared alone, without the interference of programmatic or interpretative text to mar the separate individual or cyclical visual communication. For many German Romantic artists (including Runge, on other occasions), however, the creation of visual images to function as a pregnant means of interaction with, or as an extension of, verbal texts also was an absorbing challenge. In pocket books, calendars, and almanacs small engraved illustrations were the frequent accompaniment of poems, stories, and plays reaching out to ever larger audiences. Certainly the most frequently visualized text was Goethe's drama *Faust*;[8] an initial fragment was published in 1790, the completed Part I in 1808 as the eighth volume of his collected writings, and Part II shortly after his death in 1832. Staging difficulties with Goethe's complex, often reality-defying scenes kept the play off German stages until 1828, but artists began immediately to project the play's major protagonists and episodes, although Goethe, ironically, had rejected the idea of illustrating his work: "It is so unlikely that something could be created that suits the concept and tone of the poem; copper [engravings] and poetry tend mutually to parody each other."[9] Goethe's initial published fragment had already inspired Asmus Jakob Carstens to draw the scene of *Faust in the Witch's Kitchen*, to be engraved by Wilhelm Müller in 1796; by the centennial of Part I's publication, some 1,500 paintings, prints, and other works devoted to visualizing *Faust* were counted. Among the first efforts to synopsize it in a series of visual images are the twelve drawings by Peter von Cornelius (1783–1867), begun in 1811, engraved by Julius Thaeter and Franz Ruscheweyh, and published in 1816.[10] Using a style that emulated the drawings and prints of fifteenth-

and sixteenth-century German prototypes, especially Dürer, Cornelius clothed his figures in medieval costume. For his first major appearance before the German public, Cornelius stated, "I wanted to be absolutely German, and therefore selected this form."[11] A traditional German means was used to attain modern German fame. The cycle of images—prints serving as distributable substitutes for frescoes—similarly suited both his nationalistic, historicist justification and the modern Romantic taste for an intermingling of literature and the visual arts.

Due to delays in its publication, Cornelius's *Faust cycle* was overshadowed in its impact, popularity, and also Goethe's acceptance, by the more neo-Classically conceived, more sentimental outline drawings by Friedrich August Moritz Retsch, published in 1820.[12] In the aftermath of the Napoleonic Wars, dur-

Fig. 3a Alfred Rethel (German, 1816–1859), *Title Page* from *Another Dance of Death*, 1848, woodcut $10^5/_8 \times 15^5/_8$ (27 × 39.5), Print and Drawing Purchase Fund, 1945.225.2, © 1992 The Art Institute of Chicago, All Rights Reserved

Fig. 3b *Death Rides to the City*, 1945.225.3, © 1992 The Art Institute of Chicago, All Rights Reserved

Fig. 3c *Death Before the Public House*, 1945.225.4, © 1992 The Art Institute of Chicago, All Rights Reserved

Fig. 3d *Death on the Tribune*, 1945.225.5, © 1992 The Art Institute of Chicago, All Rights Reserved

Fig. 3e *Death on the Barricade*, 1945.225.6, © 1992 The Art Institute of Chicago, All Rights Reserved

Fig. 3f *Death as Victor*, 1945.225.7, © 1992 The Art Institute of Chicago, All Rights Reserved

8. An extensive collection of *Faust* imagery is provided by Max von Boehn, "Faust und die Kunst," in Johann Wolfgang von Goethe, *Faust*, Hundertjahrsausgabe im Askanischen Verlag (Berlin: Albert Kindle, 1938). Also see Wolfgang Wegner, *Die Faustdarstellung vom 16. Jahrhundert bis zur Gegenwart* (Amsterdam: Verlag der Erasmus Buchhandlung, 1962).

9. Goethe, letter to Cotta, cited in Boehn, "Faust und die Kunst," 68–69.

10. Wegner, *Die Faustdarstellung*, 21.

11. Peter von Cornelius, quoted in Hermann Riegl, *Peter Cornelius: Festschrift zu des großen Künstlers hundertstem Geburtstag* (Berlin: R.v. Decker, 1883), 31.

a

b

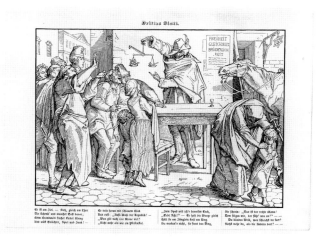

c

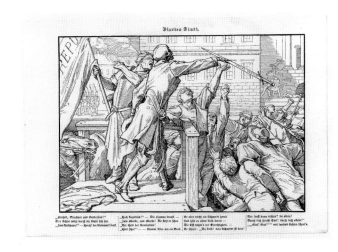

d

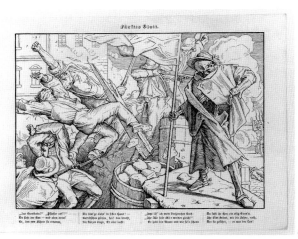

e

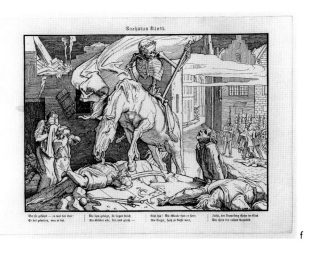

f

der Rückkehr in Braunschweig abstattete, zu der Vornahme der geheimnisvollen Handlung bestimmt und Mitglieder der Brüderschaft aus Hamburg und Hannover samt dem benötigten Apparate ebendahin verschrieben. Die Aufnahme geschah zu nächtlicher Weile, da man des Königs wegen mit großer Vorsicht verfahren mußte. Friedrich verlangte, daß man ihn ganz als einen Privatmann behandeln und keine der üblichen Zeremonien aus Rücksicht auf seinen Rang abändern sollte. So wurde er ganz in gehöriger Form aufgenommen. Man bewunderte dabei seine Unerschrockenheit, seine Ruhe, seine Feinheit und Gewandtheit ebenso, wie nach der eigentlichen Eröffnung der Loge den Geist und das Ge-

schick, mit welchem er an den maurerischen Arbeiten teilnahm. Später wurden einige Mitglieder der Brüderschaft (unter ihnen der obengenannte Bielfeld) nach Rheinsberg eingeladen, mit welchen dort, freilich wiederum im größten Geheimnis, in den Arbeiten fortgefahren wurde.

Bewegte sich solchergestalt das Leben in Rheinsberg in den verschiedensten Formen eines poetisch heiteren Genusses, suchte Friedrich denselben endlich noch durch mancherlei eigene dichterische Versuche zu erhöhen und festzuhalten, so barg sich doch zugleich unter dieser anmutvollen Hülle ein tiefer, redlicher Ernst. Die Stunden, in welchen Friedrich nicht in der Gesellschaft zum Vorschein kam — und diese umfaßten bei weitem die bedeutendere Zeit des dortigen Aufenthalts — waren der vielseitigsten geistigen Tätigkeit gewidmet. Denn wie ihm früher seine wissenschaftlichen Interessen mannigfach verkümmert waren, so suchte er jetzt eine jede freie Minute zur Gewinnung des Versäumten anzuwen-

III

a

ihm nach, aber er ritt so scharf, daß sie ihn nicht zu erreichen vermochten. Mitten in der Nacht kam er mit seinem kleinen Gefolge an das Tor von Oppeln; man fand es verschlossen. Auf den Wer-da-Ruf der Wache gab man die Antwort: Preußischer Kurier! — aber das Tor ward nicht geöffnet. Die Sache schien bedenklich. Friedrich befahl, daß einige absteigen und näher nachfragen sollten,

weshalb die Stadt verschlossen bliebe. Sowie diese sich näherten, erfolgten Flintenschüsse durch das Gattertor; — die Stadt war von einem Trupp österreichischer Husaren besetzt. Eilig wandte man nun die Pferde und jagte den Weg zurück. Mit Tagesanbruch kam Friedrich nach Löwen, einem Städtchen in der Mitte zwischen Mollwitz und Oppeln. Hier fand er die Gendarmen, die ihm am vorigen Abend gefolgt waren; außer diesen aber auch einen Adjutanten, der ihm die Nachricht von der siegreichen Beendigung der Mollwitzer Schlacht brachte. Unmittelbar von Löwen begab sich Friedrich nun auf das Schlachtfeld zurück, so daß er in einem Ritte vierzehn Meilen zurückgelegt hatte. Die Tüchtigkeit und Präzision, der Mut, die unerschütterliche Standhaftigkeit seiner Infanterie, als diese erst Raum fand, ihre Kräfte zu entwickeln, hatte den Österreichern den Sieg entrissen. Neipperg hatte sich mit bedeutendem Verluste, in der Richtung nach Neiße, zurückgezogen; den geschlagenen Feind zu verfolgen und zu vernichten hinderte teils die einbrechende Nacht, teils konnte man nicht zu einem übereinstimmenden Entschlusse kommen.

Friedrich hat nachmals, als er die Geschichte seiner Zeit schrieb, ein strenges

157

b

dem Frieden in rascher Tätigkeit verfaßt; diese wurden nun vollendet, und wieder andre reihten sich ihnen an. Den zweiten Teil der Geschichte seiner Zeit, welcher den Zweiten Schlesischen Krieg enthält, hatte Friedrich schon im Jahre 1746

geschrieben. Im folgenden Jahre hatte er seine Memoiren zur Geschichte des brandenburgischen Hauses (die Geschichte seiner Vorgänger) begonnen, deren einzelne Abschnitte in der Akademie vorgelesen, auch in den Schriften der Akademie gedruckt wurden; vollendet und in einer selbständigen Prachtausgabe erschien

237

c

ing which an initial modern nationalism emerged among the German lands, Cornelius continued his search for an identifiably German text, a heroic book of the people, to be accompanied with images, and selected the medieval saga of the Nibelung. Begun shortly after he joined the Brotherhood of the Nazarenes in Rome, the drawings—to be engraved by Amsler, Barth, Lips and Ritter—once again called on Dürer as stylistic model, but now showing influences of Michelangelo, Mantegna, and Signorelli in an effort to produce a monumental style capable of pre-

Fig. 4a Adolf Menzel (German, 1815–1905), *The Emblems of the Freemasons, According to Special Instructions* from Franz Kugler, *The History of Frederick the Great* (Leipzig: E. A. Seemann, [1940]), page 111, 9¹³/₁₆ × 6¹³/₁₆ (24.9 × 17.3), Joseph Regenstein Library, The University of Chicago

Fig. 4b Untitled illustration, page 157

Fig. 4c *Dinner Table in the Salon of Sanssouci*, page 237

12. Retsch's works drew on John Flaxman's illustrations to Homer and Dante as their stylistic source.

senting the mythic side of history painting. Published by G.A. Reimer in Berlin in 1821, after the patriotic verve of the German Wars of Liberation had ebbed, the portfolio of seven prints failed to fulfill Cornelius's yearning for popular success. Nonetheless, the Nibelung saga became a constant of German Romantic concerns, with Richard Wagner's music drama cycle *Der Ring des Nibelungen* (The Ring of the Nibelung), serving as its most memorable index. Medieval legends also were seen as a suitable means of marking the 1840 quadricentennial of Gutenberg's invention of movable type, an event marked by a deluxe, illustrated publication accompanying a modern translation of the text.[13] Following the drawings supplied by Ludwig Bendemann, Julius Hübner, and Alfred Rethel, the technique of wood engraving, then newly popular, was applied by the wood engravers Hugo Bürkner, Friedrich Ludwig Unzelmann, and Albert Vogel. Using a line-cut technique that emphasized an archaizing linear construction rather than refinements of shading and volume, as was the more general practice, they modeled their work on the woodcuts of Dürer and Hans Holbein, expecting to produce independent large-scale prints as well as smaller illustrations.

One major project resulted. With images measuring 12¼ × 10¾ (31 × 27.3), Rethel also applied the Holbein motif of a Dance of Death in a portfolio of six wood engravings *Another Dance of Death* (figs. 3a–f), cut by Bürkner and his workshop, and published in 1849.[14] Accompanied with explicatory verses by Robert Reinick, the print cycle formed a political pamphlet revealing death as the sole victor of the harshly suppressed German revolutions of 1848. Conceived as a self-contained cycle, employing a historically justified and popular technique, and injecting contemporary events into the traditional theme of the Dance of Death, Rethel's portfolio also functioned as a statement of particular concerns that dominated German art of the period and would define much of its transition from Romanticism and historicism to Modernism later in the century. By reviving a technique identified with the German past and

its masters, a popular ethnic, graphic style was also achieved that could be applied, with less incisiveness and stylistic harshness, by other German artists—for example, Moritz von Schwind in his portfolio of wood engravings *Twelve Pictures from the Lives of Bavarian Rulers* (1858), or the several contributors, again including Schwind, to Bühlau's *(German History in Pictures* (1856)—in visualizing the German past, establishing a common heritage, and affecting the national consciousness of their predominantly middle class audiences. A similar undertaking, concerned not with the German past but with a common Christian heritage, was the series of 240 wood engravings after drawings by Julius Veit Hans Schnorr von Carolsfeld that composed *The Bible in Pictures*. A late manifestation of the Nazarenes' striving for a modern religious art, published in folios beginning in 1851 and completed in 1860, it became one of the most popularly successful works of the time.

Heavily dependent on history or biblical narrative, their images numbering in the hundreds, these wood engraving portfolios functioned more as book substitutes than as independent cycles of prints, and appropriately gained even greater acceptance and circulation in reduced format reproductions inserted among the texts of history books and Bibles. In fact, the wood engraving had been adapted from its more widespread application in periodical and book illustration requiring a large number of impressions in a comparatively small format. It was in book illustration too that the linear rather than tonal wood engraving received its initial application by Adolph Menzel with his series of drawings for Franz Kugler's *History of Frederick the Great* (1840, fig. 4), a *Volksbuch*, or "people's book", designed to edify the Prussian people visually and spiritually in its presentation of

---

13. Curt Glaser, *Die Graphik der Neuzeit vom Anfang des XIX. Jahrhunderts bis zur Gegenwart* (Berlin: Bruno Cassirer, 1923), 218.

14. For an extensive discussion of Rethel's print cycle and its signification, see Peter Paret, *Art as History: Episodes in the Culture and Politics of Nineteenth-Century Germany* (Princeton: Princeton University Press, 1988), 77–130.

the deeds of the Enlightenment despot who formed the modern Prussian state.[15] With the exception of his portraits of "heroes of war and peace" for the portfolio *From King Frederick's Times* (1848–55), Menzel did not employ the wood engraving technique for the production of text-independent serial imagery. His first portfolio of prints *Experiments in Engraving* (1844), broke with the preferred wood engraving technique of late Romanticism and historicism in favor of copper engravings, modeled on the example of Rembrandt. Also rejected was the accent on overt narrative in favor of a loose grouping of contemporary genre scenes and landscapes without discursive content, focused instead on precision of observation and the dramatic effect of chiaroscuro. Experimentation and exploration of the medium, and the interconnection of images, were the portfolio's expressed goals. Such an exploitation of the material properties of the medium, in which the artist himself worked directly on the print plate rather than invoking the intermediary of the professional wood engraver, likewise characterizes Menzel's portfolio of six lithographs *Experiments on Stone with Brush and Scraper* (1851): historical costumes, self-portraiture, polished compositions, broadly conceived sketches with randomly brushed patterns, dramatic light effects, and neutral illumination all combine into a seemingly random grouping held together by the personality of the artist and his pronounced concern with material statements of the lithograph's diverse vocabulary.

Menzel's Realist experiments combine disjunctively into the portfolio format. The serial concept, other than as viewed within the physical limitations of a number of explorations of a single medium, worked counter to the priority placed by him on the artist as the material witness of a scene or object. His images therefore consisted of isolated phenomena of vision carefully and independently preserved and translated, rather than becoming part of a conceptual unit of interlocking images. As other German artists —Wilhelm Leibl and his circle of artists, Max Liebermann, and Hans Thoma—embraced the ethos of Realism and Naturalism, as well as their variant in Impressionism, during the 1870s and 1880s, Menzel's approach that prioritized the single print image was likewise adopted in their portrait and landscape engravings and lithographs. Serial imagery was retained by academically-oriented artists, who also continued to make use of wood engraving techniques, but the German artists attempting to break from established practices avoided it, just as they rejected the wood engraving technique with its intermediary technicians. When the print portfolio was taken up again, it was by artists such as Max Klinger who newly sought contact with a recognized German artistic past, a fundamentally neo-Romantic attitude, but who also accepted the accentuation on the personal production of the artist such as Menzel's Realism had espoused. With the demand that artists personally stamp each aspect of a print's production, from conception to execution, with their individuality, the preferred techniques became drypoint, engraving, and lithography. For the relief print (which in the form of linear wood engraving had been the major technique of nineteenth-century portfolios and illustrated books) to be revived, as it was in the woodcut medium by the German Expressionists, a new approach became necessary that retrieved techniques of the fifteenth-century German artists who had inaugurated Germany's printmaking tradition.

Throughout, a conscious dialogue between past and present, between preservation and rejection, between tradition and innovation, became a subtext to the portfolios' visual narratives. The artist-designed print, however, also lost the overt contact with the concerns of an extended middle class audience it had found earlier in the nineteenth century through calendars, illustrated books, book-format portfolios, and periodicals. The cost of artistic experimentation and the expansion of artistic means was the loss of broad popular support and influence, the space within which the comic strip would flourish.

15. Ibid., 26–60.

ROBIN REISENFELD

The revival, transformation, and dissemination of the print portfolio in Germany and Austria, 1890 to 1930

One of the first avid collectors of German Expressionist prints, the Hamburg judge Gustav Schiefler, recounts in *Meine Graphik-Sammlung* (My Graphic Collection) the extraordinary impact that Max Klinger's serial prints made on him when he first saw them at a Hamburg exhibition in the winter of 1889–90. The magnitude and breadth of Klinger's graphic cycles so overwhelmed him that he felt compelled to begin collecting contemporary prints.[1] As Schiefler recounted later in 1927: "Looking back I recall that to a large measure it wasn't the artistic but the objective, literary content of the leaves that thrilled me . . ."[2]

Klinger's print cycles and Schiefler's response to their imaginative possibilities serve as harbingers of the central importance that the graphic arts were to play in shaping modern German art. An ignored, marginal genre in Germany by the end of the nineteenth century, the fine art print flooded the market by the early 1920s to such an extent that the critics Curt Glaser and Walter Ley complained of the print's debasement and growing commercialization.[3] In 1879, Max Klinger was the rare example of a German artist who included prints as an integral part of his oeuvre. Similarly, Gustav Schiefler was one of the few members of the *Bildungsbürgertum* (educated middle class) to recognize the significance of the graphic arts and its role as a visual language through which the modern artist could communicate to a large contemporary audience.[4] By the end of the First World War the situation had changed so that every major German artist—and legions of minor practitioners of the medium—executed prints. The collecting of fine prints had grown to the extent that it even rivalled the importance of porcelains among the traditional collectors of fine and applied arts.[5]

Corresponding to this print revival was the increasing popularity of the print portfolio itself.[6] The print portfolio consists of a set of images—generally one per unbound sheet—conceived as a thematic unit and meant to be viewed in sequential order. The

1. The first contemporary print Schiefler acquired was Klinger's etching *Verfolgter Kentaur* (Battling Centaurs) from the 1881 portfolio *Intermezzi (Opus IV)*. See the editor's afterword in Gustav Schiefler, *Meine Graphik-Sammlung*, ed. Gerhard Schack (Hamburg: Gesellschaft der Bücherfreunde, 1927; Hamburg: Christian Verlag, 1974), 315.

2. "Rückblickend erkenne ich, daß es zu einem guten Teil nicht der künstlerische, sondern der gegenständliche, der literarische Inhalt der Blätter war, der mich packte." Schiefler, *Meine Graphik-Sammlung* (Hamburg: Gesellschaft der Bücherfreunde, 1927), 2.

3. Curt Glaser, "Vom Graphik-Sammeln," *Das Kunstblatt* 3, no. 11 (1919): 321–30, and Walter Ley, "Graphische Neuerscheinungen," *Das Kunstblatt* 3, no. 11 (1919): 331–37. For an overview of their position, see Ida K. Rigby, "The Revival of Printmaking in Germany," *German Expressionist Prints and Drawings: The Robert Gore Rifkind Center for German Expressionist Studies* (Los Angeles and Munich: Los Angeles County Museum of Art and Prestel Verlag, 1989), 60–62.

4. Schiefler, *Meine Graphik-Sammlung* (Hamburg: Christian Verlag, 1974), 319.

5. Adolph Donath makes a distinction between two kinds of collectors: those belonging to the "universal" group and those in the "specialist" group. He notes that along with porcelains, graphics have become favored items of the specialists; Donath attributes both the establishment of *Kupferstichkabinette*, or print rooms, in museums and the improvements in the art market to this new graphic interest. Furthermore, he observes that the art market is flooded with etchings, woodcuts, color woodcuts, and lithographs—prints that never before existed in such large quantities. See *Psychologie des Kunstsammelns*, 3rd ed. (Berlin: Richard Carl Schmidt & Co., 1920), 17–18.

6. Waltraut Neuerburg lists approximately three hundred examples grouped under nine different categories made by ninety artists during the first quarter of the twentieth century in her thesis on German Expressionist graphic cycles. Neuerburg then more narrowly subdivides these nine categories into seventeen. See appendices A and B in Waltraut Neuerburg, "Der graphische Zyklus im Deutschen Expressionismus und seine Typen, 1905–1925" (Ph.D. diss., Bonn, Rheinischen Friedrich-Wilhelms-Universität, 1976), 290–425.

series may incorporate inscriptions or be accompanied with a typeset introductory text, but it can also be developed as a cycle without text, forming a visual narrative. The physical presentation of German print cycles from this period ranges from deluxe portfolios frequently commissioned and produced by well-established fine arts publishers and issued in signed and numbered editions that were stored in book-like albums, to inexpensive gatherings contained in paper wrappers that were printed and distributed by the artists themselves or by small, commercial presses. The serial print's great appeal for the printmaker lay in part in its flexibility, that is, its ability to communicate or confound ideas demanding a sequential reading which likened it to the experience of reading a book. As demonstrated below, early modern German serial prints crossed a wide spectrum of themes, formats, methods of production and distribution, and (originally) cost. In addition to the fame of the artist or the appeal of the subject, the portfolio's sliding price scale made it affordable to collectors of differing financial means. Frequently turning to the serial print in their examination of such diverse subjects as artistic life and war, religion and economics, or love and politics,[7] artists adopted the multiple-image format to articulate responses to the era's complex set of cultural, social, and political issues. They, however, also employed the print portfolio in the narration of events imagined and personal. Produced in different styles and graphic media—etching, engraving, drypoint, lithography (transfer, photo, and offset), and woodcut—the cycles allowed artists an expanded treatment of a particular theme, situation, or idea.

How did a relatively ignored genre in Germany develop within such a short span of time into a highly popular and experimental medium? Initially Klinger and a few other artists were attracted to the cycle's possibilities of functioning as a *Gesamtkunstwerk*, or total work of art, in which they combined visual imagery with various artistic principles drawn from literature (poetry and drama) and music. Despite its compelling features, the print cycle remained a sec-

ondary aesthetic genre until the intervention of the dealer, who legitimized the print and print cycle as a fine art commodity, and the introduction of marketing strategies directed towards a newly-emerged prosperous middle class. Through the intentions of the artists who took up printmaking and the response of a public who understood the cycle's significance, the serial print did not merely reflect society but also helped play an active role in shaping new attitudes. Its emergence dove-tailed with structural shifts in late nineteenth-century German society that favored visual over literary forms of communication; this situation challenged the written text as the primary mode of intellectual discourse in the semi-private sphere of the living room or study.[8] Reaching a German bourgeois audience whose decision to collect had become an endorsement of creative freedom, the cycle identified a collective resistance to more traditional genres.

During the first half of the nineteenth century, the Romantic artists Peter von Cornelius, Alfred Rethel, and Moritz von Schwind, among others, produced fine art print cycles. By the 1870s, however, the role of the print as an original work of art had been largely replaced by its function as a reproductive technique for the illustration of newspapers and the reproduction of famous paintings and Old Master prints. Yet toward the end of the century, publishers, perceiving a renewed interest in Germany's cultural heritage, began to produce facsimile editions of old German prints and print cycles such as Albrecht Dürer's companion woodcut series, *Marienleben* (The Life of the Virgin) and *Große Passion* (The Large Passion), both published in 1887 as photographically reproduced images from the originals printed from zinc plates by L. Zehl in Leipzig; Georg Hirth's 1888 reproduction of

---

7. Ibid.

8. See Jürgen Habermas, "Social Structures of the Public Sphere: The Bourgeois Family and the Institutionalization of a Privateness Oriented to an Audience," *The Structural Transformation of the Public Sphere: An Inquiry into a Category of Bourgeois Society*, trans. Thomas Burger (Cambridge, Mass.: MIT Press, 1989), 49–51.

Albrecht Altdorfer's *Sündenfall und Erlösung des Menschengeschlechtes* (The Fall and Redemption of Mankind); *Kupferstiche und Holzschnitte alter Meister in Nachbildungen* (Engravings and Woodcuts of the Old Masters in Reproduction); and Rudolf Kautzsch's *Die Holzschnitte der Kölner Bibel von 1474* (The Woodcuts of the Cologne Bible of 1474). An interest in the historical print, combined with the example of the English Arts and Crafts movement (in particular William Morris's defense of craftsmanship and the hand-printed book) prompted a revival of the book arts in the 1890s in Germany. The first major late nineteenth-century German artist to appreciate the aesthetic features of the portfolio was Max Klinger. Both his 1891 theoretical treatise on painting and drawing entitled *Malerei und Zeichnung* (Painting and Drawing) and the etching cycles he produced in the last two decades of the century provided a strong stimulus for the modern graphic art movement in Germany.

Even before a general rekindled interest in the graphic arts, Klinger had revived the Romantic conception of the print as an original work. In the 1880s he executed a series of print cycles that emphasized an immediacy of expression and personal visual language. Whereas most Romantic artists had based their cycles on literary models in the illustration of epic tales or stories,[9] Klinger loosely conceived his cycles in terms of a musical score. This borrowing from the world of music opened the serial print to new formal structures outside a strict, linear narrative progression: the title page is analogous to the overture, and the sequence of printed images, variations on a theme. As scholars have observed in other works by Klinger, he also envisioned his cycles as a visual discourse that linked ideas through an associative process similar to stanzas of poetry.[10]

Although Klinger wanted to emphasize the print's unique formal features in his treatise, he was forced to subsume it in a category with a pre-established aesthetic affiliation: therefore, he included all black and white art forms, notably the print, under the heading "drawing". The use of this term in the treatise's title

instead of "printmaking" underscores the transitional status of the graphic arts in 1891. As he explained in the foreword, he chose the word "drawing" because printmaking connoted reproductive printing (*vervielfältigende Prozeduren*).[11] Instead, he sought to promote the print's role as an aesthetic medium equal to, but different from, painting.

Klinger further stated that the print cycle's sequential order allowed a programmatic statement to develop and enabled the artist to express his own world view. After arguing that the graphic cycle "allows in the narrowest space the strongest feelings to be compressed, giving up its most reluctant feelings in the quickest succession,"[12] he proceeded to define the substance of this world view as an individual's experience of life. Through the serial print's ability to sustain a sense of the passage of time through an ordered sequence of images the artist is able to develop "in quick secession a piece of life in all of its manifestations. It may expand epically; may intensify dramatically; it may look at us in dry irony. Being only shadows it even grasps the uncanny without being repellent."[13]

Klinger introduced in his print cycles a new form of viewing, or "privatization" of seeing, that paralleled the conventional act of reading a printed text. The subjectivity of Klinger's prints and the format of the folio lent themselves to presentation in an intimate space, suitable for sustained viewing and intellectual reflection, after the fashion of the traditional print connoisseur and his albums, in the drawing room, study, club, bookstore, or small gallery, either laid out for study on a table or framed on the wall.

---

9. Neuerburg, "Der Graphische Zyklus," 28.

10. See Thomas W. Gaehtgens, "Von der Ästhetik der graphischen Künste," *Max Klinger* (Bielefeld: Kunsthalle Bielefeld, 1976), 206.

11. Max Klinger, *Malerei und Zeichnung: Tagebuchaufzeichnungen und Briefe*, ed. Anneliese Hübscher (Leipzig: Verlag Philipp Reclam, 1985), 19–20.

12. Ibid., 36.

13. Ibid., 37.

Small-scale in size, prints required close-up, intimate viewing that optimally permitted an audience of one or two at a time. The rise of the print collector at the turn of the century helped validate the private sphere's increasing importance in modern bourgeois life. Klinger manipulated an expressive means dependent on acute observation and optical reality to construct a highly symbolic and subjective content. Thus, the artist's presentation forced his audience to "read" his prints in a manner similar to reading a book. Instead of using words to construct an associative pattern of thought, the artist relied on the accretion of factually presented motifs that take on symbolic meanings for the viewer in their new and unfamiliar contexts. The sequential viewing of images in a predetermined order as one examines the leaves of a portfolio demands that the observer develop his or her own interpretations in the construction of meanings that are flexible and shifting. As in the act of reading a book, viewing a print portfolio demanded a quiet, contemplative environment.

Klinger's cycles were published for a society that increasingly lacked the time for traditional literary pursuits. Reading books and letter writing, considered by the late eighteenth-century bourgeoisie as important domestic activities in the dissemination of reflections on life and man's activity in life,[14] were considered outmoded by the end of the nineteenth century. In 1920, the art historian Emil Waldmann reflected on this changed situation when he wrote in *The Collector and His Kind*:

> It is understandable, that a man of absolute modern life, an industrialist for example, who has no time to read a book or write letters or absorb himself slowly and restfully in a culture of a bygone age, and who communicates only through the telephone or telegraph, who [concerns himself] with coal, cables, ebonite, steel and machines and at the most with social welfare causes, a man . . . who possesses a passion and understanding for art of his time . . . This man from the business world represents a new type of collec-

tor, who principally deals with our artists and art dealers. And with justification.[15]

Waldmann describes here the collector who lives in the mechanized modern age and is increasingly dependent upon technological advances and visual means of communication. At a time in which individuals felt isolated from one another, the editioned print cycle provided a means of connecting the cultured middle class to its social stratum. Unlike the literary salons of the eighteenth century, however, the viewing of print cycles did not require the presence of an audience in order to forge a link between the individual and his class. The importance of the private realm is reinforced by the reproducibility of the cycle in editions, large and small, thereby enabling the private collector in his home to establish a link with a wider audience of artists, critics, and other collectors.

The constitution of a private arena for the print portfolio contrasts sharply with the initial print revolution of the fifteenth and sixteenth centuries that had created a public print culture,[16] in which handbills, pamphlets, and broadsheets were distributed

14. Habermas, "Social Structures of the Public Sphere," 49–51.

15. "Es ist begreiflich, daß ein Mensch des absolut modernen Lebens, ein Industrieller zum Beispiel, der keine Zeit hat, Bücher zu lesen und sich in eine Kultur vergangener Epochen langsam und ruhig zu versenken, der keine Briefe schreibt und sich nur noch per Telegraph oder Telephon mitteilt, der nur mit Kohlen und Kabeln, mit Hartgummi, Stahl und Maschinen und höchstens noch mit sozialer Wohlfahrtspflege zu tun hat, daß also ein Mensch mit einem solchen ganz auf das Aktuelle gerichteten Sinn sehr gut Leidenschaft und Verständnis haben kann für die Kunst seiner Zeit . . . Dieser Mann aus der Geschäftswelt, der das Wertvollste an modernen Bildern kauft, stellt einen neuen Typus des Sammlers dar, den mit dem unsere Künstler und unsere Kunsthändler vornehmlich rechen. Und mit Recht." Emil Waldmann, *Sammler und ihresgleichen* (Berlin: Bruno Cassirer Verlag, 1920), 14. For an informative overview of Berlin patronage, see Adolph Donath, "Der Berliner Kaufmann als Kunstfreund" in Max Osborn, ed., *Berlins Aufstieg zur Weltstadt* (Berlin: Reimar Hobbing, 1929). For a contemporary discussion of early modern art patronage in Berlin, see *Zeitschrift des deutscher Vereins für Kunstwissenschaft* 42 (Fall 1988).

16. Elizabeth Eisenstein, *The Printing Press as an Agent of Change*, 2 vols. (Cambridge: Cambridge University Press, 1979) and *The Printing Revolution in Early Modern Europe* (Cambridge: Cambridge University Press, 1983).

in the town market to a broad segment of the population. The nineteenth-century revival of the fine art print was intended for the consumption of a cultured, literate bourgeois audience, who had been educated in the visual arts through the public museum (which had developed in Germany in the second half of the nineteenth century). While the first print revolution stressed objective knowledge—using prints to educate an illiterate public about religion, politics, or social issues—the nineteenth-century revival emphasized a subjective world of art and aesthetics more appropriate to a privileged semi-private sphere. Disseminated in journals, books, and portfolios, the early modern print prospered through the intervention of art dealers and fine arts publishers who sought their market among an educated elite who were bound together by shared cultural values.

While Klinger's treatise was itself debated in critical and art historical circles,[17] his serial prints were commercially successful and secured his artistic reputation: the price of *Ein Leben* (A Life), for example, rose from 450 German marks in 1883 to 6,700 marks in 1908.[18] His print cycles appealed to the new collector who typically came from a middle class background. The art historian Gustav Hartlaub commented on these collectors and their interest in the print portfolio in his 1920 book *Die neue deutsche Graphik* (New German Graphics):

> We close our vast print portfolio, whose contents at the same time might give an example of how print collecting must come to be done today . . . It is no longer an art for lovers of minor masters' artistic translations of technical refinements and variations… It imperatively demands a new type of collector, who unhesitantly aims more at artistic content and less at rarity and every possible collector's value… It must come to be evaluated as the artist himself valued it in the creation…[19]

Unlike the traditional connoisseur of Old Master prints—whose interest focused on attribution, iconography, provenance, technique, quality of impression, paper type, and collectors' seals and stamps—

this new patron responded in a more personal fashion to the artistic merit and emotive content of newly printed works. The cycle's often strong literary content impressed the artist's public, as indicated by Schiefler's comment on his first viewing of Klinger's graphics. A visual counterpart to literary discourse, the print cycle became a powerful agent in the definition of a shared identity in one segment of society.

Klinger's treatise and graphics provided an influential, liberating example to other artists, including those as diverse as the Social Realist Käthe Kollwitz and the Symbolist Edvard Munch, and later Expressionist artists in Germany and Austria and Surrealists in Belgium and France. After reading Klinger's treatise, Kollwitz stopped painting and became a printmaker.[20] Instead of relying on musical motifs as Klinger had done, she turned to literary models: her first cycle *Ein Weberaufstand* (A Weavers' Revolt, Klipstein 32–37) of 1897 was based on Gerhart Hauptmann's play about the Silesian peasants' uprising in 1844, *Die Weber* (The Weavers). Even though Kollwitz had turned to a dramatic text, she was not primarily concerned, as many of her Romantic predecessors had been, with executing a visual narrative true to a specific text. Like Klinger, she utilized the print series to give free rein to her own imagination. Consisting of three etchings and three lithographs, *A Weavers' Revolt* follows the sequence of the drama, but none of the prints is an exact illustration of a scene from the play.[21] The fact that

17. For a discussion of its reception, see Gaehtgens, "Von der Ästhetik der graphischen Künste," 205.

18. Prices are quoted in Anneliese Hübscher's introduction to *Malerei und Zeichnung*, 6–7, and Robin Lenman, "Painters, Patronage and the Art Market in Germany 1850–1914," *Past and Present: A Journal of Historical Studies* no. 123 (May 1989): 123.

19. Translated in Rigby, "The Revival of Printmaking in Germany," 62.

20. Hübscher quotes Kollwitz's reaction upon viewing Klinger's work for the first time, see *Malerei und Zeichnung*, 8.

21. Frances Carey and Antony Griffiths, *The Print in Germany 1880–1933: The Age of Expressionism* (New York: Harper & Row, 1984), 61.

Kollwitz called the series *A Weavers' Revolt* rather than *The Weavers* is indicative of her intent to parallel rather than to follow literally the action of Hauptmann's play.[22]

Kollwitz also turned to Klinger's cycles as a conceptual model. She included a seventh plate in the original version of *A Weavers' Revolt*, so that the cycle would end on a symbolic note. Although she abandoned the etching in the edited cycle on the advice of her friend Julius Elias, its original place in the portfolio reveals a debt to Klinger.[23] Both the idea of ending the series with a metaphysical statement and the iconography of the etched plate itself allude to Klinger's cycle *Vom Tode, Erster Teil* (On Death, Part One) from 1889. Kollwitz's abandoned plate of a dead man stretched out Christ-like and flanked by two crucified women compares closely to Klinger's final image, entitled *Der Tod als Heiland* (Death as the Savior), in *On Death, Part One*. Similarly, the caption inscribed above Kollwitz's image, "O nation, you bleed from many wounds," echoes the text located above the outstretched dead man in Klinger's print: "We flee from the manner of death, not from death itself; for the goal of our highest desires is death." Thus, Kollwitz originally intended to use Klinger's successful formula in which specific events are combined with philosophic speculations. After realizing that it would drain her cycle of its immediacy and potency, she abandoned the idea.

Instead, she succeeded in developing a visual vocabulary that powerfully conveyed the universality and depth of human emotion that she sensed in all people. A comparison between *A Weavers' Revolt* and her second cycle *Bauernkrieg* (A Peasants' Revolt, Klipstein 94–98), published in 1908, reveals how she increasingly favored emotional impact over historical accuracy or narrative sequence. *A Peasants' Revolt* relates an event from the sixteenth century and its images are loosely derived from a literary source. Kollwitz centers her cycle around "Black Anna", a peasant woman who encouraged the revolt, as she was portrayed in Wilhelm Zimmermann's account of the uprising in *Allgemeine Geschichte des großen*

Bauernkrieges (A General History of the Great Peasants' War).[24] While retaining her use of chiaroscuro, so important in *A Weavers' Revolt*, Kollwitz concentrates in this series on the figures by giving them increased physical existence and by eliminating subsidiary details. In *Die Flüger* (The Ploughman, Klipstein 94), *Schlachtfeld* (Battlefield, Klipstein 96), *Vergewaltigt* (Raped, Klipstein 97), and *Beim Dengeln* (Whetting the Scythe, Klipstein 90) the printmaker pushes the isolated figure or figures to the front of the scene and communicates the intense emotions of rage, despair, and hatred by means of exaggerated gestures and poses. Through these formal means, the historical events become incidental to the expression of universal feelings of hopelessness and anger engendered by poverty, hunger, and violence.

While Kollwitz devoted herself to the etching technique, adapted to her critique of modern life, Munch developed his prints in an opposite direction, as exemplified in the 1880–89 cycle *Alpha und Omega* (Alpha and Omega, Schiefler 306–327). In this lithographic series of twenty-two images, Munch pursued subjective content and trance-like conditions which infer an inner mood or psychological state of mind. Drawing directly from Klinger's conception of the cycle as a summation of life's experiences while exploring the themes of Eros and Death, Munch offers a bitter satire about Alpha and Omega, the single human couple on an island inhabited by animals. Driven by her need to procreate, Omega seduces and has sexual intercourse with all the animals. The off-spring of these unions overpower Alpha and murder him. Alpha and Omega are fashioned after the original biblical couple, Adam and Eve, and Munch conceived the story as a parable

22. Ibid.

23. For a discussion of the cycle and a reproduction of the omitted image, see Otto Nagel, *Käthe Kollwitz* (Greenwich, Conn.: New York Graphic Society Ltd., 1963), 30.

24. Carey and Griffiths, *The Print in Germany*, 67.

of the unchanging relationship between Man and Woman.

The works of Kollwitz and Munch from this period exemplify Klinger's influential role in the authentication of the print cycle as a modern art form.[25] Yet the serial print was also indebted conceptually and formally to works published in the experimental illustrated journals of the 1890s, such as *Pan* (1895), *Simplicissimus* (1896), *Ver Sacrum* (1898), and *Deutsche Kunst und Dekoration* (1897). Artists and collectors became aware of the portfolio's synaesthetic possibilities through these and a growing number of other German periodicals devoted to the visual arts and culture. The publishers of these journals rejected the historical styles found in the many facsimile reproductions of the previous decade and promoted new modes of illustration. Thus Georg Hirth, who had been responsible in the 1880s for publications devoted to the reproduction of German Renaissance print cycles, began in 1896 the innovative journal *Jugend* that promoted contemporary graphics as an integral aspect of modern art. It was in the pages of *Jugend* (and *Pan*) that artists like Peter Behrens and Otto Eckmann first introduced title pages, border designs, innovative typefaces, vignettes, and fine art woodcuts. Both experimental and eclectic, *Jugend* and other newly-established journals attempted a synaesthetic approach in which text, typography, and illustration, and the style of these component elements were integrated into a unified whole.

Joseph Sattler's first cycle, produced in 1894 and consisting of thirteen prints, *Ein moderner Totentanz* (A Modern Dance of Death), likewise exemplifies the transition from historical imitation in the search for and definition of a new, inventive formal vocabulary. As a regular contributor to *Pan* and a book illustrator, Sattler made his reputation with an archaic drawing manner strongly reminiscent of works by the early German Renaissance artists Albrecht Dürer, Hans Baldung Grien, and Hans Holbein. In *Wurmstich* (Wormhole) from *A Modern Dance of Death*, Sattler presents a grim skeleton from which seals and keys dangle as he crosses over a row of medieval books.

Standing on sharply pointed stilts, he leaves a trail of worm-like holes in the pages of the manuscripts he treads over. Sattler alludes in this series of prints to his German artistic patrimony through an archaistic style based on Dürer and a theme popularized by Holbein. At the same time, he appealed to a contemporary audience through the invention of new, personal, visual conceptions of the macabre.[26]

The early print cycles produced by German Expressionist artists demonstrate how Jugendstil experiments gave rise to innovative publications. The Russian-born co-founder of Der Blaue Reiter (The Blue Rider), Wassily Kandinsky, composed *Gedichte ohne Worte* (Poems without Words) in 1903 to 1904; it constitutes the artist's first attempt to recreate a type of synaesthesia with pictures that—through a sequential rhythm—were meant to correspond to musical sounds. Conceptually, Kandinsky's cycle relates to Sattler's *Meine Harmonie* (My Harmony) from 1896[27] that employed specific colors in its compositional arrangement to register moods and notes from the musical scale. Kandinsky's woodcuts, which reverse the relationship between ground and objects, are stylistically indebted to the woodcuts of Felix Vallotton that were widely exhibited and published at the time in *Jugend* and *Pan*.[28] While Kandinsky's early cycle looks back to Jugendstil

25. The graphic cycles of Alfred Kubin likewise owe their debt to Klinger's work and advocacy of graphics as a means of exploring the realm of fantasy. See Hübscher's introduction to *Malerei und Zeichnung*, 8–9.

26. Sattler's cycle was enthusiastically received by Germans and foreigners alike. Printed in two editions by J.A. Stargardt of Berlin in 1894, the cycle was exhibited at the Paris salon, and, according to an 1894 review, published in England by H. Grevel & Co. in a limited edition of one hundred copies. See Charles Hiatt, "Joseph Sattler," *The International Studio* 4 (1894): 92–97, and Theodor Knorr, "Josef Sattler: Sein Leben und seine Kunst," *Elsaß-Lothringisches Jahrbuch* 11 (1932): 279–303.

27. An example of this cycle exists in the collection of the Museum für Kunst und Kunstgewerbe, Hamburg.

28. Vallotton's work, in fact, was exhibited at Kandinksy's *XI. Phalanx* exhibition of 1904, which was devoted to graphics. See *Die Kunst für Alle* 19 (June 1, 1904): 408, and Peg Weiss, *Kandinsky in Munich: The Formative Jugendstil Years* (Princeton, N.J.: Princeton University Press, 1979), 71.

printmaking, it also looks ahead to his more fully realized *Klänge* (Sounds), the 1912 album that combines poetry and woodcuts in an attempt to recreate without notes the sensation of a musical composition.

The 1905 print cycle *Idioten-Serie* (Idiot Series)[29] and *Zwei Menschen* (Two People) by Ernst Ludwig Kirchner, the co-founder of the Brücke (Bridge) group, derive as well from Jugendstil prototypes. The former series consists of seven woodcuts of portrait heads that resemble the caricature-like style of *Simplicissimus*, which he regularly studied.[30] The latter, comprised of seven woodcuts with title page and end plate, depicts the meeting, union, and eventual estrangement of a man and woman. *Two People* relates thematically to Klinger's pessimistic attitude to the relations between the sexes and Munch's *Alpha and Omega* series, while it adumbrates Kokoschka's lithographic cycle of 1916, *Der gefesselte Kolumbus* (Columbus Chained, cat. no. 3). Kirchner's use of black and white planar contrasts here relies on Vallotton's woodcut manner.

Brücke artists also drew on the cycle as a promotional device in their annual print portfolios, called *Jahresmappen*, published from 1906 to 1912 for distribution to their so-called passive members or subscribers.[31] Such use had previously been employed by the Jugendstil artists associated with the organ *Ver Sacrum*, who in 1902 designed the catalogue for the fourteenth Viennese Secession exhibition;[32] the catalogue consisted of woodcuts made by various contributors to the exhibition and was conceived as an extension of Klinger's three-dimensional *Gesamtkunstwerk* installation of architectural, sculptural, and painted elements dedicated to the great German Romantic composer Ludwig von Beethoven that formed the show's central exhibit. The catalogue paid tribute to Klinger's prints and cycles, but it also served as a portable promotional pamphlet for the contributing printmakers (as an extension beyond the physical restraints of the exhibition building).

What these and other early efforts in serial prints had in common was their experimentation with the cycle's ability to interact with other aesthetic forms, whether musical or literary, and to suggest the passage of time through the sequential viewing of multiple compositions. Taken together, these initial, experimental pictorial cycles with their linkage to dramatic, poetic, literary, historical, satirical, or musical forms anticipate the more fully realized portfolios that appeared after 1910. For instance, Emil Orlik executed a pictorial diary of his travels between 1896 and 1899 in the form of a portfolio called *Kleine Holzschnitte* (Small Woodcuts). Orlik published this collection of woodcuts as a permanent record of three years' daily life and customs of his native city Prague, the Slovak countryside, Holland, London, France, and England. Orlik's woodcuts look forward to Lovis Corinth's diaristic etching cycle, executed in 1919 and published the following year, entitled *Bei den Corinthern* (At the Corinths, cat. no. 4).

Although the illustrated journal, with its broad-based appeal, had provided a creative outlet for artists to experiment with the cyclical print format, official art world legitimacy and financial security for the portfolio were not attained until the art dealer, publisher, and museum director and curator concertedly promoted the serial print. Among the many artists who experimented with the serial print, Kollwitz is the only major artist who worked exclusively as a printmaker, and her consistent production of cycles at such an early date stands apart. More representative is the example of Lovis Corinth whose

29. Annemarie Dube and Wolf-Dieter Dube, *E.L. Kirchner: Das graphische Werk* (Munich: Prestel Verlag, 1967), nos. 2–8.

30. Observed by Hans Wentzel, "Zu den frühen Werken der 'Brücke'- Künstler," *Brücke-Archiv* I (1967): 16. Wentzel specifically compares Kirchner's work to Olaf Gulbransson's style.

31. Mentioned by Alexander Dückers in "Portfolios," *German Expressionist Prints and Drawings: The Robert Gore Rifkind Center for German Expressionist Studies,* 69.

32. *XIV. Ausstellung der Vereinigung Bilden der Künstler Österreichs Secession Wien, 1902 April–Juni* (Vienna: Ver Sacrum, V. Jahr [1902]). A copy of the catalogue is housed in the Robert Gore Rifkind Collection of the Los Angeles County Museum of Art.

cycle from 1893–94 *Tragikömodien* (Tragi-Comedies, Schwarz 5), which was possibly inspired by Klinger, appeared twenty years before his next two series of 1910 and 1911, both commissioned by Paul Cassirer,[33] *Das Buch Judith* (The Book of Judith, Schwarz L54) and *Das Hohe Lied* (The Song of Songs, Schwarz L82), respectively. Corinth's experience demonstrates the erratic use of cycles by artists before 1910 and suggests that this uneven output originated in part from the lack of a promotional vehicle. In 1905, Emil Nolde had produced his first etching cycle, titled *Fantasies*, while he was working in the Jugendstil, but he did not return to the print portfolio until 1917 in *Grotesques*.[34] Whereas Brücke artists were among the first to understand the cycle's potential for a wider audience and seized on the opportunity by serving as their own printer and publisher, in general, the exploration of the serial print by other artists remained fragmented as long as they lacked a promotional mechanism. It was the art dealer, later joined by the publisher, who served as a liaison between the artist and client. Acting as a broker in a new consumer-oriented market, the dealer fulfilled a role that the academies located in Germany's major urban centers refused to play: the dealer not only encouraged artists to create cycles, he in turn found an audience for them.

Movements such as the applied art workshop in Munich (constituted in 1898), the series of Secessions in Berlin, Dresden, Munich, and Vienna (comprised of artists exhibiting independent of officially sponsored exhibitions dominated by the academies in these cities), and independent artist associations had begun seriously to promote the print at the turn of the century. The Arts and Crafts artist-designers Peter Behrens and Otto Eckmann, for instance, produced woodcuts instead of paintings for inclusion in their unified decorative interiors. The Secessions sought to diversify the market for modern art by producing watercolors and prints to expand their exhibitions. For example, beginning in the winter of 1901 to 1902 the Berlin Secession held regular exhibitions devoted to graphics (*Schwarzweiß Ausstellungen*) as

one way of promoting the print as an important genre within the art they were championing. Individual societies of artists such as Phalanx, established by Kandinsky in 1901, displayed prints alongside paintings in their group exhibitions. Of course, commercial art galleries had existed in Germany before the end of the nineteenth century,[35] but they were not so much concerned with the definition as the commodification of aesthetic taste demanded by their clients.

By the turn of the century some collectors supported themselves by dealing in art; except for government commissions, the art gallery had almost completely replaced the patronage system with its direct artist–client relationship.[36] Fritz Gurlitt and Paul Cassirer epitomized the enterprising, innovative gallery owner in Germany who actively supported the graphic arts as an important medium in contemporary art. Cassirer, who opened his gallery in Berlin in 1898, assertively promoted contemporary paintings and graphics to his clientele. In defense of the modern art movement, he was the first to introduce to a German public French Impressionism and neo-Impressionism.[37] Playing an influential role in the

33. Alfred Kuhn, "Corinth als Graphiker," *Kunst und Künstler* 22 (1924): 205.

34. Nolde produced only one cycle between the years of 1905 and 1917, that of the woodcut portfolio *Zehn Holzschnitte* (Ten Woodcuts, Schiefler 6–15) from 1906.

35. Large-scale commercial dealings made their appearance later in Germany than in Holland, France, or England. Berlin had only a handful of galleries in the 1850s; Commeter in Hamburg was a long established firm. For an informative study of the early patronage and art dealing practices of Germany, see Lenman, "Painters, Patronage and the Art Market in Germany 1850–1914," 123–24.

36. Sebastian Müller, "Official Support and Bourgeois Opposition in Wilhelminian Culture," *The Divided Heritage: Themes and Problems in German Modernism*, ed. Irit Rogoff (Cambridge: Cambridge University Press, 1991), 175. For an in-depth discussion of the rise of the art dealer and development of a new patronage system, see Peter Paret, *The Berlin Secession: Modernism and its Enemies in Imperial Germany* (Cambridge, Mass.: Harvard University Press, 1980), and Nicolaas Teeuwisse, *Vom Salon zur Secession* (Berlin: Deutsche Verlag für Kunstwissenschaft, 1986) and "Bilder einer verschollenen Welt: Aufstieg und Niedergang der Berliner Privatsammlungen 1871–1933," *Der unverbrauchte Blick* (exh. cat.) (Berlin: Martin-Gropius-Bau, 1987), 13–39.

37. Ibid.

Berlin Secession and other artist societies, he educated his clientele about young artists and their work, and devoted exhibition space to the art of the print. He encouraged established artists like Corinth to make graphic cycles as a means of exposing their work to a larger audience. Others followed Cassirer's example, including Otto Dix's dealer Karl Nierendorf who suggested that Dix make a graphic cycle to publicize himself, resulting in the series *Der Krieg* (The War, cat. no. 9).

While Cassirer may be regarded as a pioneer, during the first decades of this century there began to be forged throughout Germany a new kind of relationship between the dealer of modern art, avant-garde artists, and a new collecting audience, and an integrated national (and international) art market began to develop.[38] In this context, the list of active dealers at the time included Hans Goltz and Emil Thannhauser in Munich, Commeter in Hamburg, Ernst Arnold and Emil Richter from Dresden, and Alfred Flechtheim from the Rhineland (Düsseldorf). Of special interest is the great publicist for German Expressionism, Herwarth Walden, who opened his Berlin gallery in 1912 two years after the first publication of his literary weekly, *Der Sturm*, which was devoted to literature, criticism, and the visual arts. Often the dealer and publisher of prints were the same individual, as in the case of Cassirer, who published Barlach's prints and cycles, and Fritz Gurlitt, who published Oskar Kokoschka's cycle *Columbus Chained* (cat. no. 3). In their promotion of the artists they represented, dealers regularly advertised graphic art exhibitions and the publication of new print cycles in contemporary art periodicals. In 1910, J. B. Neumann opened his Berlin gallery called Graphisches Kabinett solely for the display and sale of prints and later published over a third of Max Beckmann's work—including the portfolios *Die Hölle* (Hell, Hofmaier 139–149) and *Berliner Reise* (Berlin Journey, Hofmaier 212–222). Similarly Goltz, the Munich book dealer and gallery owner, acted as the publisher of several graphic cycles from 1910 to 1920. The Munich publisher Reinhard Piper played

the dual role of promoter and collector of Beckmann's prints. In conjunction with the art historian Julius Meier Graefe and the Marées-Gesellschaft (Marées Society), Piper published Beckmann's cycles *Gesichter* (Faces, Hofmaier 81, 84, 88–90, 105, 108, 126–137) and *Jahrmarkt* (Carnival, cat. no. 6) as well as Corinth's intaglio series *Antike Legende* (Ancient Legends, Schwarz 351).

The conditions created by the Industrial Revolution in Germany gave rise to a new art buying public as a corrollary to the advent of the new art dealer. The bourgeoisie expanded during the second half of the nineteenth century and included bankers, merchants, industrialists, higher civil servants, doctors, lawyers, and professors. Constituting a social entity bound together by the belief in freedom of production of goods and the exchange of these goods, this stratum of society saw itself as distinct from both the titled aristocracy, socially above them, and the lower middle class.[39] Historians have designated two groups within this class: the educated and professional *Bildungsbürgertum* who dominated during the first half of the nineteenth century and the monied, propertied *Besitzbürgertum* whose numbers increased with industrial expansion.[40]

While industrialization expanded the middle class, it also isolated the members of the bourgeoisie from one another as the work force shifted from the family as the unit of production to paid laborers gathered in shops and factories. Released from its economic function, the moderately well-to-do middle class family replaced labor with consumption as

38. Robin Lenman, "A Community in Transition: Painters in Munich, 1886–1924," *Central European History* 15 (March 1982): 14.

39. David Blackbourn and Richard J. Evans, eds., *The German Bourgeoisie: Essays on the Social History of the German Middle Class from the Late Eighteenth to the Early Twentieth Century* (London: Routledge, 1991), xiv–xv.

40. Ibid., xv.

the structural basis for its private life.[41] Increasingly the life of the family became more isolated not only from labor institutions but also from the public sphere. The social segregation and patterns of consumption within the middle class in late nineteenth-century Germany provide evidence for this process of polarization.[42] During the Wilhelmine era in Berlin, for example, elite businessmen relocated their families from houses near their factories to exclusive residences in the suburbs of the city. As this new economic class withdrew from the public life of the city, collecting art became a means to validate their position in society.[43] Toward the end of the century many wealthy businessmen began to acquire contemporary art in all its forms including prints. Among these are Eugen Gutmann (co-founder of Deutsche Bank), the banker Rudolf Mosse, the heavy industrialist Emil Kirdorff, and the politician and industrialist Wather Rathenau. In the early twentieth century the businessman Markus Kruss exclusively collected Brücke paintings and prints, and the Berlin manufacturer Bernhard Koehler centered his acquisitions on prints and paintings by members of Der Blaue Reiter.

Brücke's list of subscribers shows that many were located socially and economically within one or the other of the defined subsets of this new middle class, which clearly functioned as an important patron of German Expressionist graphics.[44] Although most, like Schiefler, were drawn from the professional classes, some such as the factory owner Karl M. Seifert came from the industrial sector. Still unusual for the period, a substantial part of Brücke's passive membership was composed of women, including the Jewish art historian Dr. Rosa Schapire; this aspect of the subscription roles provides compelling evidence that these patrons were newly empowered socially and financially.

Many of these collectors considered their activity as a sign of new-found prosperity but they also sought a shared experience with other like-minded members of their social and economic class through the acquisition of fine art.[45] Having come to be

regarded as a component of the developing modern art movement, the print cycle became a vehicle for the fragmented bourgeoisie to take an ideological stand against repressive official policies towards contemporary art. According to Peter Paret and, more recently, Sebastian Müller, state patronage did not look favorably upon modern art because it did not conform to an officially sanctioned idealistic view of how the German nation should be portrayed. For instance, Wilhelm I's Minister of Culture vetoed the jury's recommendation of awarding a prize to Kollwitz for her cycle *A Weavers' Revolt* because of her realistic depiction of the peasants' miseries.[46] Although many of the collectors from the bourgeois class, such as the Hagen banker Karl Ernst Osthaus, aligned themselves with nationalistic and conservative policies of the Kaiser, they nonetheless opposed the Emperor's restrictive attitude towards modern art. In their defense of the political principle of freedom, they equated the artist's freedom of expression to

41. Jürgen Habermas discusses the structural changes that produced the polarization of the public and private spheres by which the family became ever more private and the world of work and organization ever more public. The family was released from its economic task as labor shifted from within the home to the outside. Once the domain of private control, the work force moved to large industrial enterprises. When the world of work and organization was established as a sphere in its own right, the family's autonomy depended upon its function of consumption. Habermas states that "as a result there arose the illusion of an intensified privacy in an interior domain whose scope had shrunk to comprise the conjugal family only insofar as it constituted a community of consumers." See *The Structural Transformation of the Public Sphere*, 152 and 156.

42. See Dolores Augustine's study "Arriving in the Upper Class: The Wealthy Business Elite of Wilhelmine Germany," *The German Bourgeoisie*, 46–86.

43. Müller, "Official Support and Bourgeois Opposition in Wilhelminian Culture," 175.

44. Brücke's passive members included professional, educated, middle class men, such as the architects Bellmann, Wünsche, Bauer, and Schneidereit; the doctors Weiss, Waldstein, Thiele, Lippmann; and the professors Gussmann and Fehr. See the Brücke group's 1910 exhibition catalogue from the Galerie Arnold, an original example of which is in the collection of The Art Institute of Chicago.

45. Müller, "Official Support and Bourgeois Opposition in Wilhelminian Culture," 175.

46. Ibid., 165, and Paret, *The Berlin Secession*, 21

their own freedom of economic production. Just as they perceived themselves as pioneers of material production, the artist was the gatekeeper of the spiritual realm and human soul. For example, Osthaus, one of the most outstanding collectors and promoters of German Expressionist painting and graphics, called upon the middle class citizen to play an active role in supporting art at the opening of the Folkwang Museum in Essen in 1902. It was the cultural mission of the bourgeoisie, he (and others) argued, to protect artistic freedom and to integrate the spirituality embodied in aesthetic works into the social fabric of modern industrial life:

> The nineteenth century is the century of specialization. Through specialization a gap has come about in the world. Each person sits on his own branch and has no idea of the whole tree. Here is where art must come in and act as an intermediary, uniting and unleashing productive forces, and it must saturate every aspect of work. It appears as if one could no longer put any hope that such an effect will be achieved in people who primarily have been called upon to do this, that is, ruling sovereigns. And so industry must step into their place. Art must come out of the palaces and into industrial towns, and industry, which is already accustomed to working according to the laws of functionality, must be imbued with art.[47]

Osthaus called on the middle class collector to challenge the official, court taste of the Wilhelmine government. The middle class patron of the arts could assist, he asserted, in bringing together a divided, splintered society brought about by technological progress. The print cycle lent itself to this task.

The gap of almost twenty-five years between the date of the first cycle in this exhibition by Klinger (cat. no. 1) and the next, *Brücke VI* (Bridge VI) by Erich Heckel and Max Pechstein (cat. no. 2), accurately reflects the slow acceptance of the print portfolio by German society. Although artists explored the formal and iconographic possibilities of the cycle in the 1890s, they did not consistently

produce serial prints until after 1910 and often at the instigation and promotion of dealers and publishers. While a handful of artists such as Kirchner, Kokoschka, Kollwitz, Alfred Kubin, and Pechstein turned to it regularly before the First World War, others such as Beckmann, Corinth, Dix, and Grosz began to privilege it over painting only during and after the war (although Corinth stands somewhat apart in his prodigious output of paintings, drawings, *and* prints during the last five years of his life). From 1914 until the 20s the cycle increasingly became a favored format for a widening number of artists. It provided an effective means for artists to examine critically the social disasters induced by modern industrialization and mechanized warfare and to explore the attendant psychological repercussions on the human spirit. The print portfolio, as a visual discourse, rivalled the written word in its ability to convey an attitude, opinion, or subjective point of view. Artists employed it not merely to reflect upon the conditions of society but, like an essayist or journalist, to effect change through the assertion of a particular viewpoint. Indeed, from an early point in his career George Grosz saw himself as an artist and equally as a political satirist or social critic. Like Beckmann in his drypoint series *Carnival* (cat. no. 6), Grosz unmasked society's mores and exposed people's prejudices and self-delusions in his many prints, portfolios, and illustrated books from the 1920s. Motivated by the cycle's capacity to reach a widespread and diverse audience through its reproduction in editions, Grosz repudiated the notion of the unique masterpiece, and he conceived most of his cycles as photolithographs and offset lithographs—printing techniques identified with the commercial publishing world of books, journals, and newspapers.

The content of print cycles diversified after Klinger's initial experiments as artists incorporated an expanded program of subjects, themes, and personal perspectives into the production of ever increasing numbers of portfolios between 1910 and

47. Quoted in Müller, 188.

1930. For instance, Brücke artists used their annual print portfolios not only as a means to raise funds from their subscription supporters but also to share their primitivistic cultural ideas with a broad audience of collectors interested in modern art and culture. The *Lebensreform* (Reformative Living) movement in Germany and prevailing social attitudes towards youth and nudism, for instance, found their visual analogue in Brücke prints of nudes in the landscape (see cat. no. 2c).[48] Kokoschka saw the serial print as a means to express the fundamental antagonism between the sexes (see cat. no. 3). As Grosz's 1922 photolithographic series *Die Räuber* (The Robbers, cat. no. 7) demonstrates, through the support of sympathetic publishers, the print cycle became a means to circumvent state-controlled avenues of production and dissemination in the articulation of views that subverted or opposed mainstream attitudes.[49] Other printmakers, such as Rafaello Busoni in his inexpensive cycle *Börsentaumel* (Stock Market Frenzy, 1923, cat. no. 8) saw the serial print as a way to align themselves with one class while mocking another. Whereas Beckmann and Dix turned to the portfolio as a forum for their views on the dehumanizing effects of twentieth-century life, Corinth and Barlach, appealing to their viewers' patriotism, used it to invoke the spirituality that they perceived had existed in Germany's great literary and religious past (see cat. nos. 5 and 10). Likewise, the portfolio's affordability and potential for widespread distribution made it accessible to a large audience in an act of affirmation of class identity.

Anticipating certain current art films, attended by people who wish to affiliate themselves with a particular social or political view, the print cycle constituted a semi-private sphere for its liberal bourgeois audience. A product of the creative expression of the spirit, the print portfolio was recognized by the new middle class collector as the artistic counterpart to his own freedom of material means.

48.   These ideas were widely held by the middle class. Jill Lloyd relates the final three Brücke portfolios to the contemporary historical debate raging over the issue of "city versus country." See Lloyd, *German Expressionism: Primitivism and Modernity* (New Haven, Conn.: Yale University Press, 1991), 106–10.

49.   Grosz was brought to trial for his anti-military portfolio *Gott mit Uns* (God is with Us, 1920) which resulted in a fine of 300 marks and the destruction of the printing plates by the police. Later, his portfolio *Ecce Homo* of 1923 led to trial for obscenity and a fine of 6,000 marks. See Uwe M. Schneede, *George Grosz: The Artist in His Society*, trans. Robert and Rita Kimber (Woodbury, N.Y.: Barron's Educational Series, 1985), 107–108, and Carey and Griffiths, *The Print in Germany*, 181.

INTERMEZZO
ADAM UND EVA UND TOD UND TEUFEL

Cat. no. 1i

Cat. no. 1m

Cat. no. 2b

E Heckel 10

Cat. no. 2c

E Heckel 10

Cat. no. 2d

11/70   VIII

Cat. no. 9r

10/70

Cat. no. 9gg

10/70   II

Cat. no. 9m

10/70

Cat. no. 9uu

Notes on the catalogue

The catalogue consists of ten essays, one for each portfolio arranged chronologically according to the original publication date, together with illustrations of each folio. These are followed by comprehensive catalogue entries detailing the contents of each portfolio, including folio and wraparound paper covers, introductory texts, colophon pages (where relevant), and prints. Inside the cover, if extant, the print folios are ordered according to the original sequence, as can be reconstructed from contents pages or inscriptions, sometimes with reference to catalogues raisonnés. In the case of a discrepancy, the contents page has been followed.

The catalogue was researched and compiled by Richard A. Born and Stephanie D'Alessandro. Each portfolio has been assigned a number (1–10) based on chronological sequence. The individual parts of the portfolio are identified by this number, followed by a letter from the alphabet (a–z, and then aa–zz, if necessary). Each entry begins with general information about the artist, portfolio contents, publication history, and museum/lender identification. This is followed by the print entries. Unless noted under individual entries, the medium and paper type described in the general heading apply throughout the portfolio. Dates of the individual prints are the same as those described in the general entry, unless stated otherwise.

Dimensions are in inches followed by centimeters. Height precedes width. Many sheets are irregular; the measurements given are the maximum sizes. States are indicated by Roman numerals, for example, I/II means the first of two states. All annotations, inscriptions, and signatures are in pencil, unless otherwise noted. The following abbreviations are used: f. for folio, r. for recto, v. for verso, l.l. for lower left, l.c. for lower center, l.r. for lower right, u.l. for upper left, u.c. for upper center, u.r. for upper right, ed. for edition, cat. no. for catalogue number, cat. nos. for catalogue numbers, acc. no. for accession number, acc. nos. for accession numbers.

English titles in the catalogue have been provided by Reinhold Heller, Stephanie D'Alessandro, and Richard A. Born. In some instances, especially when the print is commonly known in English by another name, the alternate translation has been adhered to, for example, in the case of the catalogue raisonné entries for George Grosz's *Die Räuber* (The Robbers). Translations from the German in the essays are by Robin Reisenfeld; the initial citation of a work in an essay gives the German with English in parentheses; subsequent references are in English.

Eine Liebe (Opus X)
A Love (Opus X)

1887

Max Klinger, who initiated the modern graphic art movement in Germany, was the first major late nineteenth-century artist to regard prints as an integral part of his oeuvre. Klinger articulated his position on graphics within the visual arts in his 1891 treatise *Malerei und Zeichnung* (Painting and Drawing), in which he assigned a specific role to the print medium distinct from painting. Presenting a theoretical defense for the autonomy of the graphic arts, he promoted the status of the medium from a reproductive practice to an aesthetic form equal to, but different from, painting. In his belief that painting left nothing to the imagination, the artist assigned a twofold task to the "black and white" arts: to penetrate the subjective world of fantasy and, with the successive and narrative potential of print cycles, to explore a world view or *Weltanschauung*.[1]

According to Klinger, painting and sculpture, or works in color as he referred to them, were capable of rendering the physical world in a harmonic manner, through the avoidance of any reference to violence and passion. Collaterally, the artist assigned the depiction of the darker side of life to the graphic arts:

> The difference between the painter and the draftsman cannot be more sharply defined. The former depicts form, expression, color in a purely objective manner . . . the draftsman, in contrast, looks eternally at the unfilled holes, the yearned-for and the barely attainable; his is a personal coming to terms with a world of irreconcilable powers. Optimism speaks from the work of the painter, the enjoyment of the

world . . . the draftsman cannot escape his more negative vision, beyond appearances . . .[2]

By linking the reality that lay beneath surface appearances to an artist's unspoken thoughts, he argued for the capacity of the graphic arts to articulate the artist's most intimate feelings, to depict what "he [the artist] sees, to give what he feels."[3] For Klinger, then, the "foremost characteristic of drawing" is the "strong subjectivity of the artist. It is his world and his outlook that he represents, and they are his personal observations of the occurrences around him and in him . . ."[4] Furthermore, Klinger asserted that the art-

1. Max Klinger, *Malerei und Zeichnung: Tagebuchaufzeichnungen und Briefe*, ed. Anneliese Hübscher (Leipzig: Verlag Philipp Reclam, 1985), 34–37, with an informative introduction by Anneliese Hübscher. For a synopsis of Klinger's essay, see Waltraut Neuerburg, "Neubewertung der Graphik und des graphischen Zyklus in Deutschland unter Max Klinger," in "Der Graphische Zyklus im deutschen Expressionismus und seine Typen, 1905–1925" (Ph.D. diss., Bonn, Rheinischen Friederich-Wilhelms-Universität, 1976), 31–37 and Heidi Roch, "Das Problem des Zyklus in Klingers Graphik," in *Max Klinger* (exh. cat.) (Bielefeld: Kunsthalle Bielefeld, 1976), 209–18. A good, recent study of the artist is found in Alexander Dückers, *Max Klinger* (Berlin: Rembrandt Verlag, 1976).

2. "Schärfer kann der Gegensatz zwischen dem Maler und Zeichner nicht ausgesprochen werden. Jener bildet Form, Ausdruck, Farbe nach in rein objectiver Weise, . . . Der Zeichner dagegen steht vor den ewig unausgefüllten Lücken . . . dem Ersehnten und dem Erreichbaren, und es bleibt ihm nichts als ein persönliches Abfinden mit der Welt unvereinbarer Kräfte. Aus den Werken des einen spricht der Optimismus, der Genuß der Welt . . . Unter dem Drucke der Vergleiche, des Schauens über die Formen hinaus kann sich der andere des verneinenden Betrachtens nicht entziehen." Klinger, *Malerei und Zeichnung*, 44.

3. "Zu empfinden, was er sieht, zu geben, was er empfindet." Ibid., 33.

4. "Der hervorragendste Charakterzug der Zeichnung . . . die starke Subjektivität des Künstlers. Es ist seine Welt und seine Anschauung, die er darstellt, es sind seine persönlichen Bemerkungen zu den Vorgängen um ihn und in ihm . . ." Ibid., 37.

ist's ability to express his subjective outlook was enhanced by the print's potential seriality when several or many different compositions are gathered thematically into a loose-leaf portfolio. In its capacity for programmatic statements, the graphic cycle was the ideal means, following Klinger's reasoning, to explore the artist's critical and imaginative views of the world in a narrative, episodic sequence. As he states, the artist could associate freely and develop "in quick secession a piece of life in all of its manifestations. It may expand epically; may intensify dramatically; it may look at us in dry irony. Being only shadows it even grasps the uncanny without being repellent."[5]

Even before Klinger had formally formulated his theoretical position, he had experimented with the print's specific nature through his graphic series. Klinger had produced eleven of his fourteen completed cycles before the publication of his treatise in 1891. In each cycle the artist explores a different way of employing its programmatic feature. For example, his earliest portfolio, *Ein Handschuh* (A Glove, 1881), unfolds in a trance-like sequence of events that evokes a subjective or psychological state of mind. Klinger turns the lost glove in the print series into a fetishistic object fraught with violent subconscious sexual longings and fantasies. The first two plates, entitled *Ort* (Place) and *Handlung* (Action), introduce the dream that constitutes the rest of the series. In *Action,* a man picks up the lost glove dropped by an attractive woman who is skating away in the distance. In the third image, *Wünsche* (Yearnings), the man is in bed with head buried in his hands as he suffers agonizing carnal desire. The glove lies beneath him on the blanket, and the object of his longing stands beneath a fruit tree in the distance. Later in the series, the composition titled *Entführung* (Abduction) illustrates the man's violent succumbing to his desires. Here Klinger shows a crustaceous, bat-like creature escaping with the glove through a broken window; the winged creature flying above opened magnolia blossoms suggests sexual consummation. Equating sexual lust with the man's animal desires,

Klinger uses the prehistoric creature as a symbol of man's primal nature.

In other cyclical works, such as his 1889 *Vom Tode, Erster Teil* (On Death, Part One), Klinger offers a philosophical discourse on the theme of death. *On Death, Part One* comments on the way death comes in unexpected forms and uses the theme to provide an overriding order to otherwise unrelated images. In *Der Tod als Heiland* (Death as Savior), Klinger divides the image into picture and frame, thereby amplifying the work's contents by the introduction of a second order of meaning. In the central scene, a group of figures in classical garb flees while a lone man kneels before the apparition of Death. In the margins are scenes of sexual violation: at the lower right, a woman resists the grasp of a giant beast—part human, part toad—while at the left, another woman is raped by a giant lobster. Once again, Klinger expresses his conviction that physical love and death are interwoven within psychic life.

Eine Liebe (Opus X) (A Love [Opus X]) examines the clash between emotion and desire and social convention in late nineteenth-century European society. Conceiving the series in musical terms in ten instead of twelve plates as originally intended, Klinger emphasizes the non-verbal nature of his "text". By incorporating elements of a musical composition into his cycle, Klinger creates a language of sentiment or sensation. With Eros presented as the central theme, *A Love (Opus X)* recounts the events of an illicit relationship between a man and a woman, each presumably of high bourgeois origins: the encounter, its consummation, the woman's pregnancy and shame, her death, and the lover's belated acknowledgement of grief and responsibility.

The cycle is dedicated to the Swiss artist Arnold Böcklin (1827–1901). The etched and engraved plate on the dedication page (cat. no. 1d) locates Klinger's personal discourse without text within a larger artis-

---

5. "...im schnellen Wechsel ein Stück Leben mit allen uns zugänglichen Eindrücken. Sie mögen sich episch ausbreiten, dramatisch sich verschärfen, mit trockener Ironie uns anblicken: nur Schatten, ergreifen sie selbst das Ungeheuerliche, ohne anzustoßen." Ibid.

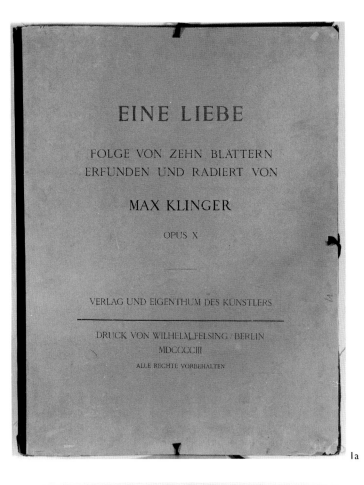

EINE LIEBE

FOLGE VON ZEHN BLÄTTERN
ERFUNDEN UND RADIERT VON

MAX KLINGER

OPUS X

_____

VERLAG UND EIGENTHUM DES KÜNSTLERS

DRUCK VON WILHELM FELSING / BERLIN
MDCCCCIII
ALLE RECHTE VORBEHALTEN

1a

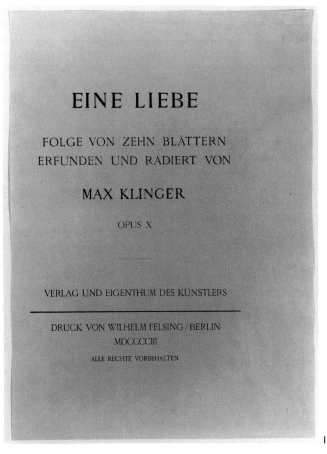

EINE LIEBE

FOLGE VON ZEHN BLÄTTERN
ERFUNDEN UND RADIERT VON

MAX KLINGER

OPUS X

_____

VERLAG UND EIGENTHUM DES KÜNSTLERS

DRUCK VON WILHELM FELSING / BERLIN
MDCCCCIII
ALLE RECHTE VORBEHALTEN

1b

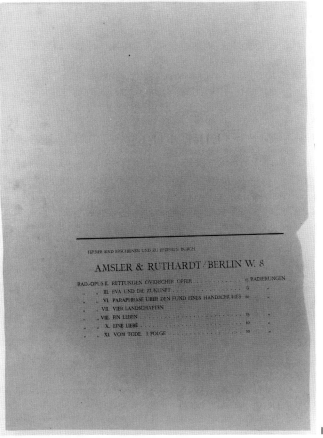

FERNER SIND ERSCHIENEN UND ZU BEZIEHEN DURCH

AMSLER & RUTHARDT / BERLIN W. 8

RAD.-OPUS II. RETTUNGEN OVIDISCHER OPFER . . . . 15 RADIERUNGEN
„ III. EVA UND DIE ZUKUNFT . . . . 6 „
„ VI. PARAPHRASE ÜBER DEN FUND EINES HANDSCHUHES 10 „
„ VII. VIER LANDSCHAFTEN . . . . „
„ VIII. EIN LEBEN . . . . 15 „
„ X. EINE LIEBE . . . . 10 „
„ XI. VOM TODE. I. FOLGE . . . . 10 „

1c

EINE LIEBE

INHALT

WIDMUNG – BEGEGNUNG – AM THOR – KUSS – NACHT
INTERMEZZO – NEUE TRÄUME – ERWACHEN
SCHANDE – TOD

1c

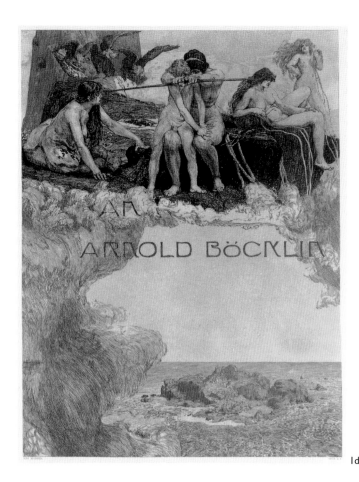

1d

1e

tic framework and offers the viewer a gradual transition from the outside world into the imaginative realm of the artist. The central allegorical group—the goddess of Fate teaching a youth to shoot an arrow—may be an autobiographic allusion to Böcklin's influence on Klinger: in their art, both artists combined classical imagery in unsettling juxtapositions, and here Klinger suggests that Böcklin's example served as an inspiration for his own fantasies. As in *A Glove*, Klinger establishes the theme of the pictorial narrative in the first two plates of the series. In the first, *Eine Bewegungen* (First Encounter, cat. no. 1e), Klinger defines place and context by the accretion of signifying motifs: from a thicket of dense foliage, a man spies an unaccompanied woman in an open carriage riding through the park; the screen of vegetation enclosing the pair suggests fertility and hints at the tragic consequences of their chance encounter. Klinger fills the foreground with unopened rosebuds—symbols of the woman's sexual potential —and he alludes to the man's sexual arousal through upright chestnut blossoms. The two potential lovers

are separated by a bush, in this context a metaphor for their as yet unconsummated love.

In *Am Thor* (At the Gate, cat. no. 1f), Klinger obliquely refers to the man's shedding of social conventions as he is driven by instinctual forces by the loss of his hat while kissing the woman's hand.[6] The woman appears at an open gate ornamented with a reptilian dragon, another allusion to physical love. Finally, Klinger makes explicit the charged erotic atmosphere by once again depicting a tree with erect chestnut blossoms thrusting through a dense foliage.

The couple embraces passionately beneath a large tree in the next plate in the series, called *Im Park* (In the Park, cat. no. 1g). The folds of the woman's dress are reminiscent of the rosebud petals in *First Encounter*, while the man's legs merge with the trunk of the tree. Playing on opposites, such as light and dark, or rounded and straight shapes, Klinger equates such pairings with the feminine and mas-

6. This is an observation by Elizabeth Streichner in an English summary of the cycle; see J. Kirk Varnedoe and Elizabeth Streichner, *Graphic Works of Max Klinger* (New York: Dover Publications, Inc., 1977), 85.

culine principles. Below the couple in the lower right is a stream with an empty boat and paddle, a motif that may be understood as the harbinger of their barren union with the passage of time. In the next scene, *Glück* (Happiness, cat. no. 1h), the two lay in an amorous embrace on a bed revealed by the light of the moon.[7] Beyond, the landscape opens into a garden and lake encircled by a white colonnade. The open blossoms on the flowering tree symbolically attest to the couple's consummated love.

Pausing with a philosophical reflection on the previous sequence of events, Klinger abruptly breaks the lyrical tempo of the love theme in the following plate, *Intermezzo* (cat. no. 1i). The artist encapsulates in one allegorical image the overall program of the cycle. With Schopenhauerian pessimism he foretells the woman's eventual death because of her sinful indulgence. Latin and German inscriptions below an unclothed male and female couple kneeling on a rocky shore proclaim: "Motto: Illico post coitum cachinnus auditur diaboli. / Intermezzo / Adam und Eva und Tod und Teufel" [Motto: Just after coitus, the

cackling of the devil is heard. / Intermezzo / Adam and Eve and Death and Devil].[8] The identification of the nude couple as Adam and Eve transposes Klinger's late nineteenth-century bourgeois story in the first four plates of the cycle into the biblical and transcendent historic framework of the first earthly couple (Gen: 2:7–3:24). The frail, naked pair bows in supplication to robed and masked Death, who points an accusatory finger towards the woman, while the Devil who clutches a sealed scroll looks on. Unlike later Expressionist graphic cycles, for example by Oskar Kokoschka (see cat. no. 3), that associate women with death and emphasize the battle of the sexes, Klinger's print series focuses on the conflict between human desire and social strictures and obligations.[9]

---

7. The image of the moon as a negative symbol is traditional and appears in other German prints from the period; see the entry for cat. no. 6.

8. Ibid.

9. Neuerburg, "Neubewertung der Graphik," 122–23.

1h

1j

See color plate 1i

1k

1l

See color plate 1m

The next image *Neue Träume von Glück* (New Dreams of Happiness, cat. no. 1j), reestablishes the love theme, but in a more meditative mood. While the woman is completely absorbed in her physical union with her partner, the man looks up into a mirror that reflects his visage—a conventional formal device for intellectual self-realization and the transiency of life. A winged angel pulls them along in an upward sweeping motion. The woman has relinquished herself to the man, placing complete faith in him, while he follows the angel's call that will lead to her death. In the subsequent image, *Erwachen* (Awakening, cat. no. 1k), the title refers not only to the woman's disturbed sleep but also to her awakening from an illusory love. She sits up in bed and looks towards the apparition of a fetus surrounded by a glowing light; between them a window, much narrower than the one in *New Dreams of Happiness,* opens onto a barren landscape and empty sky. The woman realizes that she is pregnant.

Klinger initially conceived *A Love (Opus X)* as a sequel to his 1883 print cycle *Dramen* (Dramas).[10] The latter presents a critique of nineteenth-century society and its lack of compassion towards women. With *A Love (Opus X)* Klinger shifts focus to represent a personal tragedy in which society is indicated less directly.[11] Nevertheless, in *Schande* (Shame, cat. no. 1l) the artist suggests the cruelty inflicted upon the woman as she appears abandoned by her lover. Passing beneath a mocking crowd, the woman, accompanied only by her guilt in the guise of her shadow, is no longer dressed elegantly but in plain clothes. Klinger uses the compositional arrangement, as well as the aquatint's tonal values, to reinforce her sense of isolation. A sunlit wall separates her and contrasts sharply with the shaded throng above. The woman is accompanied only by her guilt, or shame, which Klinger indicates is a psychic apparition through the figure's shadowless, weightless appearance. Adhering to the specific demands of the etching technique, Klinger communicates to his audience the substance

of the cycle's theme. With *Tod* (Death, cat. no. 1m), Klinger concludes his cycle. Death appears again, emerging from the dark shadows, holding the stillborn child in one hand while his outstretched arm summons the dying or dead woman. Her lover lays his head against hers in sorrow and remorse.

While Klinger's symbolism may appear contrived to today's viewer, his treatise and works provided powerful, liberating examples for other artists to emulate.[12] For example, the combination of subtle textural effects in the aquatint and gruesome content in *Death* is a visual device that Otto Dix would introduce in his 1924 intaglio print cycle *Der Krieg* (The War, see cat. no. 9) as a means to accentuate the macabre. Later artistic groups, such as the Expressionists in Germany and the Surrealists in Belgium and France, as well as artist contemporaries of Klinger as different in approach as the Symbolist Edvard Munch and the Social Realist Käthe Kollwitz, were influenced by Klinger's writings and works. Indeed Munch's and Kollwitz's oeuvres point to the opposing directions that Klinger assigned to the graphic arts. On the one hand, Munch promoted the print's capacity for subjective content and trance-like conditions, in which inner moods or psychological states predominate; on the other, Kollwitz pursued the suitability of printmaking in her lifelong critique of modern life through unequivocal scenes of poverty and the destruction of humanity brought about by national wars and peasant uprisings, past and present.

10. As recorded by H.H. Meier; see Hans W. Singer, *Klingers Radierungen: Stiche und Steindrucke* (New York: Martin Gordon, Inc., 1978), 61–62.

11. Varnedoe and Streichner, *Graphic Works of Max Klinger,* 84–85.

12. Klinger's influence is summarized in the introduction to Frances Carey and Antony Griffiths, *The Print in Germany 1880–1933: The Age of Expressionism* (New York: Harper & Row, 1984), 11–13. For a comparison between Klinger's *A Love (Opus X)* and Munch's work, see Reinhold Heller, *Edvard Munch: The Scream, Art in Context* (New York: Viking Press, Inc., 1973), 40–45. See also Neuerburg, "Neubewertung der Graphik," 120–22.

Max Klinger
German, 1857–1920

Eine Liebe (Opus X) (A Love [Opus X])
Portfolio of ten prints, two loose sheets
(title, content, and publisher pages),
with original cover (fourth edition)

Medium: etching, engraving, etching
with aquatint

Ink: brown

Paper: English etching paper (prints)
and two text pages on Velin

Publisher and Publication Date:
Max Klinger, 1907 (fourth edition, first
published 1887)

Printer: Wilhelm Felsing, Berlin

Reference: Singer 157–166

The David and Alfred Smart Museum
of Art, Purchase, Unrestricted Funds
Acc. nos. 1983. 49a–m

1a
Cover
Tan paper board with linen binding,
    brown and black typeset titles on
    front
Format: 27^1/$_4$ × 21 (69.2 × 53.3)(closed)
1983.49k

1b
Title Page
Brown and black typeset on Velin
Sheet: 26^5/$_8$ × 19^3/$_8$ (67.6 × 49.2)
1983.49l

1c
Contents Page (*recto*)
Publisher's List of Portfolios by Klinger
    (*verso*)
Black typeset on Velin
Sheet: 26^{11}/$_{16}$ × 19^5/$_8$ (67.8 × 49.8)
1983.49m

1d
Widmung (Dedication)
Etching and engraving
Sheet: 27^1/$_{16}$ × 20^5/$_{16}$ (68.7 × 51.6)
Plate: 17^9/$_{16}$ × 13^5/$_8$ (44.6 × 33.6)
Inscribed in plate:
    AN ARNOLD BÖCKLIN
Inscribed, l.l. and l.r. in plate:
    MAX KLINGER, and *OPUS X, 1.*
Singer 157
1983.49a

1e
Erste Begegnung (First Encounter)
Etching, engraving, and aquatint
Sheet: 27 × 20^3/$_8$ (68.6 × 51.8)
Plate: 17^1/$_4$ × 10^3/$_8$ (43.8 × 26.4)
Inscribed, l.l. and l.r. in plate:
    MAX KLINGER, and *OPUS X, 2.*
Singer 158
1983.49b

1f
Am Thor (At the Gate)
Etching and engraving
Sheet: 27^1/$_{16}$ × 20^5/$_{16}$ (68.7 × 51.6)
Plate: 17^5/$_8$ × 12^3/$_4$ (44.8 × 31)
Inscribed, l.l. and l.r. in plate:
    MAX KLINGER, and *OPUS X, 3.*
Singer 159
1983.49c

1g
Im Park (In the Park)
Etching and engraving
Sheet: 27^1/$_{16}$ × 20^3/$_8$ (68.7 × 51.8)
Plate: 17^9/$_{16}$ × 10^5/$_8$ (44.6 × 27)
Inscribed, l.l. and l.r. in plate:
    MAX KLINGER, and *OPUS X, 4.*
Singer 160
1983.49d

1h
Glück (Happiness)
Etching, engraving, and aquatint
Sheet: 27^1/$_{16}$ × 20^5/$_{16}$ (68.7 × 51.6)
Plate: 17^5/$_8$ × 12^1/$_4$ (44.8 × 31.1)
Inscribed, l.l. and l.r. in plate:
    MAX KLINGER, and *OPUS X, 5.*
Singer 161
1983.49e

1i
Intermezzo
Etching and engraving
Sheet: 20^5/$_{16}$ × 27^1/$_{16}$ (51.6 × 68.7)
Plate: 9^5/$_8$ × 17^{13}/$_{16}$ (24.4 × 45.7)
Inscribed, l.l. and l.r. in plate:
    MAX KLINGER, and *OPUS X, 6.*
Singer 162
1983.49f

1j
Neue Träume von Glück (New Dreams
    of Happiness)
Etching and engraving
Sheet: 27^1/$_{16}$ × 20^5/$_{16}$ (68.7 × 51.6)
Plate: 17^9/$_{16}$ × 13^{11}/$_{16}$ (44.6 × 34.8)
Inscribed, l.l. and l.r. in plate:
    MAX KLINGER, and *OPUS X, 7.*
Singer 163
1983.49g

1k
Erwachen (Awakening)
Etching and engraving
Sheet: 27^1/$_{16}$ × 20^5/$_{16}$ (68.7 × 51.6)
Plate: 17^5/$_8$ × 12^3/$_8$ (44.8 × 31)
Inscribed, l.l. and l.r. in plate:
    MAX KLINGER, and *OPUS X, 8.*
Singer 164
1983.49h

1l
Schande (Shame)
Etching, engraving, and aquatint
Sheet: 27 × 20^3/$_8$ (68.6 × 51.8)
Plate: 17^{11}/$_{16}$ × 12^1/$_8$ (44.9 × 30.8)
Inscribed, l.l. and l.r. in plate:
    MAX KLINGER, and *OPUS X, 9.*
Singer 165
1983.49i

1m
Tod (Death)
Etching, engraving, and aquatint
Sheet: 20^5/$_{16}$ × 27 (51.6 × 68.7)
Plate: 12^5/$_{16}$ × 17^3/$_4$ (31.3 × 45.1)
Inscribed, l.l. and l.r. in plate:
    MAX KLINGER, and *OPUS X, 10.*
Singer 166
1983.49j

ERICH HECKEL and MAX PECHSTEIN

Brücke VI Bridge VI

1911

Brücke VI (Bridge VI) is the only example in the exhibition of a portfolio produced by the collaboration of two artists. Created by Max Pechstein and Erich Heckel, it embodies the ideological program and aesthetic practices of an entire artist group known as Künstlergruppe Brücke (Bridge Artists' Group).[1] From 1906 to 1912, "active" members published annual portfolios of prints or *Jahresmappen* for their subscribers, whom they called "passive" members, for the price of 12–25 German marks.[2] Brücke artists not only conceived their annual print portfolios as a means to raise funds but also as a promotional publication to develop an audience without relying on the normal commercial venues of the art gallery and annual group shows of academic institutions. Circumventing these accepted means of production and dissemination, the Brücke group acted as its own printer, publisher, and promoter. The annual portfolios helped establish a widely-dispersed community of supporters and collectors beyond the confines of Brücke's artist commune and intimate circle of artists and friends. Until 1908, each year's portfolio contained an arbitrary selection of graphics made by different Brücke artist members, but between 1909 and 1912 the group reorganized their annual portfolio into a more systematic format:[3] each portfolio consisted of an individual wrapper with the title and design contributed by one member and a group of original prints executed by another Brücke artist contained in the paper "folder". This change signaled a growing stylistic maturity of individual artists within the communal association. At the same time, by using two artists, the portfolio's cooperative structure acknowledged the group dy-

namic that fueled their respective individual styles.

This collective working method began in 1905 when the artists first met. One of their initial joint efforts was the illustrated manuscript titled "Odi Profanum."[4] Passed among the artists, it recorded their common experiences and thoughts in the form of a communal diary. While "Odi Profanum" served as a stimulus for their collective working method, weekly evening figure-drawing classes, begun in the fall of 1905, institutionalized the practice.[5] Drawing from the female nude in fifteen-minute sessions, Fritz Bleyl, Heckel, Ernst L. Kirchner, Karl Schmidt-

1. The example of *Bridge VI* from the Marcia and Granvil Specks Collection is especially noteworthy for the quality of its printing and condition, and is historically interesting since it was originally owned by Brücke artist Karl Schmidt-Rottluff and formed a part of his estate.

2. Mentioned by Alexander Dückers in "Portfolios," *German Expressionist Prints and Drawings: The Robert Gore Rifkind Center for German Expressionist Studies* (Los Angeles and Munich: Los Angeles County Museum of Art and Prestel Verlag, 1989), 69.

3. For a recent assessment of the historical importance of the annual portfolios as collective cycles, see Stephan von Wiese, "Die Jahresmappen der Künstlergruppe Brücke als kollektiver Zyklus," in Magdalena M. Moeller, ed., *Die Jahresmappen der "Brücke" — 1906–1912* (Berlin: Brücke-Archiv Heft 17, 1989), 32–40. See also Wallraf-Richartz-Museum, *Maler suchen Freunde: Jahresmappen, Plakate und andere werbende Graphik der Künstlergruppe Brücke* (exh. cat.) (Cologne: Wallraf-Richartz-Museum, 1971) for a reconstruction of the chronology of Brücke's promotional graphics.

4. Existing today only in fragments, the book is discussed in Beat Stutzer, "Das Stammbuch 'Odi Profanum' der Künstlergruppe 'Brücke'," *Zeitschrift des Deutschen Vereins für Kunstwissenschaft* 36 (1982): 87–105, and in Leopold Reidemeister, *Künstlergruppe Brücke: Fragment eines Stammbuches mit Beiträgen von Ernst Ludwig Kirchner, Fritz Bleyl und Erich Heckel* (Berlin: Mann, 1975).

5. See Robin Reisenfeld, "The Revival of the Woodcut in Germany, 1890–1920" (forthcoming Ph.D. dissertation, Chicago, Department of Art, The University of Chicago).

Rottluff, and, later, Pechstein translated their sketches into woodcuts with shared technical and stylistic innovations. They subsequently published graphic portfolios in a group format in recognition of this communal activity. Although they were not the first group of artists to publish a yearly portfolio of prints,[6] the idea does not seem to have been borrowed but to have evolved out of their own working routine.

Fashioning themselves after the medieval guild system and nineteenth-century artist groups such as the German Romantic Nazarenes, Brücke built a self-sustaining community whose members shared each other's work, models, property, and even thoughts in a communal diary. The group's restoration of a pre-industrial social and working structure was a rejection of the segmentation bound to modern urban society and industrialized mass production, and a link to their German cultural heritage. But while the members placed a high value on shared production as part of their ideological code, they emphasized equally the importance of artistic autonomy and individuality. Their use of different graphic media stressed handcraftmanship, irregularity, and the idiosyncratic; by exploiting the inherent properties of the woodcut, lithography, and a variety of intaglio processes, they emphasized the artistry of their prints and the independence of their graphic work from nature, in order to declare their role as producers of fine art. This agenda of shared community values and individual autonomy was ultimately contradictory, and the ideological friction it engendered contributed to the demise of the association in 1912.[7]

As one of the earliest *Mappen* dedicated to the prints of one member of the group, the sixth Brücke portfolio successfully sustains this tension between structural organization and aesthetic values. While the overall grouping of works identifies Heckel within the group dynamic, the individual prints are excellent examples of his first mature style. Appropriately, the title cover (a black-inked woodcut printed on dark blue paper), which was designed by Max Pechstein, depicts a kneeling nude woman prof-

fering a bowl of fruit (cat. no. 2a). Pechstein's image alludes to earlier woodcuts of the same nude model by Heckel,[8] and as the introductory image on the wrapper of the portfolio, it refers to the previous woodcut cover by Heckel entitled *Fränzi* (Dube 177) that had been designed for the catalogue of the exhibition held at the Galerie Arnold in 1910.[9] Fränzi was the adolescent orphan frequently used as a model by Brücke artists in 1910 and 1911, and in Heckel's woodcut cover she is seen awkwardly holding a doll in her lap; Heckel's image symbolized not only the young girl's emerging sexuality but also the artistic group's growing creative powers. Like the artists of Brücke entering their first creative maturity, the girl signals an as yet uncertain future.[10] Whereas Heckel's earlier woodcut points to the aesthetic evolution of the group, Pechstein's image of a full-breasted young woman acknowledges the coming-of-age of Heckel's style.

Using this subject to draw attention to Heckel and the group, Pechstein asserts his own identity through compositional arrangement and stylistic features. The most academically trained member of the group, he retained a more conventional pictorial structure in the symmetry and axial alignment of the nude in the composition. This arrangement is reinforced by the double crescent-shaped configuration that echoes the oval form of the bowl. Manipulating the woodcut technique, he creates a rough-hewn textural pattern

6. For example, *Die Gesellschaft für Vervielfältigende Kunst* (The Society for Reproductive Art) in Vienna, an affiliate of the Viennese Secession movement, issued annual portfolios of original graphics from 1898 to 1903.

7. An account of the ideological notions underlying their communal organization is given in Reinhold Heller, "*Die Brücke* at Cornell," *Art Forum* 8 (May 1970): 39–43.

8. Wiese compares Pechstein's nude to Heckel's *Liegenden* (Nude Lying) of 1909, in "Die Jahresmappen der Künstlergruppe Brücke," 39.

9. Heckel's woodcut was, in turn, based on Kirchner's poster design for the exhibition. An original example of the catalogue is in the print and drawing department of the Art Institute of Chicago.

10. Noted in Reinhold Heller, *Brücke: German Expressionist Prints from the Granvil and Marcia Specks Collection* (exh. cat.) (Evanston, Ill.: Mary & Leigh Block Gallery, Northwestern University, 1988), 46.

2a

2b

that gives added substance to the image. Pechstein's choice of a dark palette—black on dark blue—is an aesthetic response to Heckel's comparatively poetic and lyrical prints contained within the wraparound cover. Furthermore, Pechstein's print unequivocally contrasts with Heckel's canary-yellow cover for the 1910 Brücke portfolio devoted to Kirchner's prints.[11]

In addition to the printed paper cover, *Bridge VI* consist of three prints, one per unbound sheet of paper: a woodcut, a lithograph, and a drypoint—a selection by Heckel that gives consideration to the graphic media with which he experimented. By placing it first in order among the loose sheets comprising the set, Heckel privileges the woodcut, a medium that played a decisive role in his stylistic formation. Unlike Pechstein's somber prefatory image, in *Stehendes Kind* (Standing Child, cat. no. 2b), Heckel utilized a vivid, modulated red and green backdrop to set in relief his favorite model, the young Fränzi, defined and circumscribed by intense black contours with the white reserve of the paper serving as a fourth color for the flesh. Heckel employed the trapezoid shape of the block, along with multi-colored ink, to emphasize Fränzi's youthful, over-sized head. Heckel divides the image into three horizontal bands of printed color, from black at the bottom to green and

finally red.[12] Making the colors successively brighter as the composition narrows, he draws the viewer's eye upward to Fränzi's expressive face. Heckel's flat, planar style, his simplified, angular shapes, and raw, unmixed colors constitute a synthesis of elements of modern European art and styles from non-western, so-called primitive cultures encountered and absorbed during the previous years. While Heckel and other Brücke members eagerly assimilated, among others, the innovations of French neo-Impressionist and Fauve painters, it was not until 1910 that they were able to transform these influences into a new aesthetic. Introduced to Oceanic wood carvings around 1910 while they were engaged in a series of prints of landscapes and nudes at the Moritzburg Lakes near Dresden, Brücke printmakers introduced the formal vocabulary of stick-like figures found on Palau beams to their own woodcuts of female nudes.[13] Deceptively simple, Heckel's *Standing*

11. Wiese makes a similar observation in "Die Jahresmappen der Künstlergruppe Brücke," 39.

12. Dückers, "Portfolios," 74.

13. Jill Lloyd gives a thorough and insightful examination of the impact of primitivism on Brücke members in *German Expressionism: Primitivism and Modernity* (New Haven, Conn.: Yale University Press, 1991).

2c

See color plates 2a–2d   2d

Child is an accomplished testimony to this newly forged primitivistic style, formulated through continuous experimentation over the previous six years.

The next print in the portfolio, a lithograph entitled *Szene im Wald* (Forest Scene, cat. no. 2c), attests to the importance of this planographic print medium in Heckel's graphic oeuvre. Despite the fact that all the Brücke members worked with lithography, Heckel was the most consistently fascinated by it and by the end of 1909 had produced 135 lithographs.[14] Heckel mastered the physical properties of lithography and grasped its potential for surface and compositional effect. For example, mottled effects are achieved through the dragging of the pointed tip and broad side of the greasy lithographic crayon over the surface of the prepared stone from which the final composition was ultimately printed: after wetting the stone, he charged the roller with ink, then inked the prepared stone, and finally passed the stone under pressure through the press, imprinting the design in reverse onto the sheet of paper. As was common in the lithographs of Kirchner, the composition is intentionally extended to the irregular edges of the lithographic stone as part of the design. Nonetheless, the flat, planar contrasts between white and black and the linear drawing manner derive from Heckel's

woodcuts. These varied effects demonstrate Heckel's imaginative way of producing new marking systems within a given print medium based on his experience with other print processes. For instance, his use of the broad side of the lithographic crayon in order to create a coloristic screen of foliage in *Forest Scene* recalls tonal effects seen otherwise in his chip-carved woodcuts.

Nudes relaxing in the woods constitutes one of many subjects shared by Brücke artists during their summer stay at the Moritzburg lakes.[15] With the interplay between angular and rounded forms, rectangular frame and concentric center, Heckel unites the four women's figures with the features of the landscape. Thus, the rounded buttocks of the two women with their backs to the viewer echo the rising mound of earth, and the straight tree trunks parallel the angular limbs and facial features of the other two nudes. Heckel uses the scene to comment on his perception of woman as a manifestation of nature, placing emphasis on their fertility and procreative powers. Leading the viewer deep into the forest through a

14. Noted by Bessie Tina Yarborough in her entry for *Two Lovers* (1907) in Heller, *Brücke: German Expressionist Prints*, 36.

15. See Yarborough's entry on *Forest Scene*, ibid., 40.

spiralling motion set up by the placement of nudes, Heckel creates a visual metaphor for sexual union.

Far removed from the idyllic associations of innocence and freedom Brücke artists found in nature—which for them lay outside the strict conventions of contemporary German society—as suggested in *Forest Scene*, Heckel's last print in the portfolio, a drypoint titled *Straße am Hafen (Hamburger Hafen)* (Street near the Harbor [Harbor in Hamburg], cat. no. 2d), depicts a busy street in this major port near the Binnenalster, the small lagoon formed by the Alster River that links the harbor city to the North Sea.[16] Heckel no doubt included the drypoint in the set of his prints in order to show both his technical skill and thematic range. Emil Nolde had executed a series of etchings with aquatint of Hamburg's harbor the same year. Unlike Nolde, who built his compositions through a dense network of etched line and tonal areas of aquatint, Heckel depends primarily on a sparse, unadorned scratched line to delineate space and convey movement. A restrained overall atmospheric effect is achieved in Heckel's print through the partially wiped inked plate that subsequently prints a pale gray and by a loose web of thin scratches and pitting over the surface of the plate—independent of the design—which appears in the print as a faint, ill-defined tonal scribble behind the principal motifs of the scene. The drypoint needle incised directly into the metal plate marks the contours of tree trunks and leafy masses to establish a continuous succession of trees which leads the viewer's eye back to distant apartment houses similarly defined by a bold employment of the pointed tool. He anchors the lower left-hand corner of the scene with three strolling men who pull the eye to the foreground of the urban vista. The ridges of metal thrown up along the incised drypoint lines—of the trees, rooftops, and the two closer men in the foreground—print a deep, fuzzy black since the burr has not yet worn down from repeated passes through the printing press and is still capable of retaining more ink during the wip-

ing of the plate which is imparted to the surface of the paper during the printing process. Other lines are less deeply scratched into the plate's bare metal surface: these provide a counterpoint of fine, thin lines used for interior definition of forms in the fore- and mid-grounds and the notational construction of distant objects.

Like Nolde, Heckel eschewed views of middle class leisure, fashionable cafés, and shop windows favored by the French Impressionists, for more proletarian visions of city life, as here a scene of working class life set before a distant boat or barge churning the waters of the city's commercial river as it passes under a rail bridge. In this print, Heckel portrays members of the laboring middle class, identified by their bowler hats, on their way to work on an early, misty morning.[17] The isolation and absence of social interaction among the puppet-like men in the foreground or the sketchily drawn figures beyond, the simple motif of uniform trees, the unadorned apartment buildings, and the hidden or undefined faces of the workmen convey the monotony of lower class urban life.

Heckel used *Bridge VI* to pay special tribute to one of Brücke's most important "passive" members, Gustav Schiefler. In October 1910, Heckel and Kirchner traveled to Hamburg to visit this retired judge and avid collector and promoter of contemporary graphics. *Street near the Harbor (Harbor in Hamburg)* commemorates this event and documents the personal relationship—even friendship—that formed between collector and artist. By including the drypoint—a print that recreates an everyday scene from his patron's life—Heckel offers a lasting testimony to his friendship.[18]

---

16. Discussed by Heller in his entry for *Street near the Harbor*, ibid., 48–49.

17. Ibid., 49.

18. Ibid.

Erich Heckel
German, 1883–1970

Max Pechstein
German, 1881–1955

Brücke VI (Bridge VI)
Sixth portfolio published by
Künstlergruppe Brücke, comprised
of three prints from 1910 and 1911 by
Erich Heckel loosely contained in a
folding paper wrapper with a 1911
print by Max Pechstein on the front

Medium: drypoint, lithograph,
woodcut, color woodcut

Ink: various

Paper: Velin

Publisher and Publication Date:
Künstlergruppe Brücke, Dresden, 1911

References: Davis 1021 and 2220, Dube
91 and 153

Marcia and Granvil Specks Collection,
Evanston, Illinois

2a
Max Pechstein
Knieender Akt mit Schale (Kneeling Nude with Bowl)
Woodcut (black) on blue paper, sheet folded to
   form a wrapper
Sheet: 22$\frac{7}{8}$ × 17$\frac{5}{16}$ (58.1 × 44) (closed)
Image: 14$\frac{3}{4}$ × 12 (37.5 × 30.5)
Embossed in blind stamp, l.r. of sheet: crown
Stamped twice on *verso*, l.l. of sheet: estate stamp
   of Karl Schmidt-Rottluff, inventory stamp of
   Brücke Museum, Berlin
Davis 2220

2b
Erich Heckel
Stehendes Kind (Standing Child)
Color woodcut (black, green, red)
Sheet: 21$\frac{3}{16}$ × 15$\frac{1}{4}$ (53.8 × 39.8)
Image: 14$\frac{3}{4}$ × 10$\frac{13}{16}$ (37.5 × 27.5)
Signed and dated, l.r. of image: *E. Heckel 11*
Stamped twice on *verso*, l.l. of sheet: estate stamp
   of Karl Schmidt-Rottluff, inventory stamp of
   Brücke Museum, Berlin
Davis 1021, Dube 204 B 2

2c
Erich Heckel
Szene im Wald (Forest Scene), 1910
Lithograph (black)
Sheet: 15$\frac{3}{4}$ × 21$\frac{5}{8}$ (40 × 54.2)
Image: 10$\frac{13}{16}$ × 13$\frac{3}{8}$ (27.5 × 34)
Signed and dated, l.r. of image: *E. Heckel 10*
Embossed in blind stamp, l.r. of sheet: crown
Stamped twice on *verso*, l.l. of sheet: estate stamp
   of Karl Schmidt-Rottluff, inventory stamp of
   Brücke Museum, Berlin
Dube 153

2d
Erich Heckel
Straße am Hafen (Hamburger Hafen) (Street near
   the Harbor [Harbor in Hamburg]), 1910
Drypoint (black)
Sheet: 15$\frac{3}{4}$ × 21$\frac{3}{16}$ (40 × 53.8)
Plate: 6$\frac{3}{4}$ × 7$\frac{7}{8}$ (17.1 × 20)
Signed and dated, l.r. of plate: *E. Heckel 10*
Embossed in blind stamp, l.r. of sheet: crown
Stamped twice on *verso*, l.l. of sheet: estate stamp
   of Karl Schmidt-Rottluff, inventory stamp of
   Brücke Museum, Berlin
Dube 91

OSKAR KOKOSCHKA

Der gefesselte Kolumbus
Columbus Chained
1916

Although the series print portfolio *Der gefesselte Kolumbus* (Columbus Chained) was not published until 1916, Oskar Kokoschka made the twelve drawings (from which the lithographs in the set were executed) in 1913.[1] At the time, the artist was involved in an intense and unhappy relationship with Alma Mahler, the Viennese widow of the composer Gustav Mahler, and the suite represents a universalized account of their tense and conflicted affair, with Kokoschka and his lover representing the archetypal Man and Woman. *Columbus Chained* is a visual narrative of the spiritual redemption of Woman through the martyrdom of Man.[2] Throughout the series, Man appears both heroic and independent at the same time that he is physically bound by his desire to Woman. Woman is Eve, the temptress, but similarly dependent on Man.

In *Columbus Chained* Kokoschka blends textual syntax with visual imagery in order to create his formal vocabulary. As a talented playwright and poet, as well as painter and graphic artist, Kokoschka regarded his literary and visual work as a unified expression, composed from a single symbolic language: while his lithographs read as a theatrical staging, his early dramas become an enactment of a visual series.[3] This ability to combine pictorial and literary representation stems from the artist's training in Jugendstil aesthetics. Kokoschka's graphic production began in 1905, at the Kunstgewerbeschule, or Applied Arts School, in Vienna. During his early Jugendstil period, Kokoschka gained an appreciation of the printed page as a unified work of text and design. As exemplified by his earliest illustrations to the text *Die Träumenden Knaben* (The Dreaming Youths) published in 1908 by the Wiener Werkstätte, Kokoschka rejected the illusionism of the previous generation, and instead symbolically depicts a pictorial idea through the integration of textual references, decorative border, and a flattened linear style. While retaining the practice of mixing media, in *Columbus Chained* Kokoschka departs from his Jugendstil principles of design in order to formulate his individual graphic style of expression. The artist reintroduces spatial illusionism with a distorted perspective and replaces the smooth continuous line found in *The Dreaming Youths* with a jagged, shattered line. With the print cycle now divorced from a text, the twelve lithographs become the pictorial equivalent to the broken sentences and utterances contained in his early Expressionist plays such as *Mörder, Hoffnung der Frauen* (Murderer, Hope of Women, 1907).[4]

1. Wingler and Welz, in their standard reference work to Kokoschka's graphic works, date this portfolio to 1913; see H.M. Wingler and F. Welz, *Oskar Kokoschka: Das druckgraphische Werk* (Salzburg: Galerie Welz, 1975), 81–86. Carey and Griffiths doubt the authenticity of this date as well as Wingler–Welz's identification of the drawings as transfer lithographs instead of photolithographs since no precise documentation exists for either. Carey and Griffiths, however, give no reason to date the works otherwise; Frances Carey and Antony Griffiths, *The Print in Germany 1880–1933: The Age of Expressionism* (New York: Harper & Row, 1984), 142–43.

2. For an interpretation of the symbolism of the illustrations in relation to Kokoschka's play The Burning Bush, see Henry I. Schvey, *Oskar Kokoschka: The Painter as Playwright* (Detroit: Wayne State University Press, 1982), 54–60.

3. I am following Schvey's view in *Oskar Kokoschka*.

Understanding the power of graphic expression, Kokoschka set out to create a pictorial *Gesamtkunstwerk* or total work of art.

Examination of Kokoschka's writings and graphics reveals the organic nature of his working method whereby he continuously reinvents his own imagery.[5] For example, an accompanying text to the graphic series *Columbus Chained* closely resembles his play *Der brennende Dornbusch* (The Burning Bush) from 1911.[6] At the same time, the text to *Columbus Chained* is almost identical to a prose poem titled "Der weiße Tiertöter" (The White Slayer of Animals), written in 1908 as a sequel to *The Dreaming Youths.* All three—poem, play, and graphic series with its text—share similar motifs, most prominently the identification of the woman with the moon. So powerful was this sexual metaphor for Kokoschka that he recalled it years later, in a 1966 interview: "*Columbus Chained* is me again, of course, and in this sense the title is symbolic—bound by a woman, whose features I have depicted on the title page. My Columbus ventures out not to discover America but to recognize a woman who binds him in chains. At the end she appears to him as a love-ghost, moon woman."[7]

In *Columbus Chained* Kokoschka takes advantage of the nature of the cycle, not to relate a conventional narrative but to reveal through a sequence of images the ongoing struggle between Man and Woman. The cycle unfolds in a staccato rhythm in keeping with the overall mood of dissonance. Beginning with a profile of Alma Mahler in *Das Gesicht des Weibes* (The Face of the Woman, cat. no. 3a) and ending with a transcendent portrait of the same woman in *Das reine Gesicht* (The Purified Face, cat. no. 3l), the portfolio charts Mahler's transformation from individual to archetypal Woman. While the first image depicts Mahler, isolated against a white background, as a metaphor of sexual bondage, the second print in the series, *Der neue Kolumbus und der Heilige Georg* (The New Columbus and Saint George, cat. no. 3b), elucidates the meaning of the title of the cycle. Presenting himself in the guise of Columbus, a kneeling

Kokoschka is fettered by the chains of his sexual desire. At the same time, he longingly looks over his shoulder towards St. George, a symbol of freedom. Beside Columbus like a dependent creature, Woman stoops to kiss his hand. In the background, the motif of the sun (inscribed with a cross) contained between two smoking volcanoes suggests the turbulence of the conflict between freedom and desire. The illustration reveals the paradox that the remainder of the cycle plays out: despite Man's momentary dominance, he is doomed to become a sacrifical victim to the liberation of Woman.[8]

The third and fourth lithographs of the series, *Das jüngste Gericht* (The Last Judgement, cat. no. 3c) and *Der Weg ins Grab* (The Road to the Grave, cat. no. 3d), convey Kokoschka's torment and foretell his death in the penultimate scene. In *The Last Judgement*, Death assumes the form of a nude woman who dances around a coffin holding a human skeleton. The fractured space, sharply titled perspective, barren landscape, and shining sun in the scene are outer manifestations of the perturbed, inner psychological state of Man. Similarly, in *The Road to the Grave*, a man with raised arms stands in the foreground, half in his grave; in the middle ground, a reclining couple embrace in a desolate landscape while a hyena or wolf-like creature, connoting despair, looks on.

In the next image, *Das Paar im Kerzenlicht* (The Couple in Candlelight, cat. no. 3e), Kokoschka places

4. First published in *Der Sturm* 20 (July 14, 1910); reprinted in Heinz Spielmann, ed., *Oskar Kokoschka: Dichtungen und Dramen* (Hamburg: Hans Christians Verlag, 1973), 33–41 and 43–51.

5. Most of Kokoschka's poetry and dramas from this period, with the exception of *Columbus Chained*, can be found in Spielmann, ed., *Oskar Kokoschka.*

6. See Schvey, *Oskar Kokoschka*, 54–60.

7. Kokoschka, quoted in an interview published in the Arts Council of Great Britain, *Kokoschka Lithographs* (exh. cat.) (London: Arts Council of Great Britain, 1966), 9–14.

8. Schvey, *Oskar Kokoschka*, 55.

3a

3c

3b

3d

3e

3f

3g

3h

3i

3j

3k

3l

Man and Woman in a room that resembles a stage set. The diagonal recession of the interior walls leads the viewer's eye first towards the candle, then above to the moon, and finally to Woman. With her outstretched arms, Woman (Mahler) fills the room, while Columbus (Kokoschka) stands behind. The lighted candle and the moon to which she points, symbolize spiritual and sexual fulfillment, respectively.

The drama shifts again to a desolate landscape in *Der Apfel der Eva* (Eve's Apple, cat. no. 3f). Kokoschka presents Mahler and himself as the first human couple, a new Adam and Eve, with Woman tempting Man with the biblical apple (Gen. 3:1–6). Like Klinger in *Eine Liebe (Opus X)* [A Love [Opus X], see cat. no. 1, especially *Intermezzo*, cat. no. 1i), Kokoschka uses Adam and Eve in order to convey the universality of the conflicted relationship between the sexes. However, unlike Klinger who points to society as the source of this conflict, Kokoschka locates it within Woman. In her quest for fulfillment of overriding sexual desires, she becomes a temptress and leads men to their death. Making explicit the link between the apple and her physical wants, Kokoschka places a crescent-shaped moon in the sky directly above the apple. Throughout the cycle the artist uses various lighting sources to mark the different stages of the couple's doomed struggle. Whereas the sun, symbolic of Man, reigns in the first few images, in *Eve's Apple* the moon ascends, asserting Woman's sexual power over Man. Kokoschka's personal experience of the conflict between the sexes, expressed through visual cycles such as *Columbus Chained* and in his literary works, typifies the prevailing attitude towards women among the European avant-garde at this time.[9] The portrayal of the relationship between the sexes as one of hostility, violence, and fear resounds in a variety of fields, such as psychology (Otto Weininger and Sigmund Freud), philosophy (Friedrich Nietzsche), and drama (August Strindberg and Frank Wedekind). Not the least, one discovers this ambivalence towards women expressed in the works of the Viennese painter and draftsman, Gustav Klimt, who was Kokoschka's teacher.

Am Scheidewege (At the Crossroads, cat. no. 3g) again employs the motif of light to indicate the central meaning of the image. Here Kokoschka holds a candle as he makes his way out through the door. Turning his head, he gestures towards hesitant Woman to follow. The illustration strongly resembles the opening scene to Kokoschka's play *The Burning Bush*, and this similarity demonstrates the close relationship between his various creative works. The stage directions read: "Man hesitantly starts to leave, it grows dark, she takes her candlestick from the table in order to follow him, but the open door extinguishes her light."[10]

Man's martyrdom is the subject of *Der Mann mit erhobenen Armen und die Gestalt des Todes* (The Man with Raised Arms and the Figure of Death, cat. no. 3h), in which a skeleton emerges from the grave while Columbus lies horizontally with raised arms in a gesture of hopelessness. Man is identified with the setting sun, which is placed immediately behind his shoulder. The sun's rays that form a cross refer to his martyrdom, while the moon rises high in the sky. Kokoschka established movement in the composition through concentrically drawn lines and strokes, which heighten the atmosphere of confusion and turmoil in the scene. As evinced by his print oeuvre, the lithograph was Kokoschka's preferred graphic medium.[11] The tonal range and soft chalky consistency possible in lithography allowed for a painterly treatment of his subject matter; according to the artist: "the lithograph . . . permitted me to draw colorfully what 'I' felt, without using color—just with black and tonal values."[12]

9. For a discussion of the so-called "woman problem" in the late nineteenth century and its manifestation in the visual arts, see Reinhold Heller et al., *The Earthly Chimera and the Femme Fatale: Fear of Women in Nineteenth-Century Art* (exh. cat.) (Chicago: The David and Alfred Smart Gallery, The University of Chicago, 1981).

10. Schvey, *Oskar Kokoschka*, 59.

11. Almost all of Kokoschka's graphic works, comprising around 567 prints, are lithographs. See Wingler and Welz, *Oskar Kokoschka: Das druckgraphische Werk*, and Carey and Griffiths, *The Print in Germany*, 142.

The ninth illustration in the series, *Begegnung* (Encounter, cat. no. 3i), presents the naked couple standing opposite one another in a rocky landscape. Brought to the foreground, the image of Man is darker and more modeled than that of Woman. Standing apart, they seem at once attracted and repelled, a scene of the polarity between the sexes as experienced by Kokoschka during his own ill-fated affair.

While most of the sheets comprising the print series focus on Man, in the final three illustrations of *Columbus Chained* the artist features Woman as he charts her ultimate victory over Man. Kokoschka abandons the bleak landscapes and cramped interiors of the previous scenes. Instead, he places his subjects in an empty space, in order to suggest Woman's monumentality and mythic essence. Woman bends over a phantom of her own sexual desire in *Weib über Schemen gebeugt* (Woman Bent over the Phantom Spirit, cat. no. 3j). Woman's powerful embrace of the passive male recalls not only the predatory violence of Kokoschka's play *Murderer, Hope of Woman*[13] but also Edvard Munch's color lithograph and woodcut *The Vampire* (1895, Schiefler 34). In the penultimate scene, entitled *Das Weib triumphiert über den Toten* (The Woman Triumphs over Death, cat. no. 3k), Woman secures her victory. She no longer physically resembles Alma Mahler: in her simple, undecorated robe and plain features she

has become Everywoman. With one foot placed on top of Man—who lies dead on a bier—she covers his face in a final farewell. Through Man's death she has conquered her physical desires, but nevertheless grieves over his passing away.

The cycle ends with *Das reine Gesicht* (The Purified Face, cat. no. 3l), in which Woman holds a lighted torch, the emblem of her purification and independence from Man. Kokoschka plays on the double meaning of the word *Gesicht* in the print's title, to refer back to the first portrait of Alma Mahler at the beginning of the series (cat. no. 3a).[14] Whereas in the title of the frontispiece portrait the word translates as "face", in the final illustration of the print portfolio the word is better understood as "vision". In bringing the cycle full circle, Kokoschka uses the double meaning of the word to convey how, through the seriality of his graphic work, he transforms a specific individual into an abstract symbol of the artist's complex views of love and death, freedom and constraint.

12. Kokoschka, cited in the Arts Council of Great Britain, *Kokoschka Lithographs*, 9–14.

13. Schvey, *Oskar Kokoschka*, 59.

14. Ibid.

Oskar Kokoschka
Austrian, 1886–1980

Der gefesselte Kolumbus (Columbus Chained)
Series of twelve prints, ed. 50
(unnumbered first edition)

Medium: transfer lithograph or photolithograph

Ink: black

Paper: Japan and one print on unidentified laid paper

Publisher and Publication Date: Verlag Fritz Gurlitt, Berlin 1916

Reference: Wingler–Welz 43–54

The David and Alfred Smart Museum of Art, Marcia and Granvil Specks Collection
Acc. nos. 1986.277–1986.288

3a
Das Gesicht des Weibes (The Face of the Woman)
Sheet: $17^{3}/_{16} \times 12^{7}/_{8}$ (43.7 × 32.7)
Inscribed, l.l. in image: *OK*
Signed, l.r. of sheet: *O Kokoschka*
Wingler–Welz 43
1986.277

3b
Der neue Kolumbus und der Heilige Georg
   (The New Columbus and Saint George)
Sheet: $13^{7}/_{16} \times 18^{13}/_{16}$ (34.1 × 47.8)
Inscribed, l.c. in image: *OK*
Signed, l.r. of sheet: *O Kokoschka*
Wingler–Welz 44
1986.278

3c
Das jüngste Gericht (The Last Judgement)
Sheet: $18^{3}/_{4} \times 13^{3}/_{8}$ (47.6 × 34)
Inscribed, l.r. in image: *OK*
Signed, l.r. of sheet: *O Kokoschka*
Wingler–Welz 45
1986.279

3d
Der Weg ins Grab (The Road to the Grave)
Sheet: $18^{7}/_{8} \times 13^{7}/_{16}$ (47.9 × 34.1)
Inscribed, l.r. in image: *OK*
Signed, l.r. of sheet: *O Kokoschka*
Wingler–Welz 46
1986.280

3e
Das Paar im Kerzenlicht (The Couple in Candlelight)
Sheet: $17^{1}/_{4} \times 12^{7}/_{8}$ (43.8 × 32.7)
Inscribed, l.c. in image: *OK*
Signed upside-down, u.l. of sheet: *O Kokoschka*
Wingler–Welz 47
1986.288

3f
Der Apfel der Eva (Eve's Apple)
Sheet: $18^{3}/_{4} \times 13^{3}/_{8}$ (47.6 × 34)
Inscribed, l.r. in image: *OK*
Signed, l.r. of sheet: *O Kokoschka*
Wingler–Welz 48
1986.281

3g
Am Scheidewege (At the Crossroads)
Sheet: $18^{13}/_{16} \times 13^{3}/_{8}$ (47.8 × 34)
Signed, l.r. of sheet: *O Kokoschka*
Wingler–Welz 49
1986.282

3h
Der Mann mit erhobenen Armen und die Gestalt des Todes (The Man with Raised Arms and the Figure of Death)
Sheet: $18^{3}/_{4} \times 13^{7}/_{16}$ (47.8 × 34.1)
Inscribed, l.r. in image: *OK*
Signed, l.r. of sheet: *O Kokoschka*
Wingler–Welz 50
1986.283

3i
Begegnung (Encounter)
Sheet: $18^{13}/_{16} \times 13^{7}/_{16}$ (47.8 × 34.1)
Signed, l.r. of sheet: *O Kokoschka*
Wingler–Welz 51
1986.284

3j
Weib über Schemen gebeugt (Women Bent over the Phantom Spirit)
Sheet: $13^{3}/_{8} \times 18^{3}/_{4}$ (34 × 47.6)
Signed, l.r. of sheet: *O Kokoschka*
Wingler–Welz 52
1986.285

3k
Das Weib triumphiert über den Toten (The Woman Triumphs Over Death)
Sheet: $18^{1}/_{8} \times 13^{3}/_{8}$ (46.4 × 34)
Signed, l.r. of sheet: *O Kokoschka*
Wingler–Welz 53
1986.286

3l
Das reine Gesicht (The Purified Face)
Paper: laid paper
Sheet: $13^{7}/_{16} \times 18^{3}/_{4}$ (34.1 × 47.6)
Inscribed, l.l. in image: *OK*
Signed, l.r. of sheet: *O Kokoschka*
Wingler–Welz 54
1986.287

Bei den Corinthern
At the Corinths

1920

In 1921, Lovis Corinth recorded in his diary his continuing struggle with despondency and depression brought about by the effects of a stroke in 1911 and his fight to preserve his energy and keep senility at bay.[1] During this time he questioned the meaning of life, making the transcience of nature a major theme in his work. The portfolio of fourteen etchings and drypoints entitled *Bei den Corinthern* (At the Corinths) documents this important period in the artist's life. Although the plates for the cycle were executed in 1919, they were not published until the following year. As Corinth writes in the typeset introduction to this work, the series constitutes a "kind of diary for the year 1919,"[2] and like a book of memoirs, the loose sheets are safeguarded in a book-like folio imprinted with the name of the cycle. The artist seeks to visualize his personal moments and daily habits in the images as a means of capturing the essence of his private life. A general appreciation of the artist's prints had been stimulated by the publication in 1917 of Karl Schwarz's catalogue raisonné of his graphic oeuvre,[3] and the publisher E.A. Seemann reproduced the prints from *At the Corinths* in book form as part of the promotion of the print portfolio. Appearing in 1921, *Von Corinth bei Corinth* (By Corinth About Corinth) consisted of reproductions of watercolors and etchings by Corinth with text by the art historian Wilhelm Hausenstein.

In the introduction to *At the Corinths* Corinth quotes from the apostle Paul's admonition to the people of Corinth to adhere to his teachings: "Apostle Paul wrote to the Corinthians: You drink like brush-makers, therefore Corinthians, mark my words and listen, what the devout Paul teaches."[4] Since the text refers to his familial name, the artist remarks that he identified with the biblical passage. He situates his personal life within a larger historical framework in these introductory remarks through the goal of pursuing a socially responsible Christian life. At the outset of the print cycle, then, Corinth establishes an overall world view (*Weltanschauung*) and uses the portfolio as a visual summation of his personal experiences.

The portfolio itself consists of eleven portraits of the artist, his close-knit family, and household members, as well as the locus of his private life and studio activity in three plates of his city house in Berlin and country house in Upper Bavaria. As if entering a note into his diary, Corinth records the title, month, and year of execution within the image on each plate. The cycle's seriality is a crucial factor in the progression to the core of Corinth's private life. Within the private spheres of home and atelier, the artist makes a further distinction between the family's public personae as

1. Lovis Corinth, *Selbstbiographie* (Leipzig: Verlag S. Hirzel, 1926), 147–94. Horst Uhr discusses Corinth's psychological mood and increasing disillusionment in his monograph, *Lovis Corinth* (Berkeley and Los Angeles: University of California Press, 1990), 155–296, esp. pages 232–43.

2. "Dieser Zyklus Radierungen, 'Bei den Corinthern' betitelt, . . . ist eine Art Tagebuch für das Jahr 1919."

3. Uhr, *Lovis Corinth*, 267.

4. "Apostel Paulus schrieb an die Corinther: Ihr sauft ja wie die Bürstenbinder. Drum, Corinther, merkt und hört, Was der fromme Paulus lehrt."

well-to-do members of a respected household and the more relaxed manner of the inner circle of the immediate family. Corinth begins the series with his household in Berlin as a means of formally introducing the viewer to his daily surroundings and family.

In 1919, Corinth turned sixty-one and entered his last artistic phase. During the last six years of his life the artist concentrated less on painting and focused much more of his attention on graphics, primarily lithography, in an outpouring of prints with historical, biblical, and literary subjects and themes. Between 1919–20 alone, he created six portfolios and over fifty single prints.[5] Corinth returned, however, to the etching technique along with drypoint—the first graphic medium he learned almost thirty years earlier—in this visual diary of his family and life. Corinth's selection of these intaglio processes over lithography evinces the special place the media held in his oeuvre. In the first plate in the portfolio, *Im Atelier* (In the Studio, cat. no. 4c), Corinth records himself looking into a mirror (outside the composition) as he records his deft manipulation of burin and prepared metal plate in the execution of a new print. Beside him stands his model, whose pose and nudity suggest her true identity as the artist's muse or source of inspiration—a traditional motif from antiquity that was often borrowed in allegorical works of the Renaissance and Baroque periods. On the wall behind the couple hang antlers and several of the artist's paintings, and an easel leans against the wall. By calling attention to the tools and props of his profession, and in particular the very action that had produced the present cycle, Corinth confidently and proudly reaffirms his life as an artist; the cycle, then, is to be seen as an extension of his life, an artifact of his creativity. Frozen in a creative moment in the studio, the artist looks at himself in a mirrror while he is himself simultaneously being observed by the viewer of the print, and the image boldly underscores Corinth's role within his familial circle as both member and observer. The fact that Corinth and his publisher felt that there would be an audience for such an autobiographic cycle underscores the artist's popularity and

continuing success, despite age and physical incapacity, in Germany.

The next plate, *Klopstockstraße Nr. 48*, initiates the "city" sequence of the cycle with a view of the Corinth family's apartment and the artist's studio on Klopstockstraße located in central Berlin near the Tiergarten. After moving to Berlin in 1901, Corinth acquired the artist Walter Leistikow's old studio, which originally had belonged to the painter and etcher Karl Stauffer-Bern.[6] In the print, the façade of the apartment is glimpsed through a screen of trees, a natural barrier that protects Corinth's private haven from the modern urban world symbolized by the noisy carriage passing in the street, and in this instance, it is possibly also an oblique reference to the social, economic, and political upheavals of post-war Germany. As privileged viewers of the autobiographical portfolio, however, we are allowed inside to glimpse his private world as the series continues.

In the following plate, *Petermannchen* (cat. no. 4e), Corinth gives pride of place to his wife, Charlotte, who provided him with a sense of family life that he never knew as a child. Twenty-two years younger than her husband, Charlotte Berend was among Corinth's first art students in the School for Women Painters that he opened in 1901. At Corinth's request, she stopped painting when they married. His wife played a central role in Corinth's artistic formation, both nursing him through his stroke and rehabilitation, and serving as the model for many of his works. One of Corinth's earliest oil portraits of his wife, from 1902, is titled *Petermannchen* (Private Collection). Corinth's affectionate nickname for his beloved wife refers to a story she told him shortly before their marriage: in order to dissuade an unwanted suitor, she

5. Karl Schwarz provides a chronological appendix of Corinth's graphics up to 1922; see *Das graphische Werk von Lovis Corinth* (Berlin: Fritz Gurlitt Verlag, 1922), 267–81. For his later works, see Heinrich Müller, *Die späte Graphik von Lovis Corinth* (Hamburg: Lichtwarkstiftung, 1960). One of the few treatments of Corinth's stylistic graphic development from his early period up to his last years is found in Alfred Kuhn, "Corinth als Graphiker," *Kunst und Künstler* 22 (1924): 199–208 and 244–51.

6. Uhr, *Lovis Corinth*, 127.

4a

the few images of women which portray the female sex with a sense of empowerment.

The next two prints, *Thomas studierend* (Thomas Studying, cat. no. 4f) and *Bei der Toilette (Wilhelmine)* (At the Dressing Table [Wilhelmine], cat. no. 4g), present scenes of Corinth's children, Thomas and Wilhelmine. Their place within the cycle indicates their importance to an aging, ill father. Corinth advances in these scenes of childhood work and play prevailing attitudes of the middle class and the Expressionist artist in Germany toward traditional gender roles that bound the female sex to her reproductive capabilities and thereby domestic pursuits whereas the male supposedly engages in an active public role in modern society. While Wilhelmine plays with the family cat, an animal associated with uncanny intuition and the natural world, Thomas pursues an intellectually challenging activity. Similarly, Wilhelmine quietly sits by the breakfast table at their lakeside summer retreat at Walchensee in Bavaria while her father sketches in *Beim Frühstück* (At Breakfast, cat. no. 4m). In contrast, Thomas, dressed in the traditional Bavarian *lederhosen* hiking outfit, rows a boat on the lake (cat. no. 4o) in another print from the series.

Immediately following the portrait of his daughter at her dressing table with her cat, Corinth memorializes his mother-in-law in *Ma belle mère* (My Mother-in-Law, cat. no. 4h). This juxtaposition accentuates the range of age from youth to old age circumscribed in his family circle. Excluding two self-portraits, Corinth presents twelve images that act as a calendar for the months of the year, and within the series the juxtaposition of youthfulness and old age alludes as well to the cycle of life. Corinth captured the energy and restlessness of his daughter in two vignettes in *At the Dressing Table (Wilhelmine)* as Wilhelmine crosses her legs and plays with her cat; *My Mother-in-Law* emphasizes, on the other hand, the sedentary nature of old age. The entire composition conveys the weight of his mother-in-law's years: her face emerging unassertively from shadow, the sloping back of the armchair which echoes the old

described herself as an abandoned gypsy who came from the tribe Petermann. Here again Corinth presents his wife Charlotte as "Petermannchen". Fashionably dressed and detached as she looks up from her table while smoking a cigarette—a habit still not fully acceptable for women at that time—she exudes a sense of liberality and unconventionality that belies her traditional role as wife, mother, and supporter of her husband's career. Corinth accentuates her aloofness by placing a table between her and the viewer. She possesses a commanding air, emphasized by one arm expansively resting on the chair beside her. *Petermannchen* is a testimony to Charlotte's own share of control within the marital relationship and the respect her husband accorded her. Within Corinth's oeuvre, it stands apart as one of

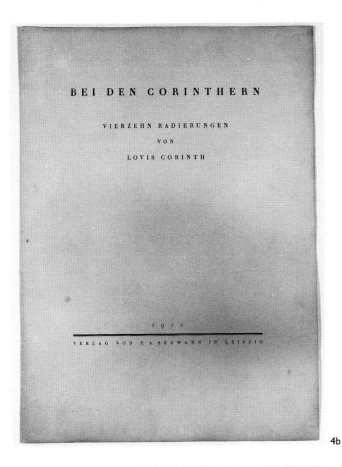

BEI DEN CORINTHERN

VIERZEHN RADIERUNGEN
VON
LOVIS CORINTH

1920

VERLAG VON E. A. SEEMANN IN LEIPZIG

4b

Es wurden von den Platten abgezogen
Nr. 1 auf Japan, Nr. 2—10 auf Geldern-Butten,
Nr. 11—100 auf Zanders-Butten.
Davon ist dies
Nr. ▮▮▮▮▮

4b

„Apostel Paulus schrieb an die Corinther:
Ihr sauft ja wie die Bürstenbinder.
Drum, Corinther, merkt und hört,
Was der fromme Paulus lehrt."

Jedes Mal, wenn der Lehrer während der Morgenandacht die Epistel Pauli an die Corinther rezitierte, versteckte ich errötend mein Haupt, nicht anders denkend: die ganze Aula mit Schülern und Lehrern müßten immer auf meine Person aufmerken. Danach verstand ich auch Goethe, wenn er sich über Herder beschwerte, der es liebte, auf seinen Namen anzügliche Worte zu verzapfen: „Der Du von den Gothen stammst oder vom Kothe!" ungefähr so ist es doch in Wahrheit und Dichtung.

Nun mache ich bereits seit geraumer Zeit Glossen über mich selbst und über meinen verehrlichen Namen. Dieser Zyklus Radierungen, „Bei den Corinthern" betitelt, ist meine neueste Arbeit. Es ist eine Art Tagebuch für das Jahr 1919. Alles, was wir erlebten, steht in diesen Kupferdrucken: die Straße in Berlin und die Sommerfrische mit dem Häuschen am wunderbaren Walchensee. Der einzige Fremde, der auf diesen Blättern erscheint, ist nebst einem weiblichen Modell unser frommer und getreuer Knecht Franz Bader: Hausverwalter, Ziegenmelker, Kutscher, Fischer, Pensionsvater unseres jungen Kätzchens „Strolch". Franz ist der Typus des Knechtes aus der Bibel. Fleißig, zuverlässig und gehorsam; manches Mal war er zerstreut, und statt auf die Tiere des Hauses aufzumerken, gingen seine Augen zu denen des Waldes, was ihn nun mit dem Gesetz in bedauerlichen Konflikt gebracht hat. Trotz seines rauhen Äußeren hat er doch das Gemüt eines Kindes. Ich hatte nicht übel Lust, das Notizbuch fortzusetzen, denn das Kätzchen ist zu einem Kater ausgewachsen. Auch eine Ziege — die Kuh des armen Mannes — meckert im Stall. Die Zeiten verändern sich, und man kann nicht wissen, was im Zeitenschoße noch schlummert. Nun, lieber Leser, wenn du Vergnügen an diesen Blättern hast, kommt vielleicht eine ganz neue Auflage für das Jahr 1922, als ein wohl verstähltes Supplement, mit erwachsenen Kindern und mir als Mummelgreis und demgemäß auch die andern.
Deß freuen wir uns baß!

Urfeld, am 13. Juni 1920   LOVIS CORINTH

4b

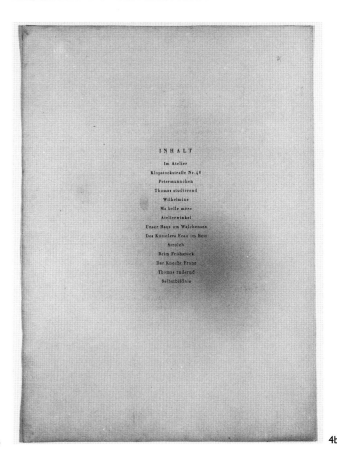

4b

woman's sloping shoulders, the accentuated sunken eyes, and clasped hands which quietly rest in her lap.

Atelierwinkel (Studio Corner, cat. no. 4i) is the last image of his city life before Corinth turns his attention to his countryside retreat, and it adds a disturbing note to the otherwise contented, familiar routine of family life. Corinth frequently portrayed men in armor as a symbol of male valor, for example, in his paintings *Rudolf Rittner als Florian Geyer* (Rudolf Rittner as Florian Geyer, Wuppertal-Elberfeld, Von der Heydt-Museum der Stadt Wuppertal) from 1906 and *Ecce Homo* (Basel, Öffentliche Kunstsammlung Basel, Kunstmuseum) executed in 1925, and the two versions of the lithograph *Ritter Jörg* (The Knight Jörg) in the 1920 *Martin Luther* cycle (see cat. nos. 5rr and 5ss). The fallen armor in *Studio Corner*, however, lays dismembered and abandoned in a corner on the floor, like the hollow shell of a once-valiant warrior, as a symbol of defeat and despair. Dated September 1919, the image is a silent, somber reminder of Germany's military surrender to the allied forces the previous year and the humiliation of defeat. The dismantled metal suit's appearance within the artist's private studio indicates Corinth's personal identification with his country's decline.

Corinth leads us to his country life in *Das Landhaus (Unser Haus am Walchensee)* (The Country House [Our House at Walchensee], cat. no. 4j). The execution of the plates for *At the Corinths* coincided with the construction of his country house, and the artist indicates both the importance of this summer residence and his pride in his successful career that enabled him to afford such an undertaking by devoting half of his cycle to the depiction of life at Walchensee. At the instigation of Charlotte and under her supervision, Haus Petermann, as their chalet forty miles south of Munich was called, was built between August and October 1919. Even more than the apartment in Berlin, Corinth's home in Urfeld am Walchensee is removed from the public realm. Shielded on either side by trees, the country house sits away from the path. There are no bustling carriages or other street noises to disturb the silence here or suggest the intrusion of city life into the rustic pleasures of the Corinth family on holiday. The house is located on a small rise, overlooking the lake that Corinth painted repeatedly in his late years. Corinth records in this plate the nestling of the new building in the landscape, as though naturally rising up from the earth like the trees and vegetation that surround it; his Haus Petermann is a remote, idyllic retreat suited to solace. In his later years, Corinth made sixteen trips to Walchensee, where he immortalized the lake and its environs in numerous paintings, drawings, and prints. Corinth devoted two subsequent print series to Walchensee (Schwarz 432 and Müller 727–732) that testify to his attachment to the area. The construction of his country home in this bucolic region in southern Germany followed his nation's recent defeat and the establishment of a new socialist government, two events that Corinth lamented in his diary.[7] The artist's decision to build a summer home at this time suggests that Corinth sought out Walchensee, in part, to remove himself from the social and political upheavals of postwar Germany.

As in the city prints, on entering the country house the first person encountered is Charlotte. Whereas *Petermannchen* had depicted his wife out in public, the portrait in *Die Frau des Künstlers im Bett (Des Künstlers Frau im Bett)* (The Artist's Wife in Bed, cat. no. 4k) presents Corinth's spouse symbolically undressed and vulnerable in her nightgown in bed. Unlike the aloofness in the first portrait of his wife, an intimacy pervades the image of Charlotte in bed, and the way the picture plane is tilted up so that the figure of his wife fills the space creates the illusion that the viewer stands at the edge of her bedside. Corinth depicts his wife's forearms twice to show her reaching out towards a mirror in the lower right-hand corner. The artist reinforces this sequential movement by describing one eye focused upward at the viewer and the other towards the mirror. In other words, Corinth portrays her in the act of turning her gaze from herself

7. Corinth, *Selbstbiographie*, 135, 140–41, and 145.

4c

4d

4e

4f

Wiesbaden Sept 1919.

Lovis Corinth (signature)

4g

Ma belle mère

Lovis Corinth (signature)

4h

Atelier Wiesbaden Sept 18 1919.

Lovis Corinth (signature)

4i

Lovis Corinth (signature)

4j

4k

4l

4m

4n

to her husband, who is fixing her likeness in the intaglio plate, and by extension, to the viewer. This record of an unguarded moment reveals the vulnerability of a private action when exposed to public view. The differences between *Petermannchen* and *The Artist's Wife in Bed* reveal two facets of this complex model and spouse: public and private, worldly and domestic, confident and vulnerable, hard and tender.

Studienblatt mit den Kindern (Strolch) (Study Sheet with the Children [Strolch], cat. no. 4l) has the immediacy and rough appeal of informal sketches as the model being jotted down on a notebook sheet quickly shifts position. The unfinished appearance of the present plate was perhaps intended by Corinth as a visual metaphor for the adolescence of his children. Dressed in an alpine dirndl and hat, Corinth's daughter sits in the middle of the composition with the family cat Strolch on her lap. To the left is a half-length portrait of Thomas, leaning his head against his arm, and to the right, another sketch of Wilhelmine;[8] each child is wearing a Tyrolean hat. Many views of the cat are scattered across the lower half of the image. In the left-hand corner Corinth identifies the cat as Strolch and dates the work August 1919. This plate is the only example in the series in which several family members are shown together. Nonetheless, he does not establish any interaction between the three figures within a unified domestic scene, but instead conceives the separate images as fragmentary thoughts, retaining the one-to-one relationship between himself and subject matter found throughout the rest of the portfolio.

The seemingly unfinished nature of this plate diverges from Corinth's earlier attitude towards printmaking as a pictorial window into illusionistic space. The collected writings of the artist published in 1920 contain the essay entitled "Wie ich das Radieren lernte" (How I Learned to Etch)[9] in which the master printmaker describes the long-standing and significant role that etching (and to a lesser extent lithography) played in his artistic oeuvre.[10] He first experimented with the etching medium in 1891,

at the suggestion of the Jugendstil graphic designer Otto Eckmann, in order to improve his draftsmanship. He became so immersed in the technique that he temporarily abandoned painting. Although he pulled only a few impressions, Corinth produced his first graphic cycle, entitled *Tragikömodien* (Tragi-Comedies, Schwarz 5) in 1893–94. The eclectic content of the series of unrelated biblical, historical, and folkloric subjects looks forward to the fully realized themes of his many later cycles. Highly finished technically, these early etchings combine naturalistic settings with flat decorative patterning that in their eccentricity may have been inspired by Max Klinger, whom Corinth had met in the winter of 1887–88.[11] Corinth continued to produce a few graphics every year, taking up lithography in 1894, but he did not seriously pursue printmaking until 1908 when he was living in Berlin and met the professional etcher Hermann Struck, who encouraged him to make another start at the medium. Although Corinth executed more prints after this meeting, it was not until 1916 that he loosened his style and grasped the full potential of printmaking as a visual language independent of painting.[12] When he abandoned the equation "print equals illustration", Corinth began to view the print more as a drawing than a painting.

One of the last prints in *At the Corinths* presents the only portrait devoted to someone outside the family (cat. no. 4n). Corinth writes in the cycle's preface:

> Franz is the very model of a laborer from the Bible. Industrious, dependable and dutiful;

---

8. Karl Schwarz misidentifies the right-hand figure as the artist's son; see Schwarz, *Das graphische Werk*, 200.

9. Lovis Corinth, "Wie ich das Radieren lernte," *Gesammelte Schriften* (Berlin: Fritz Gurlitt Verlag, 1920), 15–22.

10. Corinth briefly experimented with the woodcut, making only nine prints.

11. Uhr, *Lovis Corinth*, 84.

12. Kuhn, "Corinth als Graphiker," 244 and Uhr, *Lovis Corinth*, 223.

many times he was distracted, and instead of watching over the domestic animals, his eyes would wander to the beasts of the woods, which brought him in unfortunate conflict with the law. In spite of his rough outward appearance, he possesses the disposition of a child.

Corinth's written account of Franz as a creature of nature matches the visual record of Franz in *Der Knecht (Der Knecht Franz)* (The Servant [The Servant Franz]): the rustic day laborer stands in the woods with the straight trunk of his body aligned with a tall pine at his back. Although Franz appears tall and scruffy, his expressive eyes convey gentleness. Corinth uses an economy of line to produce a rich velvety texture that suggests the gentle fecundity of the woods. Franz is the human embodiment of nature: powerful but benevolent.

At the Corinths defines the artist in relation to his social responsibilities, his family, and nature. Progressively guiding the viewer from his most public personae—as the aging, respected, and prolific senior German painter and printmaker—into his private self as husband and father, the artist returns to where he began with a self-portrait in the last plate in the cycle. Unlike the image that introduces the series, *Selbstbildnis* (Self-Portrait, cat. no. 4p) presents the artist in a deep shadow, realized by a vigorously etched cross-hatching that obscures much of the studio and its accoutrements and the artist's face and body. The only detail that emerges clearly from the background is an easel supporting a painting of Walchensee. Isolating his eyes, hands, and the easel behind him in pools of light, Corinth visually links three crucial elements to his artistic existence in his final years. The observer is permitted one final, emotional insight into the creative life of the artist, whose personal and professional existence has been revealed and made less mysterious by the previous thirteen images and autobiographic prefatory text in the cycle. Taken in its entirety, the portfolio presents a psychological study of Corinth's relationship to the world.

Lovis Corinth
German, 1858–1925

Bei den Corinthern (At the Corinths)
Portfolio of fourteen prints, ed. 57/90

Medium: etching, drypoint

Ink: black

Paper: J.W. Zanders Bütten (prints) and
wove paper (contents page)

Publisher and Publication Date:
E.A. Seemann, Leipzig, 1920 [plates
executed 1919]

Reference: Schwarz 380 I–XIV

The David and Alfred Smart Museum
of Art, Marcia and Granvil Specks
Collection
Acc. nos. 1985.41–1985.54

4a
Cover
Yellow paper board with linen binding, with black
typeset title
Format: 21 × 15¼ (53.3 × 38.7) (closed)
1985.41a

4b
Contents Page
Bifolio of wove paper:
    f. 1r.: title page in black typeset
    f. 1v.: colophon in black typeset with the number
       57 also in black typeset
    f. 2r.: text page by Lovis Corinth in black typeset
    f. 2v.: contents page in black typeset
Format: 20⁹⁄₁₆ × 15 (52.2 × 38.1) (closed)
1985.41b

4c
Im Atelier (In the Studio)
Sheet: 17³⁄₈ × 14¼ (44.1 × 36.2)
Plate: 12⁵⁄₈ × 9¾ (32.1 × 24.8)
Inscribed, l.c. in plate: under CL cypher,
    Selbstporträt
Inscribed, l.r. in plate: *ATELIER / 1919. September.*
Signed, l.r. of plate: *Lovis Corinth*
Watermark: *JWZANDERS*
Schwarz 380 XII
1985.41

4d
Klopstockstraße Nr. 48
Sheet: 17½ × 14¼ (44.4 × 36.2)
Plate: 12⁹⁄₁₆ × 9¾ (31.9 × 24.8)
Inscribed, l.r. in plate: *Die Klopstock Str. 48./
    I. Sept. 1919.*
Signed, l.r. of plate: *Lovis Corinth*
Watermark: *JWZANDERS*
Schwarz 380 XI
1985.42

4e
Petermannchen
Sheet: 17⁵⁄₈ × 14⁵⁄₁₆ (44.8 × 36.4)
Plate: 12⁵⁄₈ × 9⁵⁄₈ (32.1 × 24.5)
Inscribed, l.c. in plate: *Petermañhen. / August 1919.*
Signed, l.r. of plate: *Lovis Corinth*
Watermark: *JWZANDERS*
Schwarz 380 IV
1985.43

4f
Thomas studierend (Thomas Studying)
Sheet: 17½ × 14¼ (44.4 × 36.2)
Plate: 12⁹⁄₁₆ × 9¹¹⁄₁₆ (31.9 × 24.6)
Inscribed, l.l.to l.c. in plate: *Thomas studierend.*
Signed, l.r. of plate: *Lovis Corinth*
Watermark: *JWZANDERS*
Schwarz 380 X
1985.44

4g
Bei der Toilette (At the Dressing Table)
    [entitled *Wilhelmine* on the contents page of the
    portfolio]
Sheet: 17⁵⁄₈ × 14³⁄₈ (44.8 × 36.5)
Plate: 12⁹⁄₁₆ × 9¾ (31.9 × 24.8)
Inscribed, l.c. in plate: *Wilhelmine Sept 1919.*
Signed, l.r. of plate: *Lovis Corinth*
Watermark: *JWZANDERS*
Schwarz 380 IX
1985.45

4h
Ma belle mère (My Mother-in-Law)
Sheet: 17⁷⁄₁₆ × 14⁵⁄₁₆ (44.3 × 36.4)
Plate: 12⁹⁄₁₆ × 9¹³⁄₁₆ (31.9 × 24.9)
Inscribed, l.l. to l.c. in plate: *Ma belle mère.*
Signed, l.r. of plate: *Lovis Corinth*
Watermark: *JWZANDERS*
Schwarz 380 XIV
1985.46

4i
Atelierwinkel (Studio Corner)
Sheet: 17½ × 14⁵⁄₁₆ (44.4 × 36.4)
Plate: 12³⁄₈ × 8¹⁵⁄₁₆ (31.4 × 22.7)
Inscribed, l.c. in plate: *Atelier-Winkel. Sept 28 1919.*
Signed, l.r. of plate: *Lovis Corinth*
Watermark: *JWZANDERS*
Schwarz 380 XIII
1985.47

4j
Das Landhaus (The Country House) [entitled
    Unser Haus am Walchensee on contents page of
    the portfolio]
Sheet: 17½ × 14⁵⁄₁₆ (44.4 × 36.4)
Plate: 12⁹⁄₁₆ × 9¹¹⁄₁₆ (31.9 × 24.6)
Inscribed, l.r. in plate: *Unser Haus / am Walchen See /
    S [backwards] ept 1919.*
Signed, l.r. of plate: *Lovis Corinth*
Watermark: *JWZANDERS*
Schwarz 380 VII
1985.48

4k
Die Frau des Künstlers im Bett (The Artist's Wife in
    Bed) [entitled *Des Künstlers Frau im Bett* on
    contents page of the portfolio]
Sheet: 17½ × 14⁵⁄₁₆ (44.4 × 36.4)
Plate: 12⁹⁄₁₆ × 9¹¹⁄₁₆ (31.9 × 24.6)
Signed, l.r. of plate: *Lovis Corinth*
Watermark: *JWZANDERS*
Schwarz 380 II
1985.49

4l
Studienblatt mit den Kindern (Study Sheet with the
   Children) [entitled *Strolch* on contents page of
   the portfolio]
Sheet: 17³/₈ × 14³/₁₆ (44.1 × 36)
Plate: 12⁹/₁₆ × 9³/₄ (31.9 × 24.8)
Inscribed, l.l. in plate: *S Milch. / August 1919.*
Signed, l.r. of plate: *Lovis Corinth*
Watermark: *JWZANDERS*
Schwarz 380 VI
1985.50

4m
Beim Frühstück (At Breakfast)
Sheet: 17¹/₂ × 14⁵/₁₆ (44.4 × 36.4)
Plate: 12¹/₂ × 9¹¹/₁₆ (31.8 × 24.6)
Inscribed, l.r. in plate: *Wilhelmine August 1919*
Signed, l.r. of plate: *Lovis Corinth*
Watermark: *JWZANDERS*
Schwarz 380 V
1985.51

4n
Der Knecht (The Servant) [entitled *Der Knecht
   Franz* on contents page of the portfolio]
Sheet: 17¹/₂ × 14⁵/₁₆ (44.4 × 36.4)
Plate: 12¹/₂ × 9¹¹/₁₆ (31.8 × 24.6)
Inscribed, l.r. in plate: *Der Knecht Franz / Sept. 1919.*
Signed, l.r. of plate: *Lovis Corinth*
Watermark: *JWZANDERS*
Schwarz 380 VIII
1985.52

4o
Thomas in Ruderboot (Thomas in a Row Boat)
   [entitled *Thomas rudernd* on contents page of
   the portfolio]
Sheet: 17³/₈ × 14⁵/₁₆ (44.1 × 36.4)
Plate: 12⁵/₈ × 9³/₄ (32.1 × 24.8)
Inscribed, l.r. in plate: *2. August 1919*
Signed, l.r. of plate: *Lovis Corinth*
Watermark: *JWZANDERS*
Schwarz 380 III
1985.53

4p
Selbstbildnis (Self-Portrait)
Sheet: 17⁵/₈ × 14³/₄ (44.8 × 36.2)
Plate: 12⁵/₈ × 9⁵/₈ (32.1 × 24.4)
Inscribed, l.c. in plate: *Selbst Porträt /
   S [backwards] eptember 1919.*
Signed, l.r. of plate: *Lovis Corinth*
Watermark: *JWZANDERS*
Schwarz 380 I
1985.54

Martin Luther,

1920

The beginning of Lovis Corinth's prolific graphic output coincides with the end of the First World War; using a number of publishers including Fritz Gurlitt Press and Propyläen-Verlag in Berlin, F. Bruckmann and Marées-Gesellschaft in Munich, and E.A. Seemann in Leipzig, the master printmaker created more than twenty portfolios and illustrated books between 1919 and 1923. Comprising nearly 400 etchings and lithographs,[1] this body of serial prints in folio format and book illustrations represents nearly half of his entire graphic production.[2] Among them is the portfolio *Martin Luther* with its thirty-eight printed images without explicatory text, one per sheet, in the regular edition. Printed in an edition of 150 by Fritz Gurlitt, many of the impressions of *Martin Luther* were destroyed during the Second World War. The remaining few, according to the artist's son Thomas, are in museums and private collections in Germany; hardly any complete sets exist in the United States.[3] The Smart Museum's example is also exceptional in that it is an artist's proof set of the transfer lithographs, a rare and possibly unique gathering of forty-six prints, including compositions not used in the edition. After the title page, in both proof and published versions, the compositions unfold as a pictorial account without supporting narrative text of the central events and essential figures in the life of the German theologian and leader of the Protestant Reformation, Martin Luther (1486–1546). The cycle was not conceived solely as a pictorialized biography of Luther's life but also as a guide which leads the viewer on a spiritual journey. In its presentation of a visual chronicle of the religious reformer's era, the series encompasses portraits of Luther's intimate acquaintances and contemporary religious, intellectual, artistic, and political personalities. Corinth intersperses among these portraits episodes from Luther's life that attest to the theologian's courage and strong moral convictions. Overall, the series of images recounts the rich cultural, yet turbulent political life during the German Renaissance and Lutheran Reformation.

Corinth's journal entries after 1918 repeatedly express disillusionment with the outcome of the war and the new socialist government in Germany.[4] A patriot who believed in the cause of war much longer than his Expressionist colleagues, Corinth supported the monarchy. Viewing himself as a Prussian, the artist suffered the Allied victory personally, although he himself was too old and infirm to have been a combatant in the conflict. Corinth turned to biblical and religious themes to find spiritual solace in the face of Germany's humiliating defeat and ensuing social and political unrest during the Weimar Republic. But

1. Horst Uhr, *Lovis Corinth* (Berkeley: University of California Press, 1990), 267.

2. The documented number of prints by Corinth varies; Maria Makela in "A Late Self-Portrait," *The Art Institute of Chicago Museum Studies* 16 (Chicago: Art Institute of Chicago, 1990), 94, n. 14, counts 1,243 prints, whereas Frances Carey and Antony Griffiths list 918 prints in *The Print in Germany 1880–1933: The Age of Expressionism* (New York: Harper & Row 1984), 81.

3. Statement by Thomas Corinth in the foreword of the facsimile edition of *Martin Luther* (Springfield, Ohio: Chantry Music Press at Wittenberg University, 1968).

4. See Lovis Corinth, *Selbstbiographie* (Leipzig: Verlag S. Hirzel, 1926), 135–94. For an English interpretation of Corinth's psychological profile as expressed through his journal entries, see Maria Makela, "A Late Self-Portrait," 57–69. Horst Uhr also discusses Corinth's patriotism and attitude towards war as expressed through his works; see *Lovis Corinth*, 232–43.

instead of choosing the universal theme of man's moral redemption as was done by his German contemporaries, such as Karl Schmidt-Rottluff in *Neun Holzschnitte* (Nine Woodcuts, 1918–19) and Max Pechstein in *Das Vater Unser* (The Lord's Prayer, 1921, Krüger H256–268), Corinth, in the selection of the life of Martin Luther as his subject, made an intentional reference to an earlier era of related social and political upheaval in the history of the German lands. Like his other cycles from this period taking historic national heroes as their subjects, including *Wilhelm Tell* (William Tell, 1923, Müller 775–787)[5] and *Fridericus Rex* (Frederick the Great, 1922, Müller 593–640), *Martin Luther* served as a vehicle for Corinth to affirm his faith in his homeland. The focus on Luther's spiritual strength in the face of earthly and demonic adversaries is an attempt by the artist to identify personally with a famous cultural hero of the German people.

The Smart Museum portfolio, consisting as it does of proof impressions approved for publication without alteration, corrected compositions with penciled notations by the artist, and images rejected in the regular edition, allows insight into the experimental nature of Corinth's working method. In the two versions of *Luther geht ins Kloster* (Luther Enters the Monastery, cat. nos. 5e and 5f), for example, Corinth chooses the brushed tusche over the drawn lithographic crayon version, favoring a treatment that more dramatically frames Luther against the raging storm. Working on transfer paper (for the later impression on stone or plate, with corrections and emendations worked directly on the reversed image, and ultimately printed to the original orientation of the transfer drawing), Corinth "paints" his images in a dissolution of form with only sparing use of delineating contour lines. The printmaker exploits lithography's technical properties for fluid, spontaneous forms impossible with most intaglio and relief print processes, when he applies the tusche loosely, with a draftsmanship normally associated with drawings and watercolors. Borrowing an aesthetic approach introduced to modern German printmaking by

Brücke members a decade earlier (see cat. no. 2),[6] Corinth reverses his conventional application of the medium in which, as late as 1916, he sought to imitate drawing at the expense of the formal possibilities allowed by lithography proper and transfer lithography.[7] Corinth's new, looser application of tusche and crayon conformed as well to his rejection of an earlier academic drawing manner featuring idealized nudes rendered in firm contours and carefully modeled surfaces. Instead, the artist adopts in his prints (and paintings and drawings) a form of expression that subordinates detailed description to the mood engendered by the experience—in this case, Luther's terror and sudden decision to leave the university and become a monk—induced by the violent thunderstorm and fear of sudden death.

After bust-length portrayals of Luther's parents, the portfolio progresses in chronological order from the reformer's youth to old age, disclosing the influential people and decisive events of the monk's life. Corinth modeled several portrait prints after paintings, copper-plate engravings, and woodcuts executed during Luther's lifetime. By alluding to the masterworks of famous artists of the late fifteenth and early sixteenth centuries, Corinth not only gives an authentic character to the age that he seeks to reconstitute, but also makes a link to his artistic patrimony, thereby implicitly connecting Germany's spiritual and religious leadership with her cultural awakening. The opening image, on the title page, of Luther as an earnest young monk with halo and hovering dove over his tonsured head (cat. no. 5a) is derived from a 1521

5. An impression of this portfolio of thirteen color transfer lithographs is in the collection of the Smart Museum (acc. nos. 1986.240–1986.252).

6. See, for example, Nathan Mason and Robin Reisenfeld's catalogue entry, "Karl Schmidt-Rottluff: House on a Hill, 1910," in Reinhold Heller et al., *Brücke: German Expressionist Prints from the Granvil and Marcia Specks Collection* (exh. cat.) (Evanston, Ill.: Mary & Leigh Block Gallery, Northwestern University, 1988), 256.

7. Compare, for example, this Luther image to Corinth's 1916 transfer lithograph, *Education of a Soldier* (reproduced in Makela, "A Late Self-Portrait," fig. 16) in which the artist uses the same wide-legged stance but symmetrically situates the figure in the middle of the page.

woodcut by Hans Baldung Grien.[8] Similarly, Corinth patterned the next two lithographs *Luthers Vater* (Luther's Father, cat. no. 5b) and *Luthers Mutter* (Luther's Mother, cat. no. 5c) after paintings by the famous artist and friend of Luther, Lucas Cranach.[9] Corinth emphasized the unaffected manners and ascetic lives of Luther's parents (shown in simple dress and with unremarkable facial features) by silhouetting them against a black background. Or again, Corinth based his *Dürer* (cat. no. 5bb) on the Dürer self-portrait painting in the Alte Pinakothek, Munich. Responding to the Renaissance artist's own confident view of himself, Corinth portrays Dürer as an intense, brooding prophet of his age, who in his 1498 *Apocalypse* woodcut series (Bartsch 40–55)[10] had anticipated the religious zeal and spiritual fire of the Reformation. Corinth instilled an immediacy and specificity in his proof edition by writing in his easily identifiable fraktur script (or occasionally a modified uncial script in the manner of a latter-day Renaissance humanist man of letters) identifying names beneath the portraits,[11] thereby suggesting that the cycle be read as a contemporaneous historical document. In the case of *Dürer*, Corinth records the former artist's diary entry on the impending imprisonment of Luther that strengthens the topical nature of the image: "O God! if Luther dies, who will henceforth preach the Holy Gospel to us so clearly."[12]

The many near-visionary story-telling vignettes of turning points in Luther's life underscore his spiritual mission and devotion to God. A print conceived for the beginning of the series, *Luther im Kloster* (Luther in the Monastery, cat. no. 5g), for example, portrays the young Catholic monk flagellating himself in the presence of his mentor, the Augustinian theologian Johann von Staupitz. It was Staupitz, shown hovering over Luther like a saintly spirit, who encouraged him to become a teacher and preacher. In *Versuchung (Tentatio)* (Temptation [Tentatio], cat. no. 5i) the heads of a fat monk and a devil with long horns emerge from the shadows from which they luridly gaze at a spotlit naked woman in bed; the device is traditional for the portrayal of dreams,

visions, or thoughts, and in this case, the devil represents the monk Luther's sexual arousal urging him to give in to his human desires. The devil appears again as a grotesque goat-like creature in *Antichrist* (cat. no. 5j) and as a winged-bat in *Teufelsspuk* (Satanic Vision, cat. no. 5cc), the latter motif familiar from Goya's *Sleep of Reason Produces Monsters* in his nightmarish series *Los Caprichos* (The Capriccios, plate 43). Luther tries to extinguish this phantasm of the mind by throwing ink in its face.

The attention in the series given to Luther's inner torments, doubts, and spiritual difficulties mirrors the important role of the concept of temptation (*Anfechtung*) in Luther's theology. However, the majority of images in *Martin Luther* feature the monk's public career as a religious reformer and the chain of events that led to the Diet of Worms, where the Roman Catholic Church condemned Luther as a heretic, and its aftermath. *Ablasshandel* (Sale of Indulgences, cat. no. 5k) and *Überfall auf Tetzel* (Ambush on Tetzel, cat. no. 5l) record the Dominican monk Johann Tetzel's abuse of the Church's sanctioned practice of the selling of indulgences to the living for salvation of the soul in the afterlife. In consequence of Tetzel's (and

8. Grien's woodcut, entitled *Bildnis Luthers mit Nimbus und Traube* (Portrait of Luther with Halo and Dove), was used to illustrate Luther's text *Acta et Res Gestae D. Martini Lutheri in Comitijs Principu Vuormaciae, Anno MDXXI*; it is reproduced in Marianne Bernhard, ed., *Hans Baldung Grien: Handzeichnungen Druckgraphik* (Munich: Südwest Verlag, 1978), 404.

9. Lucas Cranach's paintings *Bildnis des Hans Luther, Luthers Vater* (Portrait of Martin Luther's Father Hans) and *Bildnis der Margaretha Luther, Luthers Mutter* (Portrait of Martin Luther's Mother Margaretha), both *circa* 1527, are in the collection of the Wartburg Foundation, Eisenach.

10. Walter L. Strauss, ed., *Albrecht Dürer Woodcuts and Woodblocks* (New York: Abraris Books, 1980), 153–203.

11. Eight portrait prints among the Smart Museum's proofs include Corinth's inscriptional identifications in the compositions: cat. nos. 5b, 5c, 5s, 5w, 5bb, 5ee, 5ll, and 5mm. These inscriptions were removed in the regular edition.

12. "O Gott! ist Luther todt, wer wird uns hinfort das heilige Evangelium so klar vortragen." According to the unpaginated commentary by Horst Berend in the facsimile edition of *Martin Luther* (note 3, above), Dürer recorded these lines in an entry in his diary upon learning of Luther's trial for heresy.

by extension, Rome's) misuse of ecclesiastical powers, Luther wrote his famous ninety-five theses, or articles of faith. Corinth visually links these two important events by placing *Die 95 Thesen* (The Ninety-five Theses, cat. no. 5o), in which Luther nails his reform doctrine to the chapel door of Wittenberg Castle's church, in close succession in the ordering of the sheets of the portfolio to Tetzel's precipitous scandalous deeds. Corinth first recorded Luther in the 1915 painting *Martin Luther* (whereabouts unknown, Berend-Corinth, no. 655), in which the stubborn reformer prominently stands, feet squarely planted on German soil, before Wartburg Castle, defiantly looking up from the Bible in his hands. For Corinth, Luther embodied the ageless virtues of the German character: pride, courage, resolve in the face of opposition. Although Corinth does not repeat exactly the pose in his print, he copies the defiant, enraged Luther, who confronts a noisy crowd in front of the chapel door. Corinth returns to Luther's insurgency in *Luther verbrennt die Bannbulle* (Luther Burns the Papal Edict, cat. no. 5t) and *Luthers Einzug in Worms* (Luther's Entry into Worms, cat. no. 5u). After the issue of a papal edict, or bull, that threatened Luther with excommunication from the Catholic Church, he traveled to Worms to defend his beliefs before the official council of the Holy Roman Empire, whose members included the then-young Charles V. In both scenes, Luther stands above the excited crowd, distinguished from the anonymous throng by his distinctive, easily recognizable features, made courageous by his moral conviction.

Although Luther achieved a moral triumph at the Diet of Worms, the council proscribed his writings and he no longer stood under the protection of the law. For this reason, Luther's powerful friend Elector Frederick the Wise (see cat. no. 5r) arranged a mock kidnapping to remove Luther from his enemies and to escort him safely to seclusion in Wartburg Castle. Corinth's recreation of this event in *Der Überfall bei Eisenach* (The Ambush at Eisenach, cat. nos. 5z and 5aa) shows Luther on his knees in feigned terror before his carriage. The proof edition includes two

versions of this scene, affording the observer a chance to experience Corinth's varied approaches to the lithograph medium. Compositionally similar, the two images differ primarily in their spatial organization of negative and positive spaces. In the image used in the regular edition, Corinth placed Luther slightly lower in the foreground so that he appears more prominent. The use of brush and tusche in the transfer from sheet to stone or plate left little leeway for major corrections to the overall placement of the figures (although transfer lithography does allow the artist the option of emending selected areas of the transferred image directly on the stone or plate). Dissatisfied with the results of his first attempt (noted "36" in pencil in the lower right-hand corner of the sheet), Corinth reworked the scene in a second version (inscribed on the proof sheet "37"). In his search for emotional impact, Corinth pushed the lithographic technique to the point where form threatens to dissolve completely into inky, black masses. The variant composition chosen for the edition possesses a coherent pictorial logic, attained by a clearer organization of whites (blank paper) and blacks (printed image). In the rejected version, Corinth employed a sketchy brush line for the middle values and a sense of greater surface agitation, but the introduction of this element confused the spatial organization of figure and ground, so that Luther becomes lost in the scene.

Corinth commemorates Luther's lasting contribution to German culture with two illustrations that lie outside a direct narrative explication of specific contemporaneous events through the construction of symbolic and allegorical images of Luther's deeds: *Die Bibel* (The Bible, cat. no. 5hh) and *Eine Feste Burg . . .* (A Mighty Fortress [is Our God], cat. no. 5gg). During his confinement at Wartburg Castle (1521–22), Luther began his translation of the Bible from the original Greek and Hebrew texts into German. Luther's great literary accomplishment is commemorated in Corinth's adaptation of the woodcut title page of the first edition of Luther's vernacular Bible, printed by Hans Lufft in Wittenberg in 1534.

Whereas *The Bible* exemplifies Luther's literary contribution to German culture, *A Mighty Fortress (is Our God)* recognizes his musical legacy. A troop of warriors stands in front of a mounted knight, who together defend God's castle, an allegorical visualization of the sentiment expressed in the line excerpted from Luther's popular hymn and Reformation anthem, written above: "A Mighty Fortress is Our God". As part of his reform program, Luther established congregational hymn singing as an essential component of the Protestant service. Many of Luther's devotional songs, among them "A Mighty Fortress is Our God", appeared in his first, instantaneously popular, hymnbook.

In addition to the importance he placed on the public duties of political office and clerical ministry, Luther advocated domestic life as one of the three Christian vocations. Adhering to his own teachings, Luther married the former nun Catherina von Bora in 1525, and the wedding witnessed the first Protestant marriage between a "monk" and a "nun". The attending joys and sorrows of Luther's family life are condensed in *Luther und Catherina von Bora* (Luther and Catherina von Bora, cat. no. 5ff) and *Magdalenchens Sterben* (The Death of Little Magdalena, cat. no. 5pp). In the last mentioned, the couple's child sits in a white shift, like an angel who has already ascended to heaven, while her parents grieve and keep vigil in the shadows.

Corinth enriched his imagistic recreation of this tumultuous era in German history with portrait likenesses of other significant personalities who shaped the period: Luther's political foe at the Diet of Worms, Charles V, as well as his allies, Philip of Hesse and George V of Frundsberg (see cat. no. 5p); the humanist patron Emperor Maximilian I (see cat. no. 5q); and the founder of Wittenberg University at the beginning of the sixteenth century, Elector Frederick the Wise (see cat. no. 5r). He also includes bust-length portraits of great literary figures: Hans Sachs of Nuremberg (see cat. no. 5ee), the poet, Meistersinger, and disseminator of Luther's teachings; the court poet and humanist Ulrich von Hutten (see cat. no. 5y), who supported Luther in a series of pamphlets; and Luther's great rival, Erasmus of Rotterdam (see cat. no. 5s), who attacked Luther's doctrine of enslaved will in his treatise *Concerning the Free Will*. Finally, Corinth pays tribute to the great artists of the age: Albrecht Dürer (see cat. no. 5bb), and Luther's loyal friend Lucas Cranach (see cat. nos. 5w and 5x).

The cycle ends with Luther outfitted in full knightly accoutrement standing in front of his castle as the defender of the faith. Corinth frequently used medieval and Renaissance armor as a leitmotif, seen previously in several self-portrait paintings, including *Die Sieger* (The Victor) from 1910 (whereabouts unknown, Berend-Corinth 414), the 1911 *Selbstporträt als Fahnenträger* (Self-Portrait as a Standard Bearer, whereabouts unknown, Berend-Corinth 496), and the 1914 *Selbstporträt in Rüstung* (Self-Portrait in Armor, Hamburg, Hamburger Kunsthalle, Berend-Corinth 621), as well as in the 1912 etching *Der Ritter* (The Knight [Self-Portrait], Schwarz 86). Sometimes a nationalistic reference— see, for example, the contemporaneous print of an abandoned suit of armor lying in a corner of the artist's studio in his cycle *Bei den Corinthern* (At the Corinths, cat. no. 4i)—antique armor otherwise functioned for Corinth as a protective sheath for the male body: the heroic defender of Germany's religious and cultural heritage, Luther stands alone against his enemies. In *Martin Luther*, Corinth identifies his country and by extension, himself, as the modern-day embattled hero beset by foreign enemies and internal strife.[13]

---

13. In his discussion of Corinth's late graphic cycle, Horst Uhr reaches a similar conclusion (*Lovis Corinth*, 269).

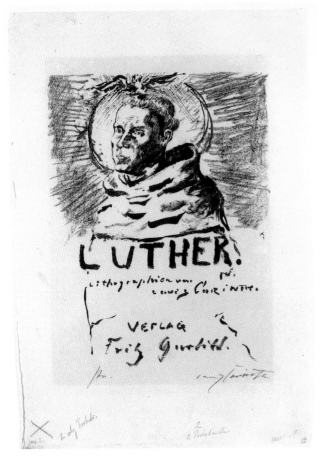

5a

5b

5c

5d

5e

5f

5g

5h

5i

5j

5k

5l

5m

5o

5p

IMPERATOR MAXIMILIANUS Germani ac.

5q

5r

Erasmus Rotterdamus

5s

5t

5u

5v

5w

5x

5y

5z

5aa

5bb

5cc

5d

5ee

5ff

5gg

5hh

5ii

5jj

5II

5mm

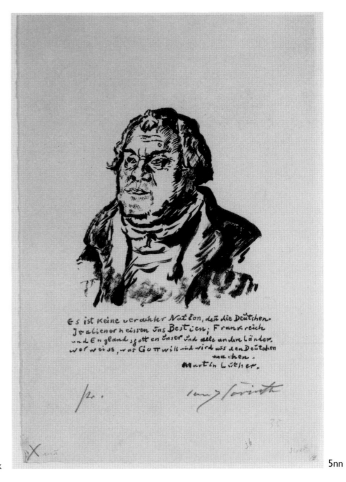

Es ist keine verachter Nation, den die Deütschen
Italiener heissen uns Bestien; Frankreich
und England, got en uns... sind alle andere Länder,
wer weiss, was Gott will und wird uns den Deütschen
machen.
Martin Lüther.

5kk

5nn

5oo

5pp

5qq

5rr

5ss

5tt

Lovis Corinth
German, 1858–1925

Martin Luther
Set of forty-six proof and trial proof
prints, with annotations by the artist,
for the 1920 portfolio edition

Medium: transfer lithograph

Ink: black

Paper: Bütten and one print on
unidentified wove paper

Publisher and Publication Date: Verlag
Fritz Gurlitt, Berlin, 1920 (regular
edition)

Printer: Gurlitte-Presse, Berlin

Reference: Schwarz L 444 II–IV, VI A,
VII–VIII, VIIIA, IX–XI, XII 1 and 2,
XIII–XXI, XXI A, XXII–XXIII A,
XXIV–XL A and B

The David and Alfred Smart Museum
of Art, Marcia and Granvil Specks
Collection
Acc. nos. 1986.194–1986.239

5a
Titelblatt (Title Page)
Sheet: 18⁷/₈ × 13¹/₁₆ (48 × 33.2)
Inscribed, at bottom in image: *LUTHER. /
   Lithographien von / LOVIS CORINTH. / VERLAG /
   Fritz Gurlitt.*
Annotated, l.l. of sheet: X
Inscribed, l.l. of image: *Pr.*
Signed, l.r. of image: *Lovis Corinth*
Miscellaneous dealer (?) or collector (?) annotations
   along bottom of sheet
Watermarks: standing bear with wheel, *1597*
Schwarz L 444 II (possibly one of two proof
   impressions described)
1986.194

5b
Luthers Vater (Luther's Father)
Sheet: 13¹/₁₆ × 9¹/₂ (33.2 × 24.1)
Inscribed, at bottom in image: *Vater Hans-Luther.*
Annotated, l.l. of sheet: X
Annotated, in image: a line around half of printed
   inscription
Inscribed, l.l. of image: *Pr.*
Signed, l.r. of image: *Lovis Corinth*
Miscellaneous dealer (?) or collector (?) annotations
   in bottom corners of sheet
Watermarks: standing bear with wheel, *1597*
Schwarz L 444 III (possibly proof impression
   described)
1986.199

5c
Luthers Mutter (Luther's Mother)
Sheet: 13¹/₁₆ × 9¹/₂ (33.2 × 24.1)
Inscribed, at bottom in image: *Mutter Luther
   Margarethe*
Annotated, l.l. of sheet: X line
Annotated, in image: a line around half of printed
   inscription
Inscribed, l.l. of image: *Pr.*
Signed, l.r. of image: *Lovis Corinth*
Miscellaneous dealer (?) or collector (?) annotations
   in bottom corners of sheet
Watermarks: standing bear with wheel, *1597*
Schwarz L 444 IV (possibly proof impression
   described)
1986.201

5d
Frau Usrula Cotta zu Eisenach
Sheet: 18¹⁵/₁₆ × 13¹/₁₆ (48.1 × 33.2)
Annotated, l.l. of sheet: X
Inscribed, l.l. of image: *Pr.*
Signed, l.r. of image: *Lovis Corinth*
Miscellaneous dealer (?) or collector (?) annotations
   in bottom corners of sheet
Watermarks: standing bear with wheel, *1597*
Schwarz L 444 V (undescribed proof impression)
1986.196

5e
Luther geht ins Kloster (Luther Enters the
   Monastery)
Sheet: 18⁵/₈ × 13¹/₈ (47.3 × 33.3)
Annotated, l.l. of sheet: X
Inscribed, l.l. of image: *Pr.*
Signed, l.r. of image: *Lovis Corinth*
Miscellaneous dealer (?) or collector (?) annotations
   in bottom corners of sheet
Watermarks: standing bear with wheel, *1597*
Schwarz L 444 VI (undescribed proof impression)
1986.200

5f
Luther geht ins Kloster (Luther Enters the
   Monastery)
Sheet: 18⁷/₈ × 13¹/₁₆ (47.9 × 33.2)
Inscribed, l.l. of image: *Pr.*
Signed, l.r. of image: *Lovis Corinth*
Miscellaneous dealer (?) or collector (?) annotations
   in bottom right corner of sheet
Watermarks: standing bear with wheel, *1597*
Schwarz L 444 VI A (possibly one of ten proof
   impressions described)
1986.197

5g
Luther im Kloster (Luther in the Monastery)
Sheet: 18⁵/₈ × 13 (47.3 × 33)
Inscribed, l.l. of image: *Pr.*
Signed, l.r. of image: *Lovis Corinth*
Miscellaneous dealer (?) or collector (?) annotations
   in bottom corners of sheet
Watermarks: standing bear with wheel, *1597*
Schwarz L 444 VII (undescribed proof impression)
1986.216

5h
Versuchung (Tentatio) (Temptation [Tentatio])
Sheet: 18⁹/₁₆ × 13¹/₁₆ (47.1 × 33.2)
Annotated in purple pencil, l.l. of sheet: X
Inscribed, l.l. of image: *Pr.*
Signed, l.r. of image: *Lovis Corinth*
Miscellaneous dealer (?) or collector (?) annotations
   in bottom corners of sheet
Watermarks: standing bear with wheel, *1597*
Schwarz L 444 VIII (undescribed proof impression)
1986.195

5i
Versuchung (Tentatio) (Temptation [Tentatio])
Sheet: 18¹⁵/₁₆ × 13¹/₁₆ (48.1 × 33.2)
Inscribed, l.l. of image: *Pr.*
Signed, l.r. of image: *Lovis Corinth*
Miscellaneous dealer (?) or collector (?) annotations
   in bottom right corner of sheet
Watermarks: standing bear with wheel, *1597*
Schwarz L 444 VIII A (possibly one of ten proof
   impressions described)
1986.215

5j
Antichrist
Sheet: 18⅝ × 13⅛ (47.3 × 33.3)
Annotated in purple pencil, l.l. of sheet: *X*
Inscribed, l.l. of image: *Pr.*
Signed, l.r. of image: *Lovis Corinth*
Miscellaneous dealer (?) or collector (?) annotations
    in bottom corners of sheet
Watermarks: standing bear with wheel, *1597*
Schwarz L 444 IX (undescribed proof impression)
1986.214

5k
Ablasshandel (Sale of Indulgences)
Sheet: 18⅝ × 13¹/₁₆ (47.3 × 33.2)
Inscribed, u.l. in image: *ABLASS. / Sobald der Gülden /
    im Becken klingt / Im Hui die Seele / im Himel
    springt.*
Annotated, l.l. of sheet: *X*
Inscribed, l.l. of image: *Pr.*
Signed, l.r. of image: *Lovis Corinth*
Miscellaneous dealer (?) or collector (?) annotations
    in bottom corners of sheet
Watermarks: standing bear with wheel, *1597*
Schwarz L 444 X (undescribed proof impression)
1986.213

5l
Überfall auf Tetzel (Ambush on Tetzel)
Sheet: 18⅞ × 13¹/₁₆ (47.9 × 33.2)
Inscribed, l.l. of image: *Pr.*
Signed, l.r. of image: *Lovis Corinth*
Miscellaneous dealer (?) or collector (?) annotations
    in bottom right corner of sheet
Watermarks: standing bear with wheel, *1597*
Schwarz L 444 XI (undescribed proof impression)
1986.212

5m
Bruder Martin (Brother Martin)
Sheet: 13¾ × 9½ (33.5 × 24.1)
Annotated in purple pencil, l.l. of sheet: *X*
Annotated, in image: a line around the frontal
    head
Inscribed, l.l. of image: *Pr.*
Signed, l.r. of image: *Lovis Corinth*
Miscellaneous dealer (?) or collector (?) annotations
    in bottom corners of sheet
Watermarks: standing bear with wheel, *1597*
Schwarz L 444 XII I/II (possibly one of ten
    proof impressions described)
1986.211

5n
Bruder Martin (Brother Martin)
Paper: thick wove paper with deckel edge
Sheet: 19⅜ × 15⅛ (49.2 × 38.4)
Inscribed, l.l. of image: *Pr.*
Signed, l.r. of image: *Lovis Corinth*
Miscellaneous dealer (?) or collector (?) annotations
    in bottom corners of sheet

Schwarz L 444 XII II/II (undescribed proof
    impression)
1986.210

5o
Die 95 Thesen (The Ninety-five Theses)
Sheet: 19 × 13 (58.3 × 33)
Annotated, l.l. of sheet: *X*
Inscribed, l.l. of image: *Pr.*
Signed, l.r. of image: *Lovis Corinth*
Miscellaneous dealer (?) or collector (?) annotations
    in bottom corners of sheet
Watermarks: standing bear with wheel, *1597*
Schwarz L 444 XIII (undescribed proof impression)
1986.217

5p
Karl V., Philip von Hessen und Georg V, Frundsberg
    (Charles V, Philip of Hesse and George V,
    Frundsberg)
Sheet: 18⅞ × 13¹/₁₆ (47.9 × 33.2)
Inscribed, at top in image: *Frundsberg, Karl V,* and
    Philipp v. / Hessen
Annotated in purple pencil, l.l. of sheet: *X*
Inscribed, l.l. of image: *Pr.*
Signed, l.r. of image: *Lovis Corinth*
Miscellaneous dealer (?) or collector (?) annotations
    in bottom corners of sheet
Watermarks: standing bear with wheel, *1597*
Schwarz L 444 XIV (undescribed proof
    impression)
1986.218

5q
Kaiser Maximilian I (Emperor Maximilian I)
Sheet: 18¹⁵/₁₆ × 13⅛ (48.1 × 33.3)
Inscribed, at bottom in image: *IMPERATOR,
    MAXIMLIANUS.* [sic] *Germani / ae.*
Annotated, l.l. of sheet: *X*
Inscribed, l.l. of image: *Pr.*
Signed, l.r. of image: *Lovis Corinth*
Miscellaneous dealer (?) or collector (?) annotations
    in bottom corners of sheet
Watermarks: standing bear with wheel, *1597*
Schwarz L 444 XV (undescribed proof
    impression)
1986.198

5r
Kurfürst Friedrick der Weise (Elector Frederick the
    Wise)
Sheet: 13¹/₁₆ × 9½ (33.2 × 24.1)
Inscribed, at bottom in image: *Friedrich der Weise.*
Inscribed, l.l. of image: *Pr.*
Signed, l.r. of image: *Lovis Corinth*
Miscellaneous dealer (?) or collector (?) annotations
    in bottom corners of sheet
Watermarks: standing bear with wheel, *1597*
Schwarz L 444 XVI (possibly proof impression
    described)
1986.202

5s
Erasmus von Rotterdam (Erasmus of Rotterdam)
Sheet: 13⅛ × 9⁷/₁₆ (33.3 × 24)
Inscribed, at bottom in image: *ERASMUS
    Rotterdamus..*
Annotated, l.l. of sheet: *X*
Annotated, in image: a line around half of printed
    inscription
Inscribed, l.l. of image: *Pr.*
Signed, l.r. of image: *Lovis Corinth*
Miscellaneous dealer (?) or collector (?) annotations
    in bottom corners of sheet
Watermarks: standing bear with wheel, *1597*
Schwarz L 444 XVII (possibly proof impression
    described)
1986.219

5t
Luther verbrennt die Bannbulle (Luther Burns the
    Papal Edict)
Sheet: 18⁹/₁₆ × 13 (47.1 × 33)
Annotated, l.l. of sheet: *X*
Inscribed, l.l. of image: *Pr.*
Signed, l.r. of image: *Lovis Corinth*
Miscellaneous dealer (?) or collector (?) annotations
    in bottom corners of sheet
Watermarks: standing bear with wheel, *1597*
Schwarz L 444 XVIII (undescribed proof
    impression)
1986.220

5u
Luthers Einzug in Worms (Luther's Entry into
    Worms)
Sheet: 18⁹/₁₆ × 13¾ (46.5 × 33.5)
Annotated, l.l. of sheet: *X*
Inscribed, l.l. of image: *Pr.*
Signed, l.r. of image: *Lovis Corinth*
Miscellaneous dealer (?) or collector (?) annotations
    in bottom corners of sheet
Watermarks: standing bear with wheel, *1597*
Schwarz L 444 XIX (undescribed proof
    impression)
1986.221

5v
Luther und Frundsberg (Luther and Frundsberg)
Sheet: 18⁹/₁₆ × 13⅛ (46.5 × 33.3)
Annotated, l.l. of sheet: *X*
Inscribed, l.l. of image: *Pr.*
Signed, l.r. of image: *Lovis Corinth*
Miscellaneous dealer (?) or collector (?) annotations
    in bottom corners of sheet
Watermarks: standing bear with wheel, *1597*
Schwarz L 444 XX (undescribed proof impression)
1986.222

5w
Lucas Cranach
Sheet: 13¹/₈ × 9¹/₂ (33.3 × 24.1)
Inscribed, at bottom in image: *Lucas Kranach.*
Annotated, l.l. of sheet: X
Annotated, in image: a line around half of printed
  inscription
Inscribed, l.l. of image: *Pr.*
Signed, l.r. of image: *Lovis Corinth*
Miscellaneous dealer (?) or collector (?) annotations
  in bottom corners of sheet
Watermarks: standing bear with wheel, *1597*
Schwarz L 444 XXI (possibly proof impression
  described)
1986.223

5x
Lucas Cranach
Sheet: 18⁵/₁₆ × 13 (48.1 × 33)
Inscribed, at bottom in image: *Lucas Cranach.*
Inscribed, l.l. of image: *Pr.*
Signed, l.r. of image: *Lovis Corinth*
Miscellaneous dealer (?) or collector (?) annotations
  in bottom right corner of sheet
Watermarks: standing bear with wheel, *1597*
Schwarz L 444 XXI A (possibly one of twenty
  proof impressions described)
1986.224

5y
Ulrich von Hutten
Sheet: 18⁵/₁₆ × 13¹/₁₆ (46.5 × 33.2)
Inscribed, around crest at bottom of image:
  Ich habs gewogt. / Ulrich von Hutten.
Annotated, l.l. of sheet: X
Inscribed, l.l. of image: *Pr.*
Signed, l.r. of image: *Lovis Corinth*
Miscellaneous dealer (?) or collector (?) annotations
  in bottom corners of sheet
Watermarks: standing bear with wheel, *1597*
Schwarz L 444 XXII (undescribed proof
  impression)
1986.225

5z
Der Überfall bei Eisenach (The Ambush at Eisenach)
Sheet: 18¹/₄ × 13³/₁₆ (46.4 × 33.5)
Annotated, l.l. of sheet: X
Annotated: a horizontal line at bottom left edge
  of image
Inscribed, l.l. of image: *Pr.*
Signed, l.r. of image: *Lovis Corinth*
Miscellaneous dealer (?) or collector (?) annotations
  in bottom corners of sheet
Watermarks: standing bear with wheel, *1597*
Schwarz L 444 XXIII (undescribed proof
  impression)
1986.226

5aa
Der Überfall bei Eisenach (The Ambush at Eisenach)
Sheet: 18⁷/₈ × 13¹/₁₆ (47.9 × 33.2)
Inscribed, l.l. of image: *Pr.*
Signed, l.r. of image: *Lovis Corinth*
Miscellaneous dealer (?) or collector (?) annotations
  in bottom right corner of sheet
Watermarks: standing bear with wheel, *1597*
Schwarz L 444 XXIII A (undescribed proof
  impression)
1986.227

5bb
Dürer
Sheet: 13¹/₈ × 9¹/₂ (33.3 × 24.1)
Inscribed, at bottom in image: *O Gott! ist Luther
  todt, wer / wird uns hinfort das heilige /
  Evangelium so klar vortragen / Dürer*
Annotated: l.l. of sheet: X
Annotated: short perpendicular lines at upper
  edge and middle of left edge of sheet, and a
  line drawn around printed inscription
Inscribed, l.l. of image: *Pr.*
Signed, l.r. of image: *Lovis Corinth*
Miscellaneous dealer (?) or collector (?) annotations
  in bottom corners of sheet
Watermarks: standing bear with wheel, *1597*
Schwarz L 444 XXIV (possibly proof impression
  described)
1986.228

5cc
Teufelsspuk (Satanic Vision)
Sheet: 17⁷/₈ × 13³/₁₆ (45.4 × 33.5)
Annotated, l.l. of sheet: X
Inscribed, l.l. of image: *Pr.*
Signed, l.r. of image: *Lovis Corinth*
Miscellaneous dealer (?) or collector (?) annotations
  in bottom corners of sheet
Watermarks: standing bear with wheel, *1597*
Schwarz L 444 XXV (undescribed proof
  impression)
1986.229

5dd
Im Schwarzen Bären zu Jena (In the Black Bear Inn
  at Jena)
Sheet: 18¹/₂ × 13 (47 × 33)
Annotated, l.l. of sheet: a horizontal line below
  image
Inscribed, l.l. of image: *Pr.*
Signed, l.r. of image: *Lovis Corinth*
Miscellaneous dealer (?) or collector (?) annotations
  in bottom corners of sheet
Watermarks: standing bear with wheel, *1597*
Schwarz L 444 XXVI (undescribed proof
  impression)
1986.203

5ee
Hans Sachs
Sheet: 18⁷/₈ × 13 (47.9 × 33)
Inscribed, at bottom in image: *Hans Sachs.*
Annotated, l.l. of sheet: X
Annotated, in image: a line drawn around half of
  printed inscription
Inscribed, l.l. of image: *Pr.*
Signed, l.r. of image: *Lovis Corinth*
Miscellaneous dealer (?) or collector (?) annotations
  in bottom corners of sheet
Watermarks: standing bear with wheel, *1597*
Schwarz L 444 XXVII (possibly proof impression
  described)
1986.230

5ff
Luther und Catherina von Bora (Luther and
  Catherina von Bora)
Sheet: 18⁵/₁₆ × 13¹/₁₆ (48.1 × 33.2)
Annotated, l.l. of sheet: X
Inscribed, l.l. of image: *Pr.*
Signed, l.r. of image: *Lovis Corinth*
Miscellaneous dealer (?) or collector (?) annotations
  in bottom corners of sheet
Watermarks: standing bear with wheel, *1597*
Schwarz L 444 XXVIII (undescribed proof
  impression)
1986.231

5gg
Eine Feste Burg . . . (A Mighty Fortress [is Our God])
Sheet: 19¹/₁₆ × 13 (48.4 × 33)
Inscribed, at top in image: *Eine feste Burg ist unser /
  Gott.*
Annotated, l.l. of sheet: X
Inscribed, l.l. of image: *Pr.*
Signed, l.r. of image: *Lovis Corinth*
Miscellaneous dealer (?) or collector (?) annotations
  in bottom corners of sheet
Watermarks: standing bear with wheel, *1597*
Schwarz L 444 XXIX (undescribed proof
  impression)
1986.232

5hh
Die Bibel (The Bible)
Sheet: 18⁵/₁₆ × 13 (48.1 × 33)
Inscribed, in image: text of the first Lutheran
  Bible printed by Hans Lufft in 1534
Annotated in purple pencil, l.l. of sheet: X
Inscribed, l.l. of image: *Pr.*
Signed, l.r. of image: *Lovis Corinth*
Miscellaneous dealer (?) or collector (?) annotations
  in bottom corners of sheet
Watermarks: standing bear with wheel, *1597*
Schwarz L 444 XXX (undescribed proof
  impression)
1986.233

5ii
Luther und sein Barbier (Luther and His Barber)
Sheet: 18¹³/₁₆ × 13¹/₈ (47.8 × 33.3)
Inscribed, l.l. of image: *Prob.* and *I. Probe.*
Signed, l.r. of image: *Lovis Corinth*
Miscellaneous dealer (?) or collector (?) annotations
    in bottom right corner of sheet
Watermarks: standing bear with wheel, *1597*
Schwarz L 444 XXXI (undescribed proof
    impression)
1986.234

5jj
Luther und der Legat Vergerio (Luther and the
    Legate Vergerio)
Sheet: 19 × 13¹/₈ (48.3 × 33.3)
Inscribed, at u.l. in image: *Da lachte er und sprach: /
    "Siehe, da fahren der deutsche Pabst und /
    Kardinal Pomeranus, die Werkzeuge Gottes."*
Annotated in purple pencil, l.l. of sheet: *X*
Inscribed, l.l. of image: *Pr.*
Signed, l.r. of image: *Lovis Corinth*
Miscellaneous dealer (?) or collector (?) annotations
    in bottom corners of sheet
Watermarks: standing bear with wheel, *1597*
Schwarz L 444 XXXII (undescribed proof
    impression)
1986.209

5kk
Luther und Cranach (Luther and Cranach)
Sheet: 18³/₈ × 13¹/₁₆ (46.7 × 33.2)
Inscribed, l.l. of image: *Pr.*
Signed, l.r. of image: *Lovis Corinth*
Miscellaneous dealer (?) or collector (?) annotations
    in bottom corners of sheet
Watermarks: standing bear with wheel, *1597*
Schwarz L 444 XXXIII (undescribed proof
    impression)
1986.204

5ll
Joachim I. von Brandenburg (Elector Joachim I,
    Brandenburg)
Sheet: 9³/₈ × 13¹/₁₆ (23.8 × 33.2)
Inscribed, at right in image: *Joachim I / Kurfürst / von /
    Branden / burg*
Annotated, l.l. of sheet: *X*
Annotated, in image: a line around printed
    inscription
Inscribed, l.l. of image: *Pr.*
Signed, l.r. of image: *Lovis Corinth*
Miscellaneous dealer (?) or collector (?) annotations
    in bottom corners of sheet
Watermarks: standing bear with wheel, *1597*
Schwarz L 444 XXXIV (possibly proof
    impression described)
1986.208

5mm
Kaiser Karl V (Emperor Charles V)
Sheet: 9³/₈ × 13¹/₁₆ (23.8 × 33.2)
Inscribed, at right in image: *Karl V*
Annotated, l.l. of sheet: *X*
Annotated, u.l. of sheet: a short horizontal line
Annotated, in image: a line around printed
    inscription
Inscribed, l.l. of image: *Pr.*
Signed, l.r. of image: *Lovis Corinth*
Miscellaneous dealer (?) or collector (?) annotations
    in bottom corners of sheet
Watermarks: standing bear with wheel, *1597*
Schwarz L 444 XXXV (possible proof impression
    described)
1986.207

5nn
Dr. Martin Luther
Sheet: 18¹⁵/₁₆ × 13 (48.1 × 33)
Inscribed, at bottom in image: *Es ist keine verachter
    Nation, deñ die Deutschen. / Italiener heissen uns
    Bestien; Frankreich / und England spotten
    unser und alle andere Länder. / wer weiss, was
    Gott will und wird aus den Deutschen / machen. /
    Martin Luther.*
Annotated in purple pencil, l.l. of sheet: *X*
Inscribed, l.l. of image: *Pr.*
Signed, l.r. of image: *Lovis Corinth*
Miscellaneous dealer (?) or collector (?) annotations
    in bottom corners of sheet
Watermarks: standing bear with wheel, *1597*
Schwarz L 444 XXXVI (undescribed proof
    impression)
1986.206

5oo
Luther errettet Melanchthon vom Tode (Luther Saves
    Melanchthon from Death)
Sheet: 18⁷/₁₆ × 13¹/₈ (46.8 × 33.3)
Inscribed, at bottom in image: *Die Beschwörung des /
    todt-kranken Melanchthon.*
Annotated, l.l. of sheet: *X*
Inscribed, l.l. of image: *Pr.*
Signed, l.r. of image: *Lovis Corinth*
Miscellaneous dealer (?) or collector (?) annotations
    in bottom corners of sheet
Watermarks: standing bear with wheel, *1597*
Schwarz L 444 XXXVII (undescribed proof
    impression)
1986.205

5pp
Magdalenchens Sterben (The Death of Little
    Magdalena)
Sheet: 18³/₈ × 13 (46.5 × 33)
Annotated, l.l. of sheet: *X*
Inscribed, l.l. of image: *Pr.*
Signed, l.r. of image: *Lovis Corinth*
Miscellaneous dealer (?) or collector (?) annotations
    in bottom corners of sheet

Watermarks: standing bear with wheel, *1597*
Schwarz L 444 XXXVIII (undescribed proof
    impression)
1986.239

5qq
Luthers Tod (The Death of Luther)
Sheet: 18³/₈ × 13¹/₁₆ (46.7 × 33.2)
Annotated, l.l. of sheet: *X*
Inscribed, l.l. of image: *Pr.*
Signed, l.r. of image: *Lovis Corinth*
Miscellaneous dealer (?) or collector (?) annotations
    in bottom corners of sheet
Watermarks: standing bear with wheel, *1597*
Schwarz L 444 XXXIX (undescribed proof
    impression)
1986.238

5rr
Ritter Jörg (The Knight Jörg)
Sheet: 18³/₈ × 13¹/₁₆ (46.7 × 33.2)
Inscribed, at bottom in image: *"Ritter Jörge"*
Inscribed, l.l. of image: *Prob.*
Signed, l.r. of image: *Lovis Corinth*
Miscellaneous dealer (?) or collector (?) annotations
    in bottom corners of sheet
Watermarks: standing bear with wheel, *1597*
Schwarz L 444 XL (undescribed proof impression)
1986.236

5ss
Ritter Jörg (The Knight Jörg)
Sheet: 18⁷/₈ × 13 (47.9 × 33)
Inscribed, at bottom in image: *Warthburg*
Inscribed, l.l. of image: *Pr.* and *I. Prüfung (nicht in
    Auflage)*
Signed, l.r. of image: *Lovis Corinth*
Miscellaneous dealer (?) or collector (?) annotations
    in bottom right corner of sheet
Watermarks: standing bear with wheel, *1597*
Schwarz L 444 XL A (proof impression
    possibly one of twenty impressions described)
1986.237

5tt
Die Herde Gottes (The Flock of God)
Sheet: 18³/₈ × 13¹/₁₆ (46.7 × 33.2)
Inscribed, l.l. of image: *Pr.*
Signed, l.r. of image: *Lovis Corinth*
Miscellaneous dealer (?) or collector (?) annotations
    in bottom right corner of sheet
Watermarks: standing bear with wheel, *1597*
Schwarz L 444 XL B (undescribed proof
    impression)
1986.235

MAX BECKMANN

Jahrmarkt Carnival

1922

Julius Meier-Graefe and Reinhard Piper commissioned and published the portfolio *Jahrmarkt* (Carnival) in 1922 (its plates having been executed the previous year) in an edition of 200 as the thirty-sixth publication of the Marées-Gesellschaft (Marées Society).[1] Pulled for the publisher before the regular edition, this exceptionally fine proof impression of the set of ten drypoints in their original sequentially numbered matts (stored in a printed folio cover and accompanied by prefatory texts and colophon) was printed on several paper types. The burr of the drypoint needle on the original plates still prints as a thick, velvety texture (normally, after repeated runs through the press, the burr wears down and some of the textural effect is lost), and special care was taken in the wiping of excess ink on each plate (prior to its run through the press) so that lines print as fine parallel channelings of ink. This undocumented example reveals the close relationship often formed between publisher, collector, and artist at this time.[2] The Munich-based Piper was Beckmann's friend as well as collector and publisher of his work. Establishing his firm in 1904, Piper promoted modern German art by devoting himself to publishing original prints and books about art, among them Wilhelm Worringer's theoretical defense of Expressionism, *Abstraktion und Einfühlung* (Abstraction and Empathy, 1908), Wassily Kandinsky's *Über das Geistige in der Kunst* (Concerning the Spiritual in Art, 1911), and *Der Blaue Reiter* (The Blue Rider Almanac, 1912). On occasion in his prints, Beckmann alludes to his publishers Meier-Graefe and Piper as a way of acknowledging their support. He dedicated the first state proof of his cycle *Gesichter* (Faces, Hofmaier 81, 84,

88–90, 105, 108, 126–137) to Meier-Graefe and illustrated Piper in *Carnival* as one of the characters represented in *Hinter den Kulissen* (Behind the Scenes, cat. no. 6f).

Beckmann worked in a late Impressionist manner until the First World War, when the shock of the war and ensuing social upheavals in Germany strongly influenced his changing view of the world and subsequently his stylistic direction. In 1915, he was discharged from the military after suffering from a nervous breakdown. Settling in Frankfurt-am-Main, Beckmann turned to drawing and printmaking (principally the medium of drypoint) and he began to paint regularly again only after 1919.[3] Between 1916 and 1923 Beckman produced approximately half of

1. The art historian and critic Julius Meier-Graefe founded the Marées Gesellschaft in 1917 with a program that included the publication of bibliophile books and portfolios with original prints, among them *Gesichter* (Faces) of 1919 by Beckmann and Lovis Corinth's *Antike Legenden* (Antique Legends) from the same year. A set of the latter, with original cover, is in the permanent collection of the Smart Museum (acc. nos. 1985.55–1985.67).

2. The colophon of this impression states that it was pulled before the edition of seventy-five as a proof for the publisher. Neither Klaus Gallwitz, ed., *Max Beckmann: Die Druckgraphik* (Karlsruhe: Badischer Kunstverein Karlsruhe, 1962) nor James Hofmaier, *Max Beckmann: Catalogue Raisonné of His Prints*, 2 vols. (Bern: Gallery Kornfeld, 1990) identifies this proof set or the small edition from which it originates. The colophon from the regular edition of 200 states that seventy-five were printed on Japan paper and 125 on Bütten, but upon examination of three different impressions, including this proof set and two portfolios in the collections of The Art Institute of Chicago, there exists a discrepancy between what the colophon and catalogue raisonné describe and the actual papers used; all three impressions are pulled on a combination of unidentified wove and laid, and various Japan and Bütten papers.

3. Frances Carey and Antony Griffiths, *The Print in Germany 1880–1933: The Age of Expressionism* (New York: Harper & Row, 1984), 157.

his graphic works,[4] out of a total oeuvre of 373 prints.[5] Of these, half are drypoints. The sustained involvement with graphics, and in particular the drypoint, played an integral part in the formation of his mature painting style. *Behind the Scenes* (cat. no. 6f), which in content and composition closely resembles his paintings *Familienbild* (Family Portrait, 1920, New York, Museum of Modern Art) and *Vor dem Maskenball* (Before the Masquerade Ball, 1922, Munich, Bayerische Staatsgemäldesammlungen), shows the reciprocal relationship between his activities as a printmaker and painter.[6] The manual dexterity and tight control demanded from the drypoint helped Beckmann develop the simplified, architectonic construction of space found in his paintings from this period. Referring to his graphics as a "very good friend,"[7] Beckmann regarded drypoint as an effective means to communicate his conception of art vis-à-vis its relationship to the world. The artist saw himself as a critic drawing upon a visual vocabulary to interpret society as it existed, rather than as an idealized presentation.[8] Thus, Beckmann's preference for the drypoint over other, more complicated intaglio processes stems from its compatibility with Beckmann's conception of artistic purpose; with its enforcement of angular forms, demand for a firm, direct statement, and dynamic quality of line, the technique lent itself to a confrontational representation of reality.

Carnival belongs to a group of print portfolios, along with *Die Hölle* (Hell, 1919, Hofmaier 139–149) and *Berliner Reise* (Berlin Journey, 1922, Hofmaier 212–222), that focuses on the modern city and, for Beckmann, its social corruption. Although Beckmann criticizes the city in these works, their sense of dynamism betrays the vitality of urban life to which he was nonetheless attracted. Beckmann articulated his ambivalent position in his 1918 essay "Creative Credo." Portraying the city as the locus of modern-day society, Beckmann saw it as a means for man's salvation, while he also acknowledged the suffering and banal existence it produces. He justified his own participation as part of his social responsibility as an artist towards mankind:

> But right now, perhaps more than before the war, I need to be with people. In the city. That is just where we belong these days. We must be a part of all the misery which is coming. We have to surrender our heart and our nerves, we must abandon ourselves to the horrible cries of pain of a poor deluded people. Right now we have to get as close to the people as possible. It is the only course of action which might give some purpose to our superfluous and selfish existence—that we give people a picture of their fate. And we can only do that if we love humanity.[9]

Whereas Beckman presents a direct indictment of society's dissolution in *Hell* and *Berlin Journey*, in the *Carnival* cycle the artist telescopes the "annual fair" into a microcosm of society. Identified in the table of contents and set forth in numbered sequence (the original matts are blind-stamped 1–10), the ten drypoints comprising the set alternate between intimate views of circus performers and panoramic vistas of the fair's overall hubbub. When viewed together, the scenes provide unconnected glimpses of various acts and roles performed by those within the circus community, and the individual sheets do not

4. Alexander Dückers discusses *Carnival* in his essay, "Portfolios," in *German Expressionist Prints and Drawings: The Robert Gore Rifkind Center for German Expressionist Studies* (Los Angeles and Munich: Los Angeles County Museum and Prestel Verlag, 1989), 113, n. 94.

5. James Hofmaier's recent two-volume catalogue raisonné of Beckmann's prints has replaced Klaus Gallwitz's partial cataloguing effort from 1962. See Hofmaier, *Max Beckmann* and Gallwitz, ed., *Max Beckmann: Die Druckgraphik*.

6. Reproduced in Carla Schulz-Hoffmann and Judith C. Weiss, eds., *Max Beckmann: Retrospektive* (exh. cat.) (Munich: Prestel Verlag, 1984), 212–13.

7. Max Beckmann, letter dated April 1917, printed in Hofmaier, *Max Beckmann*, vol. I, 8.

8. For an interpretation of Beckmann's relationship to society, see Hans Belting, *Max Beckmann: Die Tradition als Problem in der Kunst der Moderne* (Berlin: Deutscher Kunstverlag, 1984), 42ff.

9. Cited in Victor H. Miesel, ed., *Voices of German Expressionism* (Englewood Cliffs, N.J.: Prentice-Hall, 1970), 108. Beckmann's "Schöpferische Konfession" was first published in Kasimir Edschmid's *Tribüne der Kunst und Zeit*, no. 13 (1920): 66.

sequentially depend upon one another for their narrative content. In its ability to provide comprehensive and close-up views of one distinctive group on the social fringes of urban society, Beckmann's graphic cycle approximates more the structure of a play or film than a painting. At the time, in fact, Beckmann wrote plays which reveal his desire to incorporate various artistic enterprises into a single work. Indeed, the artist underscored his intention of presenting a visual drama in images such as *Behind the Scenes* (cat. no. 6f) and *Der große Mann* (The Tall Man, cat. no. 6h) which are composed as stage scenes. In *Carnival*, as elsewhere,[10] Beckmann links everyday life with the artificiality of the theater, thereby disclosing life's ephemeral existence and illusions. Explaining the use of this device, he later declared, "If one comprehends all of this, the entire war or even all of life only as a scene in the theater of the infinity, everything is much easier to bear."[11]

Adopting Max Klinger's definition of the print cycle as an extensive discourse of artistic reflection, Beckmann caustically comments upon society while conveying a moral imperative. Similarly, he developed a symbolic visual language that we are forced to decode, based upon how objects relate to one another.[12] Unlike Klinger, Beckmann conveys a greater sense of personal identification and emotional involvement by inserting himself pictorially into the cycle so that he acts as both participant in, and critic of, life's activities. Beckmann established this double role in the first plate of the portfolio, *Der Ausrufer* (The Barker, cat. no. 6d). Ringing a bell in one hand and using the other to point the way, Beckmann stands in front of a sign that reads "Circus Beckm[ann]" and summons people to the fair. Presenting himself as the stage director for the "drama" that is about to unfold, he links himself to the ensuing events by identifying his name with the circus, thus informing the viewer that it is the way *he* understands and experiences the world.[13]

As creations of his imagination, beliefs, and experience, the various circus players consist of both timeless icons and identifiable individuals close to Beckmann's own social circle. In *Der Neger* (The Negro, cat. no. 6i), Beckmann portrays a modern-day *Ecce Homo*, with the negro cast as a Christ-like martyr and an outsider—a victim of societal prejudice. The black man's generic features, notably curly hair, large nose, and thick lips, identify him as a type. While his lowered eyelids convey sorrow and oppression, his chiseled features—alluding in their angular forms to traditional African tribal sculpture—denote strength. Scholars have commented that the harlequin figure with pointed finger and laurel wreath alludes to Pontius Pilate, the Roman prefect whose decree set into motion Christ's passion and death.[14] By linking the man with the letters *keit* (the last four letters of *Ewigkeit* or eternity) inscribed behind him, Beckmann makes reference to the figure's inherent primordial spirituality and mankind's recurrent attempts to extinguish it.

Beckmann characterizes the woman in the *Schlangendame* (The Snake Lady, cat. no. 6m) as the personification of seduction. Heavily made up and adorned with a snake wrapped around her neck, she exudes sensuality and exotic danger. Gazing out at the viewer, her lowered eyes signal a sexual invitation. The man clandestinely departing or entering the doorway suggests the covert nature of their tryst. Popular in Symbolist and Expressionist art, in works

10. Dückers notes that Beckmann originally wanted to give the portfolio *Faces* the title *Welttheater* (Theater of the World) and that the series *Hell*, depicting his experience of the war and revolution in Germany, was described on the cover as a "grand spectacle in ten pictures." See Dückers, "Portfolios," 99.

11. Max Beckmann, entry for 12 September 1940, printed in *Tagebücher, 1940–50* (Munich: A. Langon–G. Müller, 1955), 11.

12. For an interpretation of Beckmann's highly personal and complex symbolism, see Friedrich Wilhelm Fischer, *Max Beckmann: Symbol und Weltbild* (Munich: Wilhelm Fink Verlag, 1972).

13. Carey and Griffiths observe that this same idea is used in the title page of Beckmann's cycle *Hell* and derives from Frank Wedekind, who uses the device of the animal-tamer to introduce the cast in his "Lulu" plays (*The Print in Germany*, 176).

14. Dückers follows Fischer's interpretation of the harlequin figure, see "Portfolios," 105.

by Oskar Kokoschka, Edvard Munch, Félicien Rops, and Franz von Stuck, for example, Woman as Temptress was not a new theme.[15] But with the innovative introduction of a male figure in the background, Beckmann points to man's complicity in the seduction. Again, in *Niggertanz* (Negro Dance, cat. no. 6l) Beckmann links women with sexuality, but this time more overtly as the object of men's carnal appetite. Wearing a transparent harem-style costume, the woman performs an erotic dance while clothed men voyeuristically observe her from below the stage. The accompanying musicians, outfitted in ethnic African costumes and playing percussion instruments, add an exotic note to the nightclub. The female dancer presented on stage, out of reach, becomes the object of male desire and enjoyment. In this context and with her back to us she is devoid of individuality and is thus reduced to a sexual object. She exemplifies the commodification of sexual relations occurring within a capitalist, urban society.

Beckmann turns inward to his world of intimate acquaintances in *Behind the Scenes* (cat. no. 6f), in which he focuses on performers waiting to go on stage. Even without the identification of members of the circus troop with specific acquaintances of Beckmann as proposed by various scholars,[16] the individual physiognomies of the entertainers betray Beckmann's intimacy with carnival people. Both the distorted spatial construction and tight composition contribute to an overall ambiance of constraint and point to the elusive nature of human relationships. Crammed into a low room, the performers belie their close proximity to one another through disengaged stares and general postures of ennui. They look past one another as they sit behind the curtain waiting for their cues. Beckmann, however, indicates that they are already on stage by constructing a three-sided room with a tilted perspective opening up to the audience. The actors are unaware that it is their anticipation that constitutes the drama of their lives. Like Franz Kafka's novels from this period, Beckmann presents life as an endless waiting game.

The Tall Man (cat. no. 6h) shifts from the close quarters of the dressing room to the stage that looks out over the carnival. The viewer enters the picture plane through the man on stage, who, in turn, looks out onto the fair, or, as the sign states, the "panopticum", or panoply, of life. The stage acts as a device which reflects the world back to the viewer, distilled through the critical lens of the artist. Beckmann often described life as *Rummel*, or hubbub,[17] and in this print the artist invokes the often-made literary definition of a fair—with all of its commotion and confusion—as a metaphor for the biblical Babylon.[18] Here then lies one key to our understanding the title of the portfolio (that literally translates as "Annual Fair"). The allusion equates the wickedness of the Old Testament city destroyed for its excessive luxury and pride with the insatiable appeal of the traveling carnival for modern man. Full of sideshow freaks, wondrous feats, exotic people and animals, strange foods, and exciting rides, Circus Beckmann exceeds the boundaries of normal experience. Adults regress into childhood,[19] as they escape from the rigid constraints of their daily lives and give in to their base desires. Beckman presents in *Das Karussell* (The Carousel, cat. no. 6j) the merry-go-round as a contemporary counterpart to the Ship of Fools, a theme well-known from sixteenth-century Northern Renaissance works by Hieronymus Bosch, Albrecht Dürer, and Hans Hol-

15. For the concept of woman in fin-de-siècle Symbolist art, see Reinhold Heller et al., *The Earthly Chimera and the Femme Fatale: Fear of Women in Nineteenth Century Art* (exh. cat.) (Chicago: The David and Alfred Smart Gallery, The University of Chicago, 1981), esp. 8–13.

16. Hofmaier identifies the man at the far left as Reinhard Piper, publisher of this portfolio and friend and patron of Beckmann. He also states that the tall man seated at the table is Erich Stichel, a doctor from Graz. See *Max Beckmann*, vol. II, 502. Scholars agree that the young woman at the right is probably Minna, Beckmann's first wife.

17. Fischer, *Max Beckmann*, 42.

18. Siegfried Kracauer, *From Caligari to Hitler: A Psychological History of the German Film* (Princeton, N.J.: Princeton University Press, 1947), 73. Kracauer analyses the meaning of the fair in the context of Robert Wiene's 1919 Expressionist film, *The Cabinet of Dr. Caligari*.

19. Ibid.

bien.[20] The mechanical vessel is filled with adults who gaily chatter away in anticipation of the ride. While two children watch from below, the master of ceremonies solemnly looks upon the vessel full of false hopes and illusions. Behind is a ferris wheel, possibly a reference to the medieval Wheel of Fortune, which traps the unfortunate riders in a dismal, endless rotation of waxing and waning luck and well-being.[21] The cyclical motion of both rides becomes for Beckmann a symbol of the chaos and forgetfulness into which the riders plunge without hope of escape.

Beckmann dedicated his *Die Seiltänzer* (The Tightrope Walkers, cat. no. 6k) to his first wife Minna as a "self-portrait of ourselves".[22] In 1925 Beckmann divorced Minna and married Mathilde "Quappi" von Kaulbach. Commemorating the union in the 1925 painting *Doppelbildnis* (Double Portrait, Städtische Galerie, Frankfurt), Beckmann portrays them close together with Quappi looking at him; each is dressed in a carnival costume. *The Tightrope Walkers* is, however, psychologically removed from this later work: Beckmann depicts Minna and himself performing separate high-wire acts on the same taut line, an autobiographical reference to the fragility of human relationships and the antithetical nature of man and woman. Beside Beckmann's veiled male tightrope walker is a crescent-shaped moon that may refer to the condition of Otherness since the motif also appears in *The Negro*.[23] Beckmann connects the female to life and its regenerative process by depicting her with an orb-like parasol, that, while echoing in shape the ferris wheel, may also refer to the sun and its life-giving properties. A similarly ambiguous motif is the petal-like splay of the female performer's dress and legs that repeats the form of the rotating spokes of the ferris wheel behind; in medieval and Renaissance depictions of the Wheel of Fortune theme, Fortuna—personified as a beautiful woman—sets the mechanical vehicle of man's fate in motion by literally turning the wheel's crank, and Minna's rotational performance seems empowered with similar control over the vicissitudes of life's endless cycle of mutable fortune.[24] Beckmann underscores their emo-

tional detachment from one another by their lack of awareness of each other's presence despite their precarious balance on the shared rope. This theme of duality between man and woman runs throughout his portfolio; in *Garderobe* (Dressing Room, cat. no. 6e), for example, he links man and woman together but places them opposite one another. Beckmann makes this parallel overt with the two plates that begin and end the portfolio: juxtaposing himself as creator and thinker in *The Barker* to the role of woman as sensual creature in *The Snake Lady*.

As a microcosm of contemporary society, the portfolio addresses both the world's daily chaos and underlying eternal truths. By unfolding the circus performers' routine in no specific narrative sequence, *Carnival* conveys the confusion of life itself while underscoring the persistence of human weakness and folly: lack of compassion, eternal lust, illusion, and irreconcilable differences between man and woman.

20. The allegorical poem *Das Narrenschiff* (The Ship of Fools) was composed in 1494 by the German scholar Sebastian Brant. Illustrated with woodcuts attributed to Albrecht Dürer, the poem describes a shipload of fools who set sail for the "fool's paradise", Narragonia, and it was intended as a satirical comment on contemporary folly and vice. Hieronymus Bosch produced, *circa* 1500, the painting *The Ship of Fools* (Paris, Louvre), and Hans Holbein created a group of engravings for Erasmus's *Enconium Moriae* (In Praise of Folly); see Erika Michael, *The Drawings of Hans Holbein the Younger for Erasmus' [sic] "Praise of Folly"* (New York: Garland Books, 1986).

21. Ibid., 74. Fortuna's Wheel is represented in manuscript painting of the High Middle Ages as a rotating spoked wheel, occasionally set into its eternal spinning cycle by Fortuna who, personified as a courtly woman, turns the crank at the wheel's hub; on the theme in medieval literature and its pictorialization in the visual arts, see Ernst Kitzinger, "World Map and Fortune's Wheel: A Medieval Mosaic Floor in Turin," *Proceedings of the American Philosophical Society* 117, no. 5 (1973): 343–73; reprinted in W. Eugene Kleinbauer, ed., *The Art of Byzantium and the Medieval West: Selected Studies by Ernst Kitzinger* (Bloomington: Indiana University Press, 1976), 327–56, esp. 343–48.

22. Fischer, *Max Beckmann*, 42.

23. Dückers, "Portfolios," 106. In classical art and Renaissance literature, the moon, as a lesser light than the sun, is imbued with sinister connotations.

24. Fortuna turning the Wheel of Fortune is seen, for example, in a late Gothic engraving by the German Master of 1464 (London, British Museum); for a reproduction of this print and discussion of the theme in relation to the art of Paul Klee, see Maurice L. Shapiro, "Klee's *Twittering Machine*," *Art Bulletin* 50 (March 1968): 67–69, fig. 3.

6a

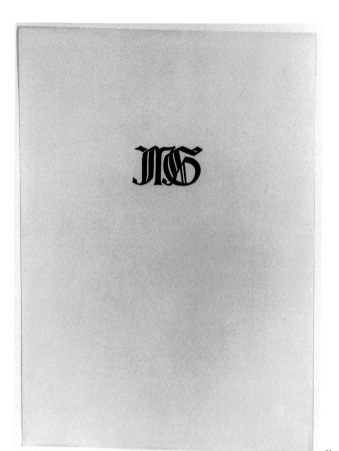

6b

Beckmann·Jahrmarkt

6c

Beckmann·Jahrmarkt

Drucke der Marées-Gesellschaft
herausgegeben von J. Meier-Graefe
Sechsunddreißigster Druck

6c

Jahrmarkt

18 Original-Radierungen von Max Beckmann

Verlag der Marées Gesellschaft/
R. Piper & Co. München, Römerstraße 1

MG

MDCCCCXXII

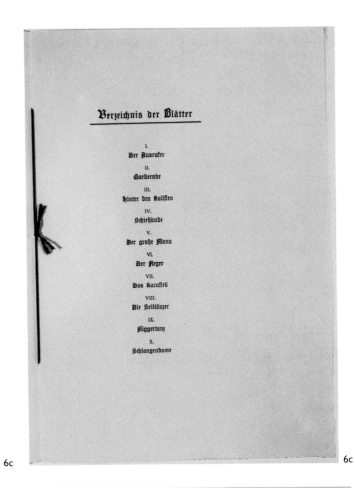

Verzeichnis der Blätter

I.
Der Ausrufer

II.
Garderobe

III.
Hinter den Kulissen

IV.
Schießbude

V.
Der große Mann

VI.
Der Neger

VII.
Das Karussell

VIII.
Die Seiltänzer

IX.
Niggertanz

X.
Schlangendame

6c

6c

Dieses Werk wurde als sechsunddreißigster Druck der
Marées-Gesellschaft
im Frühjahr 1922 hergestellt. Die Radierungen druckte Franz
Hanfstaengl, München; den Druck des Textes besorgte Otto
v. Holten, Berlin. Druckaufsicht und Überwachung des Textes:
F. H. Ehmcke. Es wurden 75 Exemplare auf Japan abgezogen;
120 Exemplare auf Bütten. Außer den 75 numerierten Exemplaren auf Japan wurde dieses Exemplar abgezogen als Beleg für
den Verlag

6d

6e

6g

6f

6h

6i

6j

6k

61

Max Beckmann
German, 1884–1950

Jahrmarkt (Carnival)
Portfolio of ten prints in original
sequentially numbered matts (1–10),
with frontispiece and introductory six-
page booklet (title and contents pages,
colophon), in original portfolio cover

Medium: drypoint

Ink: black

Paper: various

Publisher and Publication Date:
Marées Gesellschaft, Verlag R. Piper &
Co., Munich, 1922 [plates executed
1921]

References: Gallwitz 163–172,
Hofmaier 191–200

The David and Alfred Smart Museum of
Art, Marcia and Granvil Specks
Collection
Acc. nos. 1983.129–1983.138

6m

6a
Cover
Yellow paper board with vellum spine; black typeset title and embossed Marées Gesellschaft logo on front, black typeset title on spine
Format: 22 1/16 × 60 1/4 (56.1 × 41.3) (closed)
1983.129a

6b
Frontispiece (with publisher's cipher *MG* in *Altdeutsch*)
Black typeset on thick wove paper
Sheet: 21 9/16 × 15 1/2 (54.8 × 39.4)
1983.129b

6c
Text Pages
Booklet comprised of six pages (three bifolios bound as a trinion with black cord), designed by Rudolf Weiss:
f. 1r.: half title page in red typeset
f. 1v.: blank
f. 2r.: publisher's page in black typeset
f. 2v.: blank
f. 3r.: title page in red and black typeset
f. 3v.: blank
f. 4r.: contents page in black typeset
f. 4v.: colophon in black typeset
f. 5r.: blank
f. 5v.: blank
f. 6r.: blank
f. 6v.: blank
Outer folio: wove paper with watermark (crown and scroll)
Two inner bifolios: laid paper
Each Sheet: 20 5/8 × 14 5/8 (52.4 × 37.2) (folded)
1983.129c

6d
Der Ausrufer (The Barker)
Paper: Bütten paper
Sheet: 21 3/8 × 15 1/8 (54.3 × 38.4)
Plate: 13 3/16 × 9 15/16 (33.5 × 25.2)
Signed, l.r. below plate: *Beckmann*
Embossed in blind stamp below signature: logo of Marées Gesellschaft
Matt blind stamped, l.c.: *1*
Gallwitz 163, Hofmaier 191
1983.129

6e
Garderobe (Dressing Room)
Paper: laid paper with deckel edge
Sheet: 16 1/4 × 9 15/16 (41.3 × 25.2)
Plate: 7 7/8 × 5 9/16 (20 × 14.1)
Signed, l.r. below plate: *Beckmann*
Embossed in blind stamp below signature: logo of Marées Gesellschaft
Matt blind stamped, l.c.: 2
Gallwitz 164, Hofmaier 192
1983.130

6f
Hinter den Kulissen (Behind the Scenes)
Paper: wove paper with a deckel edge
Sheet: 13 × 18 3/8 (33 × 46.7)
Plate: 8 × 11 7/8 (20.3 × 27.6)
Signed, l.r. below plate: *Beckmann*
Embossed in blind stamp below signature: logo of Marées Gesellschaft
Matt blind stamped, l.c.: *3*
Gallwitz 165, Hofmaier 193
1983.131

6g
Schiessbude (Shooting Gallery)
Paper: Bütten paper
Sheet: 21 1/2 × 15 9/16 (54.6 × 39.5)
Plate: 12 9/16 × 9 9/16 (31.9 × 24.3)
Signed, l.r. below plate: *Beckmann*
Embossed in blind stamp below signature: logo of Marées Gesellschaft
Matt blind stamped, l.c.: *4*
Gallwitz 166, Hofmaier 194
1983.132

6h
Der große Mann (The Tall Man)
Paper: wove paper
Sheet: 18 5/8 × 13 (47.3 × 33)
Plate: 11 7/8 × 8 (30.2 × 20.3)
Signed, l.r. below plate: *Beckmann*
Embossed in blind stamp below signature: logo of Marées Gesellschaft
Matt blind stamped, l.c.: 5
Gallwitz 167, Hofmaier 195
1983.133

6i
Der Neger (The Negro)
Paper: Bütten paper
Sheet: 20 7/8 × 15 1/4 (53 × 38.7)
Plate: 11 1/8 × 9 15/16 (28.3 × 25.2)
Signed, l.r. below plate: *Beckmann*
Embossed in blind stamp below signature: logo of Marées Gesellschaft
Matt blind stamped, l.c.: *6*
Gallwitz 168, Hofmaier 196
1983.134

6j
Das Karussell (The Carousel)
Paper: Bütten paper
Sheet: 21 × 14 7/8 (53.3 × 37.8)
Plate: 11 1/8 × 9 15/16 (28.3 × 25.2)
Signed, l.r. below plate: *Beckmann*
Embossed in blind stamp below signature: logo of Marées Gesellschaft
Matt blind stamped, l.c.: 7
Gallwitz 169, Hofmaier 197
1983.135

6k
Die Seiltänzer (The Tightrope Walkers)
Paper: Bütten paper
Sheet: 21 3/8 × 15 1/4 (54.3 × 38.7)
Plate: 9 15/16 × 9 13/16 (25.2 × 24.9)
Signed, l.r. below plate: *Beckmann*
Embossed in blind stamp below signature: logo of Marées Gesellschaft
Matt blind stamped, l.c.: *8*
Gallwitz 170, Hofmaier 198
1983.136

6l
Niggertanz (Negro Dance)
Paper: wove paper with deckel edge (different paper from nos. 2f and 2h)
Sheet: 21 3/16 × 14 3/16 (53.8 × 36)
Plate: 9 15/16 × 9 13/16 (25.2 × 24.9)
Signed, l.r. below plate: *Beckmann*
Embossed in blind stamp below signature: logo of Marées Gesellschaft
Matt blind stamped, l.c.: *9*
Gallwitz 171, Hofmaier 199
1983.137

6m
Schlangendame (The Snake Lady)
Paper: parchment-like wove paper
Sheet: 21 3/8 × 15 1/8 (54.3 × 38.4)
Plate: 11 1/16 × 9 7/8 (28.1 × 25.1)
Signed, l.r. below plate: *Beckmann*
Embossed in blind stamp below signature: logo of Marées Gesellschaft
Matt blind stamped, l.c.: *10*
Gallwitz 172, Hofmaier 200
1983.138

GEORGE GROSZ

Die Räuber The Robbers
1922

In the years immediately after the First World War such artists as Max Beckmann and Otto Dix, both of whom had served in the German army, produced not only some of their most important print cycles but also a great number of them, including *Die Hölle* (Hell, 1919, Hofmaier 139–149), *Jahrmarkt* (Carnival, 1921, cat. no. 6), and *Berliner Reise* (Berlin Journey, 1922, Hofmaier 212–222) by Beckmann, and *Zirkus* (Circus, 1922) and *Der Krieg* (The War, 1924, cat. no. 9) by Dix. Similarly, George Grosz, who had also served in the military on two separate occasions, contributed a wealth of socially and politically critical cycles and illustrated books, including *Gott mit uns* (God is with Us, 1920), *Das Gesicht der herrschenden Klasse* (The Face of the Ruling Class, 1921), *Im Schatten* (In the Shadow, 1921), *Ecce Homo* (1922–23), and the present series *Die Räuber* (The Robbers). Although the prints of Beckmann, Dix, and Grosz vary in style, they share a sharply observed view of modern German society and its dehumanizing effects. Ironically, these prints appealed often to the very social classes they acerbicly criticized, a situation which points to the increased commodification of the print cycle in the 1920s. Purchased by the bourgeoisie as a hedge against the ruinous inflationary spiral that plagued the German economy during the Weimar Republic, the print portfolio became a form of investment: individuals daily converted the precipitously devalued mark into material goods before the next monetary slide of the near worthless banknotes (*Notgeld*) that were printed in ever larger denominations. Observing this situation, Grosz wrote in 1925:

> Today's art is dependent on the bourgeois class and shall die with it; the artist, possibly without

wishing to be so, is a banknote factory and an investment machine of which the rich exploiter and the aesthetic fop make use in order to invest his money more or less advantageously, in order to appear both to himself and to society as a patron of culture, which also seeks him out.[1]

In an attempt to sabotage the operation of the "investment machine", Grosz, a member of the German Communist party (KPD) since 1918, reproduced his drawings primarily through offset lithography. His acceptance of a commercial printing process as a suitable medium for his prints in turn was a rejection of the Expressionist (principally Brücke) artists' involvement with the making, printing, and distribution of original prints and their attendant ideological proclamation of the fine arts as an expression of individual creativity and artistic freedom. Grosz repudiated the avant-garde equation of an artist's individual creativity with a society in which all freedoms are protected and cherished.[2] As a corollary, modern painting and graphics, which emphasized authenticity, had assumed during the first two decades of the century the function of modern icons of individualism. Instead, Grosz valued collective human identity over individual creative genius and tai-

1. Cited in Stephanie D'Alessandro's entry (no. 49) for Grosz's *Die Familie* (The Family) and translated by Reinhold Heller in Heller et al., *Art in Germany 1909–1936: From Expressionism to Resistance: The Marvin and Janet Fishman Collection* (exh. cat.) (Munich: Prestel Verlag in association with the Milwaukee Art Museum, 1990), 180.

2. Carol Duncan discusses the myth of the avant-garde in her article "Virility and Domination in Early Twentieth-Century Vanguard Painting," in Norma Broude and Mary D. Garrard, eds., *Feminism and Art History: Questioning the Litany* (New York: Harper & Row, 1982), 294.

lored his art work during the early 1920s to his own left-wing political agenda.[3] His art was meant to reveal the repulsive traits he felt characterized the dominant (and domineering) social classes: decadence, perversity, and hypocrisy.[4] Grosz's paintings, prints, and drawings contrast the prosperity of the petit bourgeoisie and upper class with the depredations of the proletariat worker brought about by a predatory capitalism controlled by big business and supported by the policies of the state.

In collaboration with Wieland Herzfelde, the publisher of the Marxist press Malik Verlag, Grosz published the bulk of his prints in small, inexpensive editions that were earmarked for distribution to the general public, in particular the working class.[5] *The Face of the Ruling Class* from 1921, for example, is the fourth volume of Malik's *Little Revolutionary Library* and was the first of the polemical or educational books designed by Grosz and others to raise the class consciousness of the proletariat;[6] Grosz followed this work with illustrations for such politically militant books as *Der Dank des Vaterlandes* (The Gratitude of the Fatherland, 1921). In order to finance this propagandistic thrust of the Malik press, Herzfelde published more expensive fine art portfolios affordable only by wealthy collectors.[7] *The Robbers*, for instance, appeared in an edition of one hundred, printed on three grades of paper and priced accordingly: nos. 1–5 on handmade Japan paper contained in a vellum portfolio; nos. 6–10 on handmade Japan paper in a half-vellum portfolio with the base price of 300 marks; nos. 11–45 on handmade paper in a half-silk portfolio priced at 150 marks; and nos. 46–100 on handmade paper and stored in a linen portfolio for the price of 100 marks.[8] Following Grosz's and Malik Verlag's true intentions, a large, unsigned "organization edition" targeted for the working class was printed in 1923 and sold for a mere 3 marks.[9]

Like Ernst Barlach's 1927 woodcut series *Schiller, An die Freude* (Schiller, Ode to Joy, cat. no. 10) and Lovis Corinth's 1923 color lithographic cycle *Wilhelm Tell* (William Tell),[10] Grosz's *The Robbers* draws on the literary work of the great eighteenth-century writer and dramatist Friedrich von Schiller. The titles

of the cycle and the individual prints are borrowed from Schiller's first drama, entitled *Die Räuber* (The Robbers, 1781). In so doing, Grosz consciously refers to his German cultural heritage, but unlike Barlach and Corinth, he does not seek to evoke a past, golden age of German intellectual enlightenment and religiousness. Whereas Corinth looked to Schiller's 1804 comedy *Wilhelm Tell* (William Tell), Grosz elected to draw his inspiration from a tragedy that relates the story of the educated son of a wealthy man who turns to banditry as a protest against society's corruption. Grosz seeks to condemn, not celebrate, a continuation of social evil in Germany as he calls for an overthrow of the existing order.

As a counterpart to his series *God is with Us*, which had exposed greed and stupidity in the military sector of modern German society, *The Robbers* attacks the capitalist entrepreneur. Consisting of nine photolithographs reproduced from pen and brush drawings, the cycle is a visual exposé of the inequality between the upper and working classes. As in all

---

3. See D'Alessandro's entry (no. 50) for Grosz's *Kaschemme* (Dive) in Heller, *Art in Germany*, 180.

4. D'Alessandro, entry (no. 49) for Grosz's *Die Familie* in Heller, *Art in Germany*, 180.

5. Beth Irwin Lewis, *George Grosz: Art and Politics in the Weimar Republic*, rev. ed. (Princeton, N.J.: Princeton University Press, 1991), 124. See esp. chapter five, "Books and Portfolios," which gives a good summary of Grosz's cycles from this period and their relationship to his politics.

6. Ibid., 132–33.

7. Ibid.

8. During the height of the inflationary period from 1922 to 1923, Malik Verlag set a base price for each book. To arrive at the current sale price, the bookseller multiplied this base price by a key figure that was sent out by the press at increasingly frequent intervals (Lewis, *George Grosz*, 273). For a breakdown of the different published impressions, see Alexander Dückers, *George Grosz: Das druckgraphische Werk* (Frankfurt: Propyläen Verlag, 1979), 197.

9. The designation "organization" made reference to the German trade unions or *Gewerkschaftsorganisation*, for whom the work was intended (Dückers, *George Grosz*, 197).

10. The Smart Museum possesses an impression of Corinth's cycle *William Tell* (Müller 775–786, acc. nos. 1986.240–1986.252).

of Grosz's work, his imagery is founded on antithesis[11]—in this case the comfortable life and smugly callous attitude of the ruling, capitalist class opposite the downtrodden misery and hopelessness of the laboring worker. The sequence of vignettes of contemporary urban life (each numbered in the lower left corner of the composition) provided a forum for the elaboration of this social and economic dichotomy in the form of a causal visual narrative without a written story line: the first images dwell on the ruthlessness and despicable actions of the bourgeoisie and set the stage for the final two scenes devoted to the inevitable suffering of the proletariat and his dream of violent revolt against an unfair economic and social system.

The series begins with the portrait of an ugly industrialist, holding in one hand a phallic cigar next to his genitals (clearly indicated by the bulge in his pants) while he tickles his fleshy stomach (see cat. no. 7a). Gloating and self-satisfied, he oversees the workers who toil in the soot and dirt of his factory. Fat, round-shouldered, flat-headed, and formally dressed, the industrialist is familiar from Grosz's stable of characters. Providing a connection between the two divergent worlds depicted, the image's title reads: "*Ich will alles um mich her ausrotten, was mich einschränkt, daß ich nicht Herr bin"* ("I will root up from my path whatever obstructs my progress toward becoming the master"). Like Schiller's villain Francis, who originally spoke these words (act 1, scene 1), the factory owner uses other human beings as instruments of his will. Grosz, however, does not make a one-to-one correspondence between the characters from Schiller's play and his own prints. Instead, he transcribes Schiller's text in order to heighten the impact of his own imagery—the startling juxtaposition and irony. Since Schiller's play had been performed recently in Hamburg, the literary reference would have been recognizable to Grosz's contemporaries.[12]

The second image proposes a direct relationship between the exploiters and the exploited (see cat. no. 7b). Crippled war veterans and an old woman and child dressed in tatters—industry's laborers and their dependents—stand behind three bloated capitalists, who sit and gamble in the foreground. Caught

between the capitalist and his factory, which is guarded by two policemen, the working class remains trapped and powerless, prisoners of the economic system. Once again, Grosz uses Schiller's words to connect the disparate parts of the composition as he focuses on the heartlessness and brutality of the rich businessmen: "Under my rule it shall be brought to pass, that potatoes and small-beer shall be considered a holiday treat; and woe to him who meets my eye with the audacious front of health. Haggard want, and crouching fear, are my insignia; and in this livery will I clothe ye" (act 2, scene 2). The industrialists' well-being is inversely proportionate to the physical state of the workers whom they exploit; the capitalist is viewed by Grosz as a parasite who makes himself fat as the worker exhausts himself and dies.

The third print in the series offers a domestic scene in which a well-dressed, disdainful capitalist verbally abuses a worker (see cat. no. 7c), and Grosz quotes from Schiller, "Poor hare! Thou playest but a sorry part in this world's drama, but your worshipful lords must needs have hares!" (act 1, scene 1).[13] The two men stand in an upper class parlor on opposite sides of a small, round whiskey table; their poses accentuate their different stations in life.[14] The wealthy man holds his clean-shaven face high and raises his arm as if to drive home a point, while the downtrodden worker keeps his unshaven head bowed in deference and his arms stiffly at his sides. Grosz also emphasized the unequal economic and social positions of the two men through his manner of drawing: a thin, clean line evokes the sleekness and sophistication of the bourgeoisie, while a thicker, ragged contour suggests the disheveled destitution of the lower working class. Grosz reintroduced this

11. Alexander Dückers, "Portfolios," in *German Expressionist Prints and Drawings: The Robert Gore Rifkind Center for German Expressionist Studies* (Los Angeles and Munich: Los Angeles County Museum of Art and Prestel Verlag, 1989), 88.

12. Stated by Ida K. Rigby in *An alle Künstler: War-Revolution-Weimar* (exh. cat.) (San Diego: San Diego State University Press, 1983), 63.

13. The word "hare" is a derogatory term that refers to abject submission and cowardice. See the note to "The Robbers" in Bohn's Standard Library, *Schiller's Early Dramas and Romances* (London: George Bell and Sons, 1907), 9.

7a

image in a later book of drawings, entitled *Abrechung folgt!* (The Day of Reckoning Will Come!), in which he changed the title to *A Half Century of Progress* and again in the 1930 work *Die Gezeichneten* (The Marked Men) as *Laid Off*. The artist often reused earlier compositions as well as individual motifs, slightly altering their meaning as he shifted them from one context to another. This practice is consistent with the artist's desire to devalue the uniqueness or privileged position of single works of art.

The fourth image resonates with irony (see cat. no. 7d). The war cripple seems to utter, "I have done my part . . . the plunder is your affair!" (Schiller, act 2, scene 3). In this work, Grosz confronts the dejected, demoralized castoff of society with the excessive consumption of the upper class. In his 1946 autobiography *A Little Yes and a Big No* (original version published as *Ein kleines Ja und ein großes Nein* in 1955) the artist described the common sight in German cities during the 1920s of crippled veterans of the First World War:

Real or fake war casualties were sitting at every street corner. Some of them sat there dozing until somebody came by, then they would twist their heads and start convulsively shaking. Shakers, we called them. "Look Ma, there's another one of those funny shakers." We had become quite immune to all the weird and disgusting sights.[15]

In Grosz's print, the maimed soldier, who had sacrificed his leg in defense of his homeland, is contemptuously regarded or ignored by the very people whom he had protected. Schiller's text assumes a second level of irony here when compared to its original context: Charles, the leader of the bandits in Schiller's tragedy, made this remark after killing a lawyer.[16] The outlaw leader is not interested in the dead man's wealth and leaves the spoils for his followers. In Schiller's play, the self-imposed exile's act of murder is symbolic of freedom and a disregard for moral law. In Grosz's illustration, the caption alludes to the hypocrisy of unjust laws, for the words are spoken by one who trusted the underlying principles of modern society and suffered greatly, only to be discarded once he was no longer considered useful. Grosz implies that his sacrifices have made safe the predatory economic pillaging of the middle class.

Schiller's words and Grosz's image in the next print examine the bestiality of the capitalist (see cat. no. 7e). Seated between his factories and a skeletal, starving child, the industrialist hoards his profits in his fat hands as he enjoys an expensive cigar and champagne. Swollen from malnutrition, the child implores him to share some of the wealth. The powerful captains of industry, the print's title suggests, lack the compassion of even the wild beasts that care for their offspring, as Grosz sarcastically quotes from the

14. For the handling of a similar composition and subject, see D'Alessandro and Heller in the entry (no. 54) for Grosz's *Straßencafe* (Sidewalk Café) in Heller, *Art in Germany*, 182.

15. George Grosz, *George Grosz: An Autobiography*, trans. Nora Hodges (New York: Macmillan Publishing Co., 1983), 122. Although the English version of the autobiography was published in 1946, it was an abbreviated translation of the original German manuscript, which was not published in its entirety until 1955. Hodges' translation is based on the 1955 text. For an account of the publication history, see Lewis, *George Grosz*, 281–82.

16. D'Alessandro and Heller, *Art in Germany*, 49.

7b

7c

exemplar of German Enlightenment: "Even lions and leopards nourish their young. Ravens feast their brood on carrion" (act 1, scene 2).

The sixth image in the series, entitled *"Gottes sichtbarer Segen ist bei mir"* ("The blessing of heaven is visibly upon me," Schiller, act 2, scene 3), ostensibly portrays a pleasant domestic Christmas scene (see cat. no. 7f) but is really designed to convey the spiritual emptiness of wealth. The father sits with closed eyes in the midst of his family and puffs contentedly on a cigar. Satiated, he has lavished material goods on his family — new toys for one son and boots for his wife — but there is no spiritual warmth as father, mother, and children appear to be oblivious to one another's presence. The hypocrisy of the scene is underscored by the mother's singing of the German hymn, "Silent Night," in the middle of such an ostentatious display of gifts and self-absorbtion.

Grosz shifts from the distorted observance of an ostensibly religious holiday to the hypocrisy of organized religion itself in the seventh print in which the Church is indicted as an instrument of capitalism and militarism (see cat. no. 7g). A cleric stands on a heap of dead soldiers' bodies and weapons in front of a bloody cross; he wears over his blood-stained vestments an Iron Cross medallion bestowed by a grateful military for his "bravery". "They thunder forth from their clouds about gentleness and forbearance while they sacrifice human victims to the God of love," Schiller's dramatic line reads (act 2, scene 3), and in light of this text, the scene of human carnage takes on an alternative meaning: the minister's heroism consists of his goading his congregation — under his protection as the Good Shepherd of his flock — to their death, like sacrificial lambs to the slaughter, for the capitalist cause.

After these condemnations of bourgeoisie selfishness brought about by industrialization and capitalism, Grosz focused sympathetically in the last two photolithographs on the plight of the laboring lower class and the appalling living conditions of the urban worker. The artist and social critic originally executed the drawing for the eighth print (see cat. no. 7h) in the series as one of nine illustrations for Franz Jung's revolutionary novel *Die Rote Woche* (The Red Week), which was published in 1921 in Malik's *Red*

7d

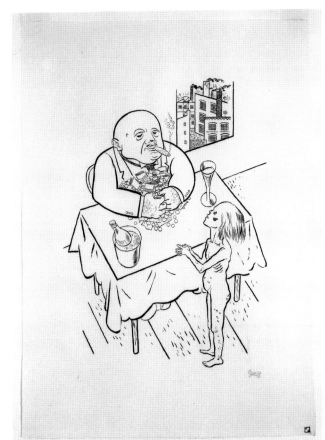

7e

Novel Series.[17] Initially titled *It Is the Proletarian Weakness*, the image was reused in the last edition of *The Face of the Ruling Class* as *And Grants to the Unemployed his Daily Death Benefits*, and later as *Triumph of the Machine* in *The Marked Men*.[18] In *The Robbers* the new title reads: "*Schwimme, wer schwimmen kann, und wer zu plump ist geh' unter!*" ("Let those who swim can – the heavy may sink!", Schiller, act 1, scene 1). Although the meaning of the image has changed slightly with each text, all these captions relate to the worker's inability to survive under the living and working conditions dictated by his boss. In sharp contrast to the luxurious, object-cluttered, comfortable living room portrayed in the sixth print (see cat. no. 7f), the isolated factory laborer lives alone in a sparsely furnished room. His head is buried in his arm, and he looks emaciated and prematurely aged.

For left-wing critics this disparity between the classes dictated action, and in the final print in the cycle Grosz entreats the proletariat to fight back (see cat. no. 7i). The bloodied worker resolutely stands with a raised fist among the graves of his comrades and the shabby working-class tenements with their cross-hatched windows that resemble the barred windows of prisons; he threatens eventual revenge on and victory over the capitalist oppressor. With the invocation of Schiller's words, "Right is with the strongest," Grosz establishes his platform of violent revolution. John Heartfield (brother of Wieland Herzfelde) later incorporated the raised fist into a photomontage that was used as an insignia for the Red Frontfighters' League, a mass workers organization, and a later variation of the motif was adopted as their official symbol.[19] The final illustration in *The Robbers* provides the rare example of how a work of art successfully side-stepped commodification and had an impact, albeit indirect, on a mass revolutionary movement.[20]

17. Lewis, *George Grosz*, 141.

18. Ibid., 141–42.

19. A description of this drawing's aftermath is to be found in ibid., 146–47.

20. Ibid., 147.

7f

7g

7h

7i

George Grosz
German, 1893–1958

Die Räuber (The Robbers)
Portfolio of nine prints

Medium: photolithograph

Ink: black

Paper: J.W. Zanders Bütten

Publisher and Publication Date: Malik-Verlag, Berlin, 1922

Reference: Dückers MV, 1–9

Marcia and Granvil Specks Collection, Evanston, Illinois

7a
"Ich will alles um mich her ausrotten, was mich einschränkt, daß ich nicht Herr bin." ("I will root up from my path whatever obstructs my progress toward becoming the master.")
Sheet 28 × 20¹/₁₆ (71.1 × 51)
Inscribed, l.l. of image: *1*
Signed, l.r. of image: *Grosz*
Watermark: *JWZANDERS 1920*
Stamped in black ink, l.r. of sheet: unidentified mark
Stamped on *verso* of sheet: *Grosz Nachlass*
Dückers M V, 1

7b
"In meinem Gebiet soll's soweit kommen, daß Kartoffeln und Dünnbier ein Traktament für Festtage werden, und wehe dem, der mir mit vollen feurigen Backen unter die Augen tritt! Blässe der Armut und sklavische Furcht sind meine Leibfarbe: in dieser Livrei will ich euch kleiden." ("Under my rule it shall be brought to pass, that potatoes and small-beer shall be considered a holiday treat; and woe to him who meets my eye with the audacious front of health. Haggard want, and crouching fear, are my insignia; and in this livery will I clothe ye.")
Sheet: 27¹³/₁₆ × 20³/₁₆ (70.6 × 51.3)
Inscribed, l.l. of image: *2*
Signed, l.r. of image: *Grosz*
Stamped in black ink, l.r. of sheet: unidentified mark
Stamped on *verso* of sheet: *Grosz Nachlass*
Dückers M V, 2

7c
"Es ist doch eine jämmerliche Rolle, der Hase sein zu müssen auf dieser Welt–Aber der gnädige Herr braucht Hasen." ("Poor hare! Thou playest but a sorry part in this world's drama, but your worshipful lords must needs have hares!")
Sheet: 27⁵/₁₆ × 20¹/₁₆ (71 × 51)
Inscribed, l.l. of image: *3*
Signed, l.r. of image: *Grosz*
Stamped in black ink, l.r. of sheet: unidentified mark
Stamped on *verso* of sheet: *Grosz Nachlass*
Dückers M V, 3

7d
"Ich habe das Meine getan . . . Das Plüdern ist eure Sache!" ("I have done my part . . . the plunder is your affair!")
Sheet: 27⁷/₈ × 20 (70.8 × 50.8)
Inscribed, l.l. of image: *4*
Signed, l.r. of image: *Grosz*
Stamped in black ink, l.r. of sheet: unidentified mark
Stamped on *verso* of sheet: *Grosz Nachlass*
Dückers M V, 4

7e
"Löwen und Leoparden füttern ihre Jungen, Raben tischen ihren Kleinen auf . . . " ("Even lions and leopards nourish their young. Ravens feast their brood on carrion . . . ")
Sheet: 27¹³/₁₆ × 20 (70.6 × 50.8)
Inscribed, l.l. of image: *5*
Signed, l.r. of image: *Grosz*
Stamped in black ink, l.r. of sheet: unidentified mark
Stamped on *verso* of sheet: *Grosz Nachlass*
Dückers M V, 5

7f
"Gottes sichtbarer Segen ist bei mir." ("The blessing of heaven is visibly upon me.")
Sheet: 27⁷/₈ × 20¹/₁₆ (70.8 × 51)
Inscribed, l.l. of image: *6*
Signed, l.r. of image: *Grosz*
Stamped in black ink, l.r. of sheet: unidentified mark
Stamped on *verso* of sheet: *Grosz Nachlass*
Dückers M V, 6

7g
"Da donnern sie Sanftmut und Duldung aus ihren Wolken und bringen dem Gott der Liebe Menschenopfer." ("They thunder forth from their clouds about gentleness and forbearance, while they sacrifice human victims to the God of love.")
Sheet: 27⁷/₁₆ × 19¹³/₁₆ (69.7 × 50.3)
Inscribed, l.l. of image: *7*
Signed, l.r. of image: *Grosz*
Stamped in black ink, l.r. of sheet: unidentified mark
Stamped on *verso* of sheet: *Grosz Nachlass*
Dückers M V, 7

7h
"Schwimme, wer schwimmen kann, und wer zu plump ist, geh' unter!" ("Let those swim who can – the heavy may sink!")
Sheet: 28 × 20¹/₈ (71.1 × 51.1)
Inscribed, l.l. of image: *8*
Signed, l.r. of image: *Grosz*
Stamped in black ink, l.r. of sheet: unidentified mark
Stamped on *verso* of sheet: *Grosz Nachlass*
Dückers M V, 8

7i
"Das Recht wohnet beim Überwältiger." ("Right is with the strongest.")
Sheet: 27⁵/₁₆ × 19⁵/₁₆ (71 × 50.6)
Inscribed, l.l. of image: *9*
Signed, l.r. of image: *Grosz*
Stamped in black ink, l.r. of sheet: unidentified mark
Stamped on *verso* of sheet: *Grosz Nachlass*
Dückers M V, 9

Börsentaumel
Stock Market Frenzy

1923

It is somewhat surprising that Rafaello Busoni, remembered today as the author and illustrator of such children's classics as *Somi Builds a Church* (1943), *Stanley's Africa* (1944), and *The Man Who was Don Quixote* (1958), should have executed *Börsentaumel* (Stock Market Frenzy), a biting commentary on inflation in Germany during the Weimar Republic.[1] Born and reared in Berlin, and emigrating to the United States in 1939, he was the son of a Swedish mother and the well-known Italian composer, pianist, and conductor active in Berlin, Ferruccio Busoni. No doubt the cultural and cosmopolitan life introduced to him through his father's profession encouraged his own artistic ambitions; he painted from an early age, experimented with the graphic techniques of lithography, etching, and woodcut, and held his first one-man show in Zurich at age seventeen. Although one may attribute his precociousness to his family environment, Busoni's decision to become a graphic artist places him in the enduring tradition of social caricature and illustration in Germany from the mid nineteenth century.

In the 1840s, two satirical *Witzblätter* or illustrated periodicals, *Kladderadatsch* in Berlin (1848–1944) and *Fliegende Blätter* in Munich (1844–1944), were founded to provide suitable outlets for social and political criticism to a large, literate audience living under a repressive regime. The editors of *Fliegende Blätter* commissioned artists, among them Moritz von Schwind, Carl Spitzweg, Adolf Oberländer, and Wilhelm Busch, to submit humorous drawings that were then translated into prints by skilled craftsmen

for reproduction in issues of the journal. Like Busoni, these artists also illustrated children's books. In 1896, Albert Langen's *Simplicissimus* and its counterpart *Jugend*, published by Georg Hirth, commenced publication in Munich as satirical weekly journals rivalling the by-then somewhat staid *Fliegende Blätter*. The most significant innovation of these new weekly periodicals was the emphasis on original illustrations—specifically the cartoon—which changed the character of the journal from an essentially written or verbal to pictorial or visual satirical format.[2] This shift reflected the late nineteenth-century development of a widespread readership situated in a fast-moving urban setting who had less time to absorb the complexities of an intellectualized literary style.[3]

Simplicissimus patronized a generation of illustrators, such as Olaf Gulbransson, Thomas Theodor Heine, Bruno Paul, and Eduard Thöny, who lampooned military life, the pompous and pretentious manners of the Kaiser and the aristocracy, marriage

1. For biographical information on Busoni, I have consulted Beulah Folmsbee, Louise P. Latimer, and Bertha M. Miller, comps., *Illustrators of Children's Books, 1744–1945* (Boston: The Horn Book Inc., 1947), 287; Marcia Dalphin, Bertha M. Miller, and Ruth H. Viguers, comps., *Illustrators of Children's Books* (Boston: The Horn Book Inc., 1958), 85; Howard Haycraft and Stanley Kunitz, eds., *The Junior Book of Authors* (New York: H.W. Wilson Company, 1951), 63, and *New York Times*, 19 March 1962.

2. For an historical account of the *Witzblätter* in nineteenth-century Germany, see Ann Taylor Allen, *Satire and Society in Wilhelmine Germany* Kladderadatsch & Simplicissimus 1890–1914 (Lexington: The University Press of Kentucky, 1984), 37.

3. Ibid.

and changing sexual mores, the philistine behavior of the middle class, slum-life, and many other facets in Wilhelmine culture and society.[4] As in the fin-de-siècle French poster, the style of the innovative drawings behind the reproductive print images published in the pages of the journal was simple, bold, and direct, giving the illustrations greater visual impact and power than possible in the minutely detailed, tonal wood engravings used in newspapers. *Simplicissimus* helped establish, among others, the career of the Berlin graphic artist Heinrich Zille (1858–1929), who became famous for his acerbic lithographic images that exposed the poverty and inhuman conditions of the urban working class in Germany. Combining a spontaneous drawing style with humorous captions written in a sharp Berlin dialect, Zille conveyed an authenticity and "eyewitness" immediacy in his work that found widespread appeal among the middle class. A generation younger than Zille, Busoni adopted a similar lively, realist style with vernacular legends but dispensed with the single-image format.[5]

In *Stock Market Frenzy*, Busoni extends Zille's strident, satiric caricatures into a serial format to address a sophisticated audience accustomed to visual parody. Focusing on the spiralling inflation that created economic havoc and widespread financial panic during the Weimar Republic, Busoni illustrates the pervasive disenchantment and paralysis felt by all segments of society at the alarming rate in the drop of the mark's value: in July 1914, immediately before the outbreak of the First World War, 4,20 marks bought one American dollar; by the end of the war in July 1919, this exchange had fallen to 14,0, and from January 1923 to November it slipped at a precipitous rate, until it finally depreciated to 4.200.000.000.000,00 marks to a dollar by 15 November 1923.[6] A fictional account, related by the protagonist of Erich Maria Remarque's *Drei Kameraden* (Three Comrades, 1938), captures the absurdity of the situation:

> In 1923, I was advertising chief of a rubber factory. That was during the inflation. I had a monthly salary of 200 billion marks. We were paid twice a day, and then everybody had a half-hour's leave so that he could rush to the stores and buy something before the next quotation on the dollar came out, at which time the money would lose half its value.[7]

The instability created a rapid downward social mobility within the middle class and a corruption of moral standards. Since the ordinary worker's wages did not keep pace with the devaluation of money, most families were unable to afford adequate food and clothing. Anyone in the middle class who possessed liquid assets was financially ruined. Apart from cash deposits in banks, most of their property was held in insurance policies and government bonds, which were now worthless.[8] Because they had converted their jewels and other valuables into cash in support of the war effort, many from the large middle class felt betrayed by the government and the banks whose policies were responsible for accelerating the pace of inflation. Social instability increased with the disenfranchisement of this segment of the

---

4. A brief history of *Simplicissimus* and its artists may be found in the introduction to Stanley Appelbaum, ed., *Simplicissimus: 180 Satirical Drawings from the Famous German Weekly* (New York: Dover Publications, Inc., 1975), vii–xii and xv–xxx.

5. The print cycle, made up of a series of "still" images, anticipated and served as a prototype for early film-makers. Zille's work, for example, inspired a number of films made in the twenties and early thirties, beginning with Gerhard Lamprecht's *Die Verrufenen* (Slums of Berlin, 1925). See Frances Carey and Antony Griffiths, *The Print in Germany 1880–1933: The Age of Expressonism* (New York: Harper & Row, 1984), 267. Lovis Corinth also connected the print portfolio with the cinema, but reversed the relationship, using the film as an inspiration for his *Anna Boleyn* (Anne Boleyn) lithographic cycle (Schwarz L428, L429) as well as a series of lithographs centered on the court life of Henry VIII (Schwarz L430). Both were inspired by the filming of a movie in the Babelsberg Studios (UFA) in Potsdam, with Henny Porten and Emil Jannings in the leading roles, to which Corinth had been invited; noted in Horst Uhr, *Lovis Corinth* (Berkeley: University of California Press, 1990), 267.

6. These numbers are given in a chart by Gordon C. Graig, *Germany: 1866–1945* (New York: Oxford University Press, 1978), 450.

7. Quoted in Craig, *Germany,* 451.

8. Hajo Holborn, *A History of Modern Germany: 1840–1945* (Princeton, N.J.: Princeton University Press, 1969), 599.

8a

8b

population. On the one side was loss of status—matrons selling family heirlooms, fathers losing their sons' respect, staggering suicide rates, and despair and ruin. On the other, there were adolescents wallowing in luxury, the nouveau-riche spending money recklessly in a hedonist quest for living for the moment.[9]

The title page (cat. no. 8b) establishes the theme of the loose-leaf cycle of six lithographs that comprise *Stock Market Fenzy*: the impact of the stock exchange on the bourgeoisie. Busoni's depiction of the façade of the stock exchange as a classical temple transforms this symbol of capitalism into a modern-day religious icon. Crowds rush to enter or groups eagerly wait on the entrance steps, and the business concern is transformed into the locus of a distorted world all-

consumed with economic survival. The title of the cycle, along with the name of the publisher that commissioned the work (Verlag für Börsen- und Finanzliteratur), appears below the image. This informs the viewer that Busoni's original audience was a specialized readership interested in economic and financial affairs of the day. Busoni's intention is clear: directing his modest portfolio at members of the middle class, the artist sets up a dichotomy between his intended audience—the official members of the stock market—and its profiteers and victims. Illustrating the meteoric rise and swift, precipitous fall of greedy schemers who played the market,

9. Henry M. Pachter, "From Bankruptcy to Stabilization," in *Modern Germany: A Social, Cultural and Political History* (Boulder, Col.: Westview Press, 1978), 111.

Busoni's satiric images caustically poke fun at the small-time speculator. In vengeance for their decline in fortunes, the middle class told jokes about the lack of education and table manners of these entrepreneurs, whom they nicknamed *Raffkes* and *Schieber* (low-born go-getters, profiteers, uncultured, nouveau-riche).[10]

The first image in the series after the title page illustration opens with three men on a city corner conversing together on a drab, rainy day (see cat. no. 8c). A sign reading "Schlächt[er]", or butcher, identifies the one wearing an apron as the shop-keeper. His profession links him to the petit bourgeoisie, while the bowler hats worn by the other two men suggest that they too belong to the same class. The group discusses the dead man whose funeral procession passes them; gesturing, the butcher remarks,

"There he goes and he still owes me the tips he promised," ironically oblivious to the condition of the man and his misfortune. The second lithograph takes the viewer inside a hotel bar, down the street from the corner in the first work (see cat. no. 8d). A barmaid and waiter stand by the counter listening to a waiter, named "Piccolo" because of his diminutive size, boast over his winnings. He confidently announces, as they look on in skepticism: "Another market like that, and I'll be the boss here!" On the next loose-leaf sheet, two cab drivers scheme on the corner in front of another bar (see cat. no. 8e). The first says to the second, "My motto is: First jump in!" Afraid of being overheard, the other responds, "Shut up, or you'll have to give 'em [stock market shares] up."

10. Ibid., 112.

DA FÄHRT ER HIN, UND DIE VERSPROCHENEN TIPS IS ER MICH SCHULDIG
JEBLIEBEN.

8c

Piccolo: Noch eene sone Börse und ick bin hier Chef!

8d

Meine Devise is: Immer Rindestiegen!
Mensch sei stille, sonst musste se abliefern.

8e

Sie: Geliebter, schau wie die Lerchen steigen!
Er: Jotte doch, und ick hab' keene jekooft!

8f

EINE VERZWEIFELTE STÜTZUNGSAKTION!

8g

MEIN SOHN, HAST DU NOCH EINEN WUNSCH?
JEBEN SIE MIR DEN KURSZETTEL.

8h

DIESES WERK WURDE IN EI-
NER EINMALIGEN AUFLAGE VON
300 EXEMPLAREN AUF ECHT-
HANDGESCHÖPFTEM ZANDERS
BÜTTEN IM AUFTRAGE DES VER-
LAGES FÜR BÖRSEN UND FINANZ
LITERATUR A.G. BERLIN GE-
DRUCKT. DEN DRUCK BESORGTE
DIE HANDPRESSE VON A.ROGALL
BERLIN. JEDES EXEMPLAR IST
NUMERIERT. JEDES BLATT VOM
KÜNSTLER EIGENHÄNDIG SIGNIERT.
DIESES IST NUMMER = 179/70

8i

Busoni shifts the viewer's attention away from the opportunist in the next cartoon-like scene in which a couple shares an afternoon together in the park (see cat. no. 8f). The wife has momentarily put her book aside and remarks to her husband, "Look sweetheart, how the larks are soaring!" The husband transposes the word *steigen*, which literally translates as "climbing", into a reference on the market's activity. Still absorbed in the stock column of the newspaper, he absent-mindedly responds, "Damn, and I didn't buy any!"

While the previous images—in order of their appearance in the portfolio—focus on the seductive power of the market, the last two concentrate on the ruination of those who have succumbed to its force. In the sixth composition, a man who has gambled and lost everything has hanged himself (see cat. no. 8g). Adding to the macabre spirit of the tragic scene are playful birds in flight above the suicide's head. In the caption, "A desperate support measure [*Stützungsaktion*]!," Busoni makes a word play on *aktien*, which refers to the stock exchange. In the last image in the series Busoni returns to subject matter about the outcome of selfish greed and the unremitting hold the market has on its victims (see cat. no. 8h). A priest has come to a jail cell one last time to visit a prisoner sentenced to death for his crimes. When asked if he has one final wish, the hardened, unrepentant criminal retorts, "Give me a stock report!"

The cycle ends on the same note as it began—death. Thus, Busoni reveals how the various get-rich-quick schemes illustrated within the series come inevitably to nothing. Directing his parody at a middle class audience who saw their wealth diminished, Busoni comforts them with a moral fable that punishes the unethical speculator for his greed and disregard for the misfortune of others.

Rafaello Busoni
German, 1900–1962

Börsentaumel (Stock Market Frenzy)
Portfolio of seven prints, ed. 290/300,
with original cover

Medium: transfer (?) lithograph or
photolithograph

Ink: black

Paper: J.W. Zanders Bütten

Publisher and Publication Date: Verlag
für Börsen- und Finanzliteratur A.G.,
Berlin, 1923

Printer: A. Rogal, Berlin

The David and Alfred Smart Museum
of Art, Gift of Mr. and Mrs. Berthold
Regensteiner
Acc. nos. 1984.21a-i

8a
Cover
Thick blue wove paper with printed title on white
wove paper affixed to front
Format: 15¹¹/₁₆ × 11¹³/₁₆ (39.9 × 30) (closed)
1984.21i

8b
Title Page
Sheet: 15⁷/₁₆ × 11¹/₂ (39.2 × 29.2)
Signed, l.r. below image and above title: *Busoni*
Watermark: *JWZANDERS*
1984.21a

8c
*Da fährt er hin, und die Versprochenen Tips is er mich
jeblieben.* (There he goes and he still owes me
the tips he promised.)
Sheet: 15³/₁₆ × 11⁹/₁₆ (38.6 × 29.3)
Inscribed, at bottom of image: title of work
Signed, l.r. below image and above legend: *Busoni*
1984.21b

8d
Piccolo: Noch eene sone Börse und ick bin hier Chef!
(Piccolo: Another market like that, and I'll be the
boss here!)
Sheet: 15¹/₄ × 11⁹/₁₆ (38.7 × 29.3)
Inscribed, at bottom of image: title of work
Signed, l.r. below image and above legend: *Busoni*
Watermark: *JWZANDERS*
1984.21c

8e
*Meine Devise is: immer rinjestieden! Mensch sei stille,
sonst musste se abliefrn.* (My motto is: First jump
in! Shut up, or you'll have to give 'em up.)
Sheet: 15³/₁₆ × 11³/₈ (38.6 × 28.9)
Inscribed, at bottom of image: title of work
Signed, l.r. below image and above legend: *Busoni*
1984.21d

8f
*Sie: Geliebter, schau wie die Lerchen steigen! Er: Jotte
doch, und ick hab' keene jekooft!* (She: Look
sweetheart, how the larks are soaring!
He: Damn, and I didn't buy any!)
Sheet: 15¹/₂ × 11¹¹/₁₆ (39.4 × 29.7)
Inscribed, at bottom of image: title of work
Signed, l.r. below image and above legend: *Busoni*
Watermark: chained unicorn
1984.21e

8g
Eine verzweifelte Stützungsaktion! (A desperate
support measure!)
Sheet: 15¹¹/₁₆ × 11⁹/₁₆ (39.9 × 29.3)
Inscribed, at bottom of image: title of work
Signed, l.r. below image and above legend: *Busoni*
Watermark: *JWZANDERS*
1984.21f

8h
*Mein Sohn, hast du noch einen Wunsch? Jeben sie mir
den Kurszettel.* (My son, is there anything else
you would like? Give me a stock report.)
Sheet: 15³/₈ × 11⁷/₁₆ (39 × 29)
Inscribed, at bottom of image: title of work
Signed, l.r. of image and above legend: *Busoni*
1984.21g

8i
Colophon
Sheet: 15¹/₄ × 11¹/₂ (38.7 × 29.2)
Numbered in blue ink at end of colophon: *290*
1984.21h

OTTO DIX

Der Krieg The War

1924

Already along the way to the front the impressions were horrible. Wounded and the first gas casualties with hollowed-out yellow faces were already being brought back. Then we proceeded into the "confused" trench system of static warfare, into the fomented, deathly pale trenches of Champagne, where one was tortured by the fetid corpses of the surrounding dead. The day before they had been piled up in a muddy corrugated iron dugout and the highest had emerged during the night. In boundless and tangled confusion the network of subterranean posts crisscrossed the earth, with its . . . kilometer-long concealed communication dugouts. A white, grayish-yellow death landscape, rising and falling like waves, stretched itself out, endless and deserted and only broken up by a pair of bullet-ridden, blackened pines. Later, at the Somme, it was a sea of dust and fire from the exploding grenades.[1]

Otto Dix published his graphic cycle *Der Krieg* (The War) in 1924, nine years after this written account of his first impressions of trench warfare as a German gunner on the western front in the First World War. The extensive series of prints in mixed intaglio techniques stands apart as the single graphic cycle among numerous depictions of war to which Dix regularly returned throughout his life. Consisting of fifty images assembled in five consecutive portfolios of ten plates each (generally inscribed below the plate in pencil, I to X), it constitutes, along with his 1920–23 painting *Der Schützengraben* (Trenches, destroyed), the first summation of his military experiences in the war. Dix did not determine the full size of

the cycle until he was in the midst of its execution and produced the portfolio in three working periods while in the Black Forest and in St. Goar am Rhein between 1923 and 1924.[2]

While many accounts interpret the cycle as a pacifist statement against war,[3] an examination of the prints in the portfolio and Dix's own comments suggest a more ambivalent interpretation. Dix's seductive technical mastery in the working of the metal plates from which the prints were printed and the obsessive manner in which he explores war's annihilating effects in the imagery reveal not only his

1. "Schon die Eindrücke auf dem Weg zur Front waren furchtbar. Verwundete und die ersten Gaskranken mit eingefallenen gelben Gesichtern wurden gerade nach hinten gebracht. Dann ging es hinein in das 'verbiesterte' Grabensystem des Stellungskrieges, in die aufgeweichen kreideweißen Graben der Champagne, wo man, vom Leichengestank der herumliegenden Toten gepeinigt, den Tag über in einem schlammigen Wellblechunterstand hockt und höchstens in der Nacht herauskommt. Grenzenlos und verwirrend durchzeiht das Netz der unterirdischen Stellungen die Erde mit seinen Kampf- und Nebengräben, mit seinen Unterständen, Sappen und Stollen, kilometerlangen überdeckten Laufgräben. Endlos und öde, auf- und abwogend, höchstens von ein paar zerschossenen schwarzen Kiefern unterbrochen, dehnt sich davor eine weiße, graugelbe Totenlandschaft. Später, an der Somme, war es ein Meer von Staub und Feuer, von platzenden Granaten." Cited in Otto Conzelmann, *Der andere Dix: Sein Bild vom Menschen und vom Krieg* (Stuttgart: Klett-Cotta, 1983), 78.

2. Fritz Löffler, *Otto Dix und der Krieg* (Leipzig: Philipp Reclam, 1986), 25.

3. For example, Linda F. McGreevy, *The Life and Works of Otto Dix: German Critical Realist* (Ann Arbor: UMI Research Press, 1981), 19 and 50, claims that Dix did not volunteer, but was drafted, and suggests that Dix fashioned the cycle as antiwar propaganda. The catalogue accompanying the 1991 recreation of the so-called Degenerate Art exhibition organized by the Nazis in Munich in 1937 also alludes to Dix's *War* as "pacifist etchings" and incorrectly attributes their origins to his wartime sketchbooks. See Stephanie Barron, ed., *Degenerate Art: The Fate of the Avant-Garde in Nazi Germany* (exh. cat.) (Los Angeles and Munich: Los Angeles County Museum of Art and Prestel Verlag, 1991), 224.

horror but also a corresponding fascination with the theme. Dix, who received an Iron Cross and the Friedrich-August medal for his war service, claimed that he was no pacifist[4] and that he volunteered for service because "I'm a man who is concerned with reality. I have to see everything. I have to plumb the depths of life. And so I go to war."[5] Later he stated: "I didn't paint war images in order to prevent war. That I would never presume. I painted them in order to exorcise the war. All art is exorcism."[6]

Dix's fascination with the theme of war predates his mustering into the German army as demonstrated by two Futurist-derived paintings, *Der Kreig* (The War, 1914, Düsseldorf, Kunstmuseum) and *Selbstbildnis als Mars* (Self-Portrait as Mars, 1915, Freital, Haus der Heimat), which eulogize the concept of military aggression and force. Tempered by first-hand knowledge and the war's sobering aftermath, Dix's postwar depictions are less celebratory of war's explosive and dynamic energy as they shift in style to a grim realism in which objects are minutely described in a manner reminiscent of Northern Renaissance and nineteenth-century Romantic painting in Germany. His explicit chronicling of modern warfare in the many prints, paintings, and over four hundred drawings devoted to his military service points to Dix's preoccupation with the theme. His controversial 1920–23 painting *The Trench* records the terrible consequences of battle in which dismembered corpses decay in a muddy trench splattered with blood. Dix may have taken advantage of the notoriety generated by the painting—which established his reputation in Germany—when he undertook his massive print cycle as a pictorial record of the horrors of the recent past. Both he and his dealer Karl Nierendorf were conscious of the increasing popularity of print collecting as a hedge against the ruinous inflation of postwar Germany, and collaboratively they decided upon the cycle as a means to widen the artist's audience.[7]

Published in an edition of seventy, the series appeared in 1924. Nierendorf, who supervised the publication, deleted two images known from proof impressions, *Soldat und Nonne* (Soldier and Nun) and *Soldat und Hure* (Soldier and Whore),[8] in the edited version because he feared that the public would find the explicit content too offensive. Each group of ten sheets originally sold for 300 marks; however, because of Germany's uncontrollable inflation, only one complete portfolio sold. As if expecting commercial failure, Nierendorf also produced an inexpensive, offset lithographic book edition of the portfolio for 2,40 marks.[9] Widely distributed at the time, it consisted of a selection of twenty-four images from the published cycle. The second edition of the book included an introduction by the French pacifist Henri Barbusse. Nierendorf exhibited a set of the original print portfolio in Berlin in 1924, and subsequently in fifteen other German cities. As a result of Nierendorf's promotional efforts the *War* cycle became an immediate popular success. Recognized as one of the most powerful encapsulations of the realities of modern warfare, the series received positive notices and reviews in important German newspapers, as well as in Spanish and Belgian art journals. At the time, Nierendorf wrote to Dix, "Never has

4. Conzelmann, *Der andere Dix*, 67

5. Cited in Alexander Dückers, "Portfolios," in *German Expressionist Prints and Drawings: The Robert Gore Rifkind Center for German Expressionist Studies* (Los Angeles and Munich: Los Angeles County Museum of Art and Prestel Verlag, 1989), 80.

6. "Ich habe nicht Kriegsbilder gemalt, um den Krieg zu verhindern. Das hätte ich mir niemals angemaßt. Ich habe sie gemalt, um den Krieg zu bannen. Alle Kunst ist Bannung." Quoted in Löffler, *Otto Dix und der Krieg*, 14.

7. Ibid., 24–25.

8. Conzelmann cites two images that were deleted from the portfolio (*Der andere Dix*, 180). Frances Carey and Antony Griffiths, on the other hand, mention only one image, *Soldat und Nonne* (Soldier and Nun, Karsch 120) as having been deleted; see Carey and Griffiths, *The Print in Germany 1880–1933: The Age of Expressionism* (New York: Harper & Row, 1984), 184.

9. Dix's exhibition catalogue contains an advertisement announcing the price of the offset book edition as 2,40 marks; this is slightly lower than the 2,50 mark price that Carey and Griffiths give for the work (ibid.). See also Gustav Eugen Diehl, ed., *Austellung Otto Dix: Katalog mit Verzeichnis der gesamten Graphik bis 1925* (exh. cat.) (Berlin: Kunstarchiv Verlag, 1926), 15.

a larger advertising campaign been made for a portfolio, and you can with justification say that you are famous."[10]

As Dix well knew, the themes of destruction and death in military conflicts had precedents in earlier graphic cycles, single prints, and drawings: Jacques Callot's etched series *Les Grands Misères de la Guerre* (The Large Miseries of War, 1633), Francisco Goya's intaglio prints from *Desastres de la Guerra* (Disasters of War, 1808–20), and Urs Graf's 1521 pen-and-ink drawing *Schlachtfeld* (Battlefield, Basel, Kunst-museum).[11] Closer in date to the execution of Dix's portfolio are several Expressionist graphic works, in particular Käthe Kollwitz's *Sieben Holzschnitte zum Krieg* (Seven Woodcuts of the War, 1924, Klipstein 177–183), Ludwig Meidner's *Krieg* (War, 1913–14), and Max Pechstein's *Somme 1916* (Krüger R96–104) and *Lithos 1917* (Krüger L190–202), all of which deal with war subjects in portfolio format. Unlike his Expressionist colleagues, Dix elected not to examine the emotional response of suffering and despair induced by the conditions of war, but instead clini-cally to dissect war's varying phases of physical devastation and desecration. And unlike Goya, whose *Disasters* was meant as an ironic commentary upon the rational principles espoused by Enlighten-ment philosophy, Dix accepted war in Nietzschean fashion as a "natural phenomenon" and "external law" of nature.[12] This is not to say that Goya and Dix in their cycles do not share similarities, but rather that they articulate world views representative of their respective eras.

Dix made a special study of the aquatint pro-cess under the instruction of Professor Wilhelm Herberholz in Düsseldorf before beginning his series, which suggests that be intended to equal Goya's technical mastery of the medium and to present a modern response to Goya's famous nineteenth-century series. Both artists underscore the senselessness and destructiveness of war, and neither favors a particular political or national view in their recapitulation of historical events (although Goya's *Disasters* is a vituperative comment on the

Napoleonic invasion of Spain by French troops). But while Goya focused on the humiliation and desecra-tion of different classes of Spanish society as the out-ward manifestation of mankind's moral malaise, Dix went one step further: he saw war as a process of spiritual and moral disintegration in which human worth and individual dignity are annihilated. The theme of Dix's *War* is dehumanization.[13]

Aside from the numbered order of the sheets (I to X) within each of the five portfolios that form the over-all cycle, there exists no readily apparent order—chronological, geographic, topical—to Dix's *War* series. Instead, imagery alternates among decaying, multilated corpses and skeletons, ravaged land-scapes and cities, scenes of madness and prostitu-tion, and wounded and battered soldiery. Dix distrib-uted the varying subjects and themes of brutalized soldiery and civilian populations randomly through-out the five portfolios, thereby suggesting that each image may be viewed independently or as an integral component within a larger, unified work. Dispensing with verbal narration, Dix took advantage of the cycle's sequentiality in order to visualize a relentless, even generic account of the overall numbing horror of the First World War on the battlefield and home front. On the other hand, the sporadic use of place names in print titles lends a specificity that in many ways anticipates cinematic war documentaries. With the exception of *Die Sappenposten haben nachts das Feuer zu unterhalten* (The Trench Sentries Must Maintain the Fire during the Night, cat. no. 9vv),

10. "Eine größere Werbung ist nie für ein Mappenwerk gemacht worden, und nun kannst Du mit Recht sagen, daß Du berühmt bist." Quoted in Conzelmann, *Der andere Dix*, 180.

11. These sources are mentioned by Dix in Florian Karsch, ed., *Otto Dix: Das graphische Werk* (Hannover: Fackelträger-Verlag Schmidt-Küster, 1970), 18.

12. Dix, cited in Museum Villa Stuck, *Otto Dix 1891–1969* (exh cat.) (Munich: Stuck-Jugendstilverein, 1985), 273.

13. Eva Karcher makes a similar point in "Alle Kunst ist Bannung" in Alfred Hagenlocher, ed., *Otto Dix: Bestandskatalog* (exh. cat.) (Albstadt: Städtischen Galerie Albstadt, 1985), 21

he seldom shows active combat; Dix does not seek to ennoble war but to unfold it in all of its stages of death and putrefying decay. In several prints of the wounded, dying, and killed (cat. nos. 9f, 9p, 9w, 9z, 9cc and 9pp), Dix manipulated the acid bath's corrosiveness in the realization of compositions (in reverse) on etching and aquatint plates as an analogue to the stages of decomposition of mutilated corpses when the completed plates were inked, wiped, and passed through the press during the printing of the approved designs. Describing his satisfaction with the etching and aquatint processes, the artist wrote: "Acid is washed away, aquatint is applied, in short, a wonderful technique, in which you can work the phases of the process in whatever way you please."[14]

The evolution of the compositions and the figure style is indebted to sketches of medieval frescoes showing the ravages of the Black Death in the Camposanto in Pisa and drawings and watercolors of ancient mummies in the Catacombs of Palermo made during his journey to Italy in 1923. The marriage of a technique that required patience and skill to an obsessive interest in the stages of human decay established the means by which Dix turned memories of his encounters with tragic, meaningless death into a willful, creative act. The remarkable nuanced tones and textural effects in many of the mixed intaglio prints recall primordial life forms—giving expression to Dix's vitalistic belief in death and regeneration— and entice the viewer into the pictorial space. In terms of traditional print connoisseurship vis-à-vis this major graphic cycle, an unambiguous dichotomy exists, then, between the seductiveness of the surface of the print and the repulsiveness of the imagery depicted.

Dix dryly commented upon the aftermath of German imperialistic ambition that had sent a sizable number of Germany's male population to be slaughtered in the shattered landscapes, desolate battlefields, and devastated cities (see cat. nos. 9b, 9d, 9i, 9k, 9q, 9x and 9y). Instead of the anticipated victorious return with its attendant glory and spoils of war, the conflict left a defeated Germany on the verge of economic, social, and political collapse and a ravaged countryside disfigured by the skulls, bones, cadavers, and other carnage and wreckage of protracted trench and aerial warfare. Using a positive and negative linear manner reminiscent of Urs Graf's sixteenth-century woodcuts, Dix, in *Leuchtkugel erhellt die Monacu-ferme* (A Rocket Flare Lights Up the Monacu-ferme, cat. no. 9q) and *Trichterfeld bei Dontrien, von Leuchtkugeln erhellt* (Field of Craters near Dontrien, Illuminated by Rocket Flares, cat. no. 9d) reveals despoiled fields through brilliant artillery flashes against a pitch-black night sky. Dix's view of bomb craters as "eyesockets of the earth"[15] is given pictorial definition in *Field of Craters near Dontrien, Illuminated by Rocket Flares.* The result of incessant bombing is an uninhabitable, rubble-strewn, pockmarked land, a vista reminiscent more of a lunar, than earthly, landscape.

Dix's topographical subjects are an ironic comment on the German landscape tradition in the visual arts originating with Albrecht Altdorfer, Albrecht Dürer, and other sixteenth-century Northern Renaissance artists. One of Altdorfer's most famous paintings, *Die Alexanderschlacht* (The Battle of Issus, 1529, Munich, Alte Pinakothek), recounts the ancient battle between the forces of Alexander the Great and the Persian king Darius in a panoramic, cosmic view of nature: diminutive armies play out their historic struggle in a low-lying countryside under a vast cloud-strewn sky. In the nineteenth century this landscape tradition was revitalized by German Romantic painters such as Caspar David Friedrich, whose views of nature were intended as a means for man's transcendence from earthly existence in his longing for the spiritual essence that vivifies visible nature. Dix's nihilistic vision of a raped and wasted land subverts the traditional benevolent world view

14. "Säure abwaschen, Aquatint drauf, kurz, wunderbare Technik, mit der man die Stufungen ganz nach Belieben arbeiten kann." Quoted in Karsch, *Das graphische Werk*, 15.

15. Cited in Dückers, "Portfolios," 82.

of northern painting. The settings in *Zerfallender Kampfgraben* (Destroyed Combat Trench, cat. no. 9i), *Verlassene Stellung bei Neuville* (Abandoned Position near Neuville, cat. no. 9k), *Verlassene Stellung bei Vis-en-Artois* (Abandoned Position near Vis-en-Artois, cat. no. 9o), and *Die Trümmer von Langemarck* (The Ruins of Langemarck, cat no. 9y) recall the background landscape in Matthias Grünewald's *Isenheim Altarpiece* (Colmar, Museum Unterlinden) but Dix turns the visionary countryside of his German predecessor into an apocalyptic graveyard. In the wasted expanses of *Granattrichter mit Blumen (Frühling 1916)* (Grenade Trench with Flowers [Spring 1916], cat. no. 9x) and *Die Trümmer von Langemarck* (The Ruins of Langemarck, cat. no. 9y) oppressively empty skies convey, according to Dix, the nothingness after life.

Dix relies on distortion and caricature to evoke the dehumanized routine of the soldier at the front. The bestial faces of troopers in many of the sheets dealing with the subhuman living conditions in the trenches (see cat. nos. 9n, 9u, 9oo, 9qq, 9rr and 9ss) reflect the degradation of the human spirit: jutting jaws, snarling mouths and bared teeth, sunken cheeks, and bulging eyes. In *Die II. Kompanie wird heute Nacht abgelöst* (The Second Company Will Be Relieved Tonight, cat. no. 9t) Dix so aggressively attacks the surface of the metal plate from which the print was pulled that the finished image matches the brutal intensity of the subject depicted: after outlining the protruding, animal-like profiles of the advancing soldiers, he filled the background with vigorous crosshatching, which was followed by dense aquatint that was subsequently scraped, finally yielding a nearly palpable expanse of mud and blackness in the printed image.

At times, Dix imitated photographic effects in his search for immediacy and a documentary-like view of war's harshness; war photos supplied to him by his friend Hugo Erfurth of Dresden were his point of reference. In etchings such as *Appell der Zurückgekehrten* (Roll Call of the Survivors, cat. no. 9ww) and *Verwundetentransport im Houthulster Wald* (Trans-

port of the Wounded in the Houthulster Wood, cat. no. 9uu), Dix conveys the suffering of a retreating army not only through grotesque facial expressions but also by dull, flat, gray tones that simulate the effects of hastily processed, over-exposed photographs. Alternatively, Dix relied on unembellished etching and drypoint lines to conjure the mood of terror and madness experienced by helpless civilians and innocent animals during military conflict (see cat. nos. 9j, 9gg, and 9ii): belly exposed, legs wildly splayed against a remorseless sky (emphasized by the stark contrast of the inked etched line of the design against uninked ground), the hapless beast in *Pferdekadaver* (Horse Cadaver, cat. no. 9e) has suffered an humiliating death. Here, jerky, jagged lines convey some of the frenzied mood of the animal's last thrashing, futile struggle for survival. Similarly, in *Die Irrsinnige von St. Marie-à-Py* (The Insane Woman of St. Marie-à-Py, cat. no. 9ii), needle-like contour lines construct a taut image of madness brought about by total despair. In this portrayal of the ravings of a woman whose child is a senseless casualty of war, the mother kneels, with one hand holding the nipple of her exposed breast in a futile attempt to nurse her dead and bloodied child. Hair disheveled, eyes wide open, and teeth bared, the mad woman cannot comprehend the destruction of her family; the sharp, scraping trace of the etching and drypoint needle on the metal plate (when inked and printed) is the outward means used by Dix to convey her hysterical psychological state of mind.

Images dealing with prostitution fostered by the extended conflict record the depravity of war carried over to the noncombatant population. As a respite from battle and death, troops on leave satiate their physical wants, or, as Dix wrote, "The soldier devours, boozes, and fornicates."[16] The prostitute in *Besuch bei Madame Germaine in Méricourt* (A Visit to Madame Germaine in Méricourt, cat. no. 9jj) is grotesquely oversized and gaudily made up; she is a creature who thrives on the climate of war. The client

---

16. "Die Soldat frißt, säuft und hurt." Quoted in Löffler, *Otto Dix und der Krieg*, 31.

in her lap gazes lustfully while wedging his arm underneath her huge breast. The relationship between the sexes is devoid of personal attachment and understood as a business transaction, in other words, sexual gratification for money.

For Dix then the war spares no one from its deforming effect. No grand gesture or noble act relieves the viewer from Dix's bitter testimony of war's dehumanizing process. Even death becomes a protracted, humiliating, and undignified experience. Systematic and indiscriminate in its extermination, warfare reduces humanity to its common denominator in the will to survive. Using the print cycle format to give form to his nightmarish remembrances of the First World War from the vantage point of a frontline soldier, he offers ultimately in the fifty prints, separately and as a group, a universal statement of the horrors of all warfare, ancient and modern. For Dix, death is war's constant companion, and he presents in many of his works a twentieth-century recasting of the traditional Dance of Death theme.[17]

17. The Dance of Death theme developed in the first half of the fourteenth century, appearing first in the form of processions and dramatic performances, then in murals in churches and cemeteries of Northern Europe, and finally in paintings, book illustrations, and independent prints, Illustrating the idea that all are equal before Death, images of the dance generally consisted of a procession or continuous chain of couples, who were led by Death, represented as a skeleton or as a decaying corpse. In the 1520s, Hans Holbein adopted the theme for two series of woodcuts as self-contained images. The theme enjoyed a revival during the Romantic era in the nineteenth century although it had never completely died out after the Middle Ages. Among well-known examples from the nineteenth century, Alfred Rethel's *Auch ein Totentanz* (Another Dance of Death) of 1849 was patterned after Holbein's series, and was intended as a critique of the suppression of the German revolutionaries of 1848. In 1894, the German graphic artist and book illustrator Joseph Sattler produced a new version of the theme, updating it for Jugendstil taste. For a brief history of the nineteenth century and a treatment of Rethel's cycle, see Peter Paret, *Art as History: Episodes in the Culture and Politics of Nineteenth-Century Germany* (Princeton, N.J.: Princeton University Press, 1988), 79–130. James Hall makes a distinction between the *Danse macabre* and the Dance of Death, identifying the latter as a popular medieval belief in which ". . . the dead rose from their tombs at midnight and performed a dance in the graveyard before setting off to claim fresh victims from among the living" (see James Hall, *Dictionary of Subjects and Symbols in Art* [London: John Murray, 1974], 94). Dix applied this alternate definition to his print *Totentanz anno 17* (Dance of Death, the Year 17, cat. no. 9s), with a macabre twist in the depiction of a circle of dead human figures caught in a tangle of barbed wire.

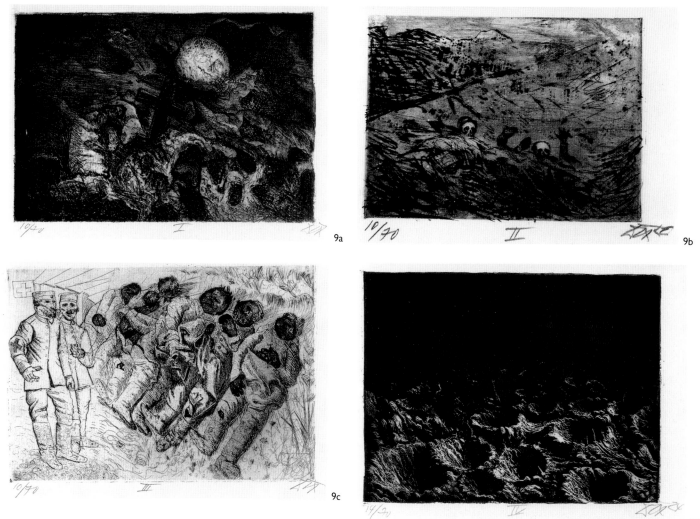

9a

9b

9c

9d

10/70   V   9e

9/70   VI   9f

10/70   VII   9g

10/4?   VIII   9h

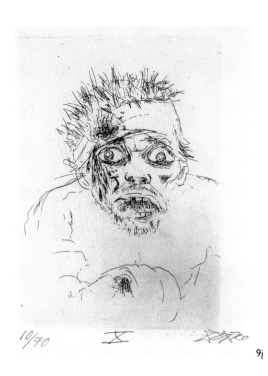

9i

9j

9k

9l

See color plate 9m

9n

9o

9p

9q

See color plate 9r

9s

9t

9u

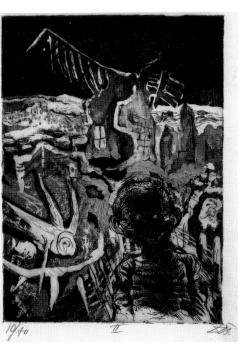

9v

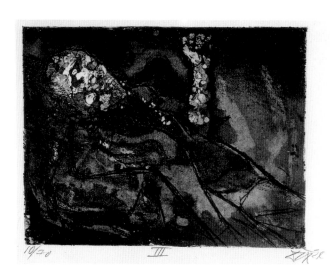

10/70   III   ZOX4   9w

10/70   IV   ZOX4   9x

10/70   V   9y

10/70   II   ZOX4

9z

9aa

9bb

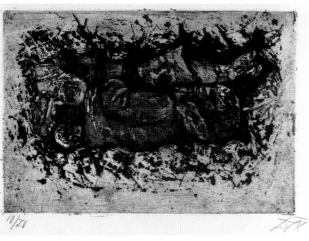

9cc

9dd

10/70   I   9ee

10/70   II   9ff

10/70

See color plate 9gg

10/70   9hh

10/70 9ii

10/70 9jj

10/70 9kk

10/70 9ll

10/70

9mm

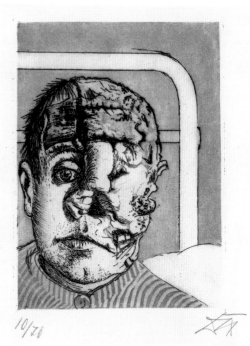

10/70

9nn

10/70

9oo

10/70   II

9pp

9qq

9rr

9ss

9tt

See color plate 9uu

9vv

9ww

9xx

Otto Dix
German, 1881–1969

Der Krieg (The War)
Fifty prints from the portfolio, ed. 10/70

Medium: etching, drypoint, aquatint

Ink: black

Paper: B.S.B. Commercial Bütten and nine prints on wove paper

Publisher and Publication Date: Karl Nierendof, 1924

Printer: Otto Felsing, Berlin

Reference: Karsch 70–119

The David and Alfred Smart Museum of Art, Marcia and Granvil Specks Collection
Acc. nos. 1984.46–1984.71 and 1986.253–1986.276

9a
Soldatengrab zwischen den Linien (Soldier's Grave between the Lines)
Etching and aquatint
Sheet: 14³/₁₆ × 18⁵/₁₆ (36 × 48.1)
Plate: 7⁵/₈ × 11¼ (19.3 × 28.6)
Signed, l.r. of plate: *Dix*
Numbered, l.l. and l.c. of plate: *10/70* and *I*
Karsh 70
1984.46

9b
Verschüttete (Januar 1916, Champagne) (Buried Alive [January 1916, Champagne])
Etching
Sheet: 14¼ × 18⁷/₈ (36.3 × 47.9)
Plate: 5½ × 7⁵/₈ (14 × 19.3)
Signed and dated, l.r. of plate: *Dix 24*
Numbered, l.l. and l.c. of plate: *10/70* and *II*
Watermark: *BSB* encircled
Karsh 71
1984.47

9c
Gastote (Templeux-La-Fosse, August 1916) (Death by Gas [Templeux-La-Fosse, August 1916])
Etching
Sheet: 14¹/₈ × 18¹³/₁₆ (35.9 × 47.8)
Plate: 7½ × 11³/₁₆ (19.1 × 28.4)
Signed, l.r. of plate: *Dix*
Numbered, l.l. and l.c. of plate: *10/70* and *III*
Watermark: *BSB* encircled
Karsh 72
1986.253

9d
Trichterfeld bei Dontrien, von Leuchtkugeln erhellt (Field of Craters near Dontrien, Illuminated by Rocket Flares)
Aquatint
Sheet: 14¹/₈ × 18⁷/₈ (36 × 48)
Plate: 7½ × 10 (19 × 25.8)
Signed and dated, l.r. of plate: *Dix 24*
Numbered, l.r. and l.c. of plate: *14/70* and *IV*
Karsh 73
1984.48

9e
Pferdekadaver (Horse Cadaver)
Etching
Sheet: 14¹/₈ × 18⁷/₈ (35.9 × 48)
Plate: 5⁹/₁₆ × 7⁵/₈ (14.1 × 19.4)
Signed and dated, l.r. of plate: *Dix 24*
Numbered, l.l. and l.c. of plate: *10/70* and *V*
Karsh 74
1984.49

9f
Verwundeter (Herbst 1916, Baupaume) (Wounded Man [Spring 1916, Baupaume])
Etching and aquatint
Sheet: 14 × 19 (35.6 × 48.3)
Plate: 7½ × 11 (19.1 × 27.9)
Signed and dated, l.r. of plate: *Dix 24*
Numbered, l.l. and l.c. of plate: *6/70* and *VI*
Karsh 75
1986.254

9g
Bei Langemarck (Februar 1918) (Near Langemarck [February 1918])
Etching
Sheet: 14¼ × 18¹⁵/₁₆ (36.3 × 48.2)
Plate: 9⁹/₁₆ × 11¹¹/₁₆ (24.2 × 29.4)
Signed and dated, l.r. of plate: *Dix 24*
Numbered, l.l. and l.c. of plate: *10/70* and *VII*
Karsh 76
1984.50

9h
Relaisposten (Herbstschlacht in der Champagne) (Relay Station [Autumn Battle in Champagne])
Etching and aquatint
Sheet: 14¹/₈ × 18⁷/₈ (35.9 × 47.9)
Plate: 5⁵/₈ × 7⁵/₈ (14.3 × 19.4)
Signed and dated, l.r. of plate: *Dix 24*
Numbered, l.l. and l.c. of plate: *10/70* and *VIII*
Watermark: *BSB* encircled
Karsh 77
1984.51

9i
Zerfallender Kampfgraben (Destroyed Combat Trench)
Etching and aquatint
Sheet: 18³/₄ × 14¹/₈ (47.6 × 36.2)
Plate: 11½ × 9³/₈ (29.2 × 23.8)
Signed and dated, l.r. of plate: *Dix 24*
Numbered, l.l. and l.c. of plate: *10/70* and *IX*
Karsh 78
1986.255

9j
Fliehender Verwundeter (Sommeschlacht 1916) (Wounded Man Fleeing [Battle of the Somme 1916])
Etching and drypoint
Sheet: 18¹³/₁₆ × 14¹/₈ (47.8 × 35.9)
Plate: 7½ × 5⁵/₁₆ (19.1 × 13.5)
Signed and dated, l.r. of plate: *Dix 24*
Numbered, l.l. and l.c. of plate: *10/70* and *X*
Karsh 79
1986.256

9k
Verlassene Stellung bei Neuville (Abandoned
    Position near Neuville)
Etching
Sheet: 19 × 14¹/₁₆ (48.3 × 35.9)
Plate: 7⁵/₈ × 5⁵/₈ (19.3 × 14.3)
Signed and dated, l.r. of plate: *Dix 24*
Numbered, l.l. and l.c. of plate: *10/70 and I*
Karsch 80
1984.52

9l
Stormtruppe geht unter Gas vor (Storm Troops
    Advance under a Gas Attack)
Etching, aquatint, and drypoint
Sheet: 14 × 18³/₄ (35.6 × 47.6)
Plate: 7¹/₂ × 11¹/₄ (19.1 × 28.6)
Signed, l.r. of plate: *Dix*
Numbered, l.l. of plate: *10/70*
Karsch 81
1986.257

9m
Mahlzeit in der Sappe (Lorettohöhe) (Mealtime in the
    Trenches [Loretto Heights])
Etching, aquatint, and drypoint
Sheet: 14³/₁₆ × 19 (36 × 48.2)
Plate: 7⁹/₁₆ × 11³/₁₆ (19.2 × 28.4)
Signed and dated, l.r. of plate: *Dix 24*
Numbered, l.l. and l.c. of plate: *10/70 and III*
Watermark: *BSB* encircled
Karsch 82
1986.258

9n
Ruhende Kompanie (Resting Company)
Etching and aquatint
Sheet: 18¹³/₁₆ × 14¹/₈ (47.8 × 35.8)
Plate: 10 × 7⁹/₁₆ (25.4 × 19.2)
Signed, l.r. of plate: *Dix*
Numbered, l.l. of plate: *10/70*
Karsch 83
1984.53

9o
Verlassene Stellung bei Vis-en-Artois (Abandoned
    Position near Vis-en-Artois)
Etching and aquatint
Sheet: 13¹⁵/₁₆ × 19 (35.4 × 48.2)
Plate: 7⁹/₁₆ × 10¹/₁₆ (19.2 × 25.5)
Signed, l.r. of plate: *Dix*
Numbered, l.l. of plate: *10/70*
Watermark: *BSB* encircled
Karsch 84
1984.54

9p
Leiche im Drahtverhau (Flandern) (Corpse in a Wire
    Entanglement [Flanders])
Etching and aquatint
Sheet: 19 × 14 (48.3 × 35.6)
Plate: 11¹/₂ × 9¹/₂ (29.2 × 24.1)
Signed and dated, l.r. of plate: *Dix 24*
Numbered, l.l. and l.c. of plate: *10/70 and VI*
Karsch 85
1986.259

9q
Leuchtkugel erhellt die Monacu-ferme (A Rocket
    Flare Lights Up the Monacu-ferme)
Aquatint
Sheet: 14¹/₈ × 18⁷/₈ (35.9 × 47.9)
Plate: 5¹¹/₁₆ × 7⁵/₈ (14.4 × 19.4)
Signed and dated, l.r. of plate: *Dix 24*
Numbered, l.l. and l.c. of plate: *10/70 and VII*
Watermark: *BSB* encircled
Karsch 86
1984.55

9r
Toter Sappenposten (A Dead Trench Sentry)
Etching and drypoint
Sheet: 18¹⁵/₁₆ × 14¹/₈ (48.1 × 35.9)
Plate: 7⁹/₁₆ × 5⁹/₁₆ (19.2 × 14.1)
Signed and dated, l.r. of plate: *Dix 24*
Numbered, l.l. and l.c. of plate: *10/70 and VIII*
Karsch 87
1986.260

9s
Totentanz anno 17 (Höhe Toter Mann) (Dance of
    Death, the Year 17 [Dead Man's Hill])
Etching, aquatint, and drypoint
Sheet: 19 × 14 (48.3 × 35.6)
Plate: 9¹/₂ × 11¹/₂ (24.1 × 29.2)
Signed, l.r. of plate: *Dix*
Numbered, l.l. and l.c. of plate: *10/70 and IX*
Karsch 88
1986.261

9t
Die II. Kompanie wird heute Nacht abgelöst (The
    Second Company Will Be Relieved Tonight)
Etching and aquatint
Sheet: 14¹/₄ × 18⁷/₈ (35.9 × 48)
Plate: 7⁵/₈ × 10 (19.3 × 25.4)
Signed and dated, l.r. of plate: *Dix 24*
Numbered, l.l. and l.c. of plate: *10/70 and X*
Karsch 89
1984.56

9u
Abgekämpfte Truppe geht zurück (Sommeschlacht)
    (Exhausted Troops Fall Back [Battle of the
    Somme])
Etching on wove paper
Sheet: 14¹/₄ × 18⁷/₈ (35.9 × 48)
Plate: 7¹/₂ × 11³/₁₆ (19 × 28.4)
Signed, l.r. of plate: *Dix*
Numbered, l.l. and l.c. of plate: *10/70 and I*
Karsch 90
1984.57

9v
Nächtliche Begegnung mit einen Irrsinnigen (A
    Nocturnal Encounter with an Insane Man)
Etching, aquatint, and drypoint
Sheet: 19 × 14 (48.3 × 35.6)
Plate: 10 × 7¹/₂ (25.4 × 19.1)
Signed, l.r. of plate: *Dix*
Numbered, l.l. and l.c. of plate: *10/70 and II*
Karsch 91
1986.262

9w
Toter im Schlamm (Dead Man in Mud)
Etching and aquatint
Sheet: 14³/₁₆ × 18¹⁵/₁₆ (36 × 48.1)
Plate: 7¹/₂ × 10 (19.1 × 25.4)
Signed, l.r. of plate: *Dix 24*
Numbered, l.l. and l.c. of plate: *10/70 and III*
Karsch 92
1986.263

9x
Granattrichter mit Blumen (Frühling 1916) (Grenade
    Trench with Flowers [Spring 1916])
Etching
Sheet: 14¹/₁₆ × 18¹⁵/₁₆ (35.7 × 48.1)
Plate: 5⁹/₁₆ × 7⁹/₁₆ (14.2 × 19.2)
Signed and dated, l.r. of plate: *Dix 24*
Numbered, l.l. and l.c. of plate: *10/70 and IV*
Karsch 93
1984.58

9y
Die Trümmer von Langemarck (The Ruins of
    Langemarck)
Etching and aquatint
Sheet: 18³/₄ × 14 (47.6 × 35.6)
Plate: 11¹/₄ × 9¹/₂ (28.6 × 24.1)
Signed, l.r. of plate: *Dix*
Numbered, l.l. and l.c. of plate: *10/70 and V*
Karsch 94
1986.264

9z

Sterbender Soldat (Dying Soldier)
Etching, aquatint, and drypoint
Sheet: 19 × 14 (48.3 × 35.6)
Plate: 7¹/₂ × 5⁵/₈ (19.1 × 14.3)
Signed and dated, l.r. of plate: *Dix 24*
Numbered, l.l. and l.c. of plate: *10/70* and *VI*
Karsch 95
1986.265

9aa

Abends in der Wijtschäte-Ebene (Evenings on the
    Wijtschäte Plain)
Etching and aquatint
Sheet: 14 × 19 (35.6 × 48.3)
Plate: 9¹/₂ × 11¹/₂ (24.1 × 29.2)
Signed and dated, l.r. of plate: *Dix 24*
Numbered, l.l. and l.c. of plate: *10/70* and *VII*
Karsch 96
1986.266

9bb

Gesehen am Steilhang von Cléry-sur-Somme (The
    View from the Precipice of Cléry-sur-Somme)
Etching, aquatint, and drypoint
Sheet: 18⁷/₈ × 14¹/₈ (47.9 × 35.9)
Plate: 10 × 7⁹/₁₆ (25.4 × 19.2)
Signed and dated, l.r. of plate: *Dix 24*
Numbered, l.l. and l.c. of plate: *10/70* and *VIII*
Watermark: *BSB* encircled
Karsch 97
1986.267

9cc

Gefunden beim Grabendurschstich (Auberive)
    (Discovered During Trench Break-Through
    [Auberive])
Etching and aquatint
Sheet: 14¹/₈ × 18¹⁵/₁₆ (35.9 × 48.1)
Plate: 7⁹/₁₆ × 11¹/₈ (19.2 × 28.3)
Signed, l.r. of plate: *Dix*
Numbered, l.l. of plate: *10/70*
Watermark: *BSB* encircled
Karsch 98
1984.59

9dd

Drahtverhau vor dem Kampfgraben (Wire
    Entanglement before the Trench)
Etching
Sheet: 18¹⁵/₁₆ × 14¹/₄ (48.1 × 36.2)
Plate: 10 × 7⁹/₁₆ (25.4 × 19.2)
Signed, l.r. of plate: *Dix*
Numbered, l.l. of plate: *10/70*
Watermark: *BSB* encircled
Karsch 99
1984.60

9ee

Schädel (Skull)
Etching on wove paper
Sheet: 18⁵/₈ × 13¹³/₁₆ (47.3 × 35.1)
Plate: 9⁷/₈ × 7⁷/₁₆ (25.1 × 18.9)
Signed, l.r. of plate: *Dix*
Numbered, l.l. and l.c. of plate: *10/70* and *I*
Karsch 100
1984.61

9ff

Matrosen in Antwerpen (Sailors in Antwerp)
Etching and aquatint on wove paper
Sheet: 13⁷/₈ × 18⁵/₈ (35.2 × 47.3)
Plate: 9¹/₂ × 11³/₈ (24.1 × 28.9)
Signed, l.r. of plate: *Dix*
Numbered, l.l. and l.c. of plate: *10/70* and *II*
Karsch 101
1984.62

9gg

Lens wird mit Bomben belegt (Lens Is Destroyed by
    Bombing
Etching and drypoint on wove paper
Sheet: 18³/₄ × 14¹/₈ (47.6 × 35.9)
Plate: 11¹/₂ × 9³/₈ (29.2 × 23.8)
Signed, l.r. of plate: *Dix*
Numbered, l.l. and l.c. of plate: *10/70*
Karsch 102
1986.268

9hh

Frontsoldat in Brüssel (Frontline Fighter in Brussels)
Etching and drypoint
Sheet: 19 × 14 (48.3 × 35.6)
Plate: 11 × 7³/₄ (28.8 × 19.8)
Signed, l.r. of plate: *Dix*
Numbered, l.l. of plate: *10/70*
Karsch 103
1986.269

9ii

Die Irrsinnige von St. Marie-à-Py (The Insane
    Woman of St. Marie-à-Py)
Etching and drypoint
Sheet: 18³/₄ × 14 (47.6 × 35.6)
Plate: 11¹/₁₆ × 7¹/₂ (28.1 × 19.1)
Signed, l.r. of plate: *Dix*
Numbered, l.l. and l.c. of plate: *10/70* and *V*
Watermark: *BSB* encircled
Karsch 104
1986.270

9jj

Besuch bei Madam Germaine in Méricourt (A Visit to
    Madame Germaine in Méricourt)
Etching, aquatint, and drypoint
Sheet: 19 × 14 (48.3 × 35.6)
Plate: 10 × 7¹/₂ (25.4 × 19.1)
Signed l.r. of plate: *Dix*
Numbered, l.l. and l.c. of plate: *10/70* and *VI*
Karsch 105
1986.271

9kk

Kantine in Haplincourt (Canteen in Haplincourt)
Etching on wove paper
Sheet: 14³/₁₆ × 18⁷/₈ (36 × 47.9)
Plate: 7¹/₂ × 10 (19 × 25.4)
Signed, l.r. of plate: *Dix*
Numbered, l.l. and l.c. of plate: *10/70* and *VII*
Karsch 106
1984.63

9ll

Zerschossene (Shot to Pieces)
Etching and aquatint on wove paper
Sheet: 14³/₁₆ × 18⁷/₈ (35.7 × 47.9)
Plate: 5⁵/₈ × 7⁵/₈ (14.3 × 19.4)
Signed, l.r. of plate: *Dix*
Numbered, l.l. and l.c. of plate: *10/70* and *VIII*
Karsch 107
1984.64

9mm

Durch Fliegerbomben zerstörtes Haus (House
    Destroyed by Aerial Bombs)
Etching and aquatint
Sheet: 18⁷/₈ × 14¹/₈ (47.9 × 35.7)
Plate: 11¹/₂ × 9⁹/₁₆ (29.2 × 24.3)
Signed, l.r. of plate: *Dix*
Numbered, l.l. of plate: *10/70*
Watermark: *BSB* encircled
Karsch 108
1984.65

9nn

Transplantation (Transplant)
Etching and aquatint
Sheet: 18³/₄ × 14 (47.8 × 35.8)
Plate: 7⁵/₈ × 5⁵/₈ (19.4 × 14.2)
Signed, l.r. of plate: *Dix*

Numbered, l.l. of plate: *10/70*
Karsch 109
1984.66

9oo

*Maschinengewehrzug geht vor (Somme, November
    1916)* (Machine-Gun Troop Advance [Somme,
    November 1916])
Etching and aquatint on wove paper
Sheet: 14¹/₈ × 18⁷/₈ (35.9 × 47.9)
Plate: 9⁷/₁₆ × 11³/₈ (24 × 28.9)
Signed, l.r. of plate: *Dix*
Numbered, l.l. of plate: *10/70*
Karsch 110
1984.67

9pp
Toter (St. Clément) (Dead Man, St. Clément)
Etching, aquatint, and drypoint
Sheet: 18⁷/₈ × 14¹/₁₆ (47.9 × 35.7)
Plate: 11⁹/₁₆ × 10 (29.3 × 25.4)
Signed, l.r. of plate: *Dix*
Numbered, l.l. and l.c. of plate: *10/70* and *II*
Watermark: *BSB* encircled
Karsch 111
1986.272

9qq
Essenholer bei Pilkem (Food Reconnoiterer near
   Pilkem)
Etching and aquatint
Sheet: 14 × 18¹/₄ (35.6 × 46.3)
Plate: 9¹/₂ × 11¹/₄ (24.1 × 28.6)
Signed, l.r. of plate: *Dix*
Numbered, l.l. of plate: *10/70*
Karsch 112
1986.273

9rr
Überfall einer Schleichpatrouille (Surprise Attack of
   a Reconnoitering Patrol)
Etching and aquatint on wove paper
Sheet: 18⁷/₈ × 14³/₁₆ (47.9 × 36)
Plate: 7⁵/₈ × 5⁵/₈ (19.4 × 14.3)
Signed, l.r. of plate: *Dix*
Numbered, l.l. of plate: *10/70*
Karsch 113
1984.68

9ss
Unterstand (Fox Hole)
Etching, aquatint, and drypoint
Sheet: 14¹/₁₆ × 18¹⁵/₁₆ (35.7 × 48.1)
Plate: 7⁹/₁₆ × 11¹/₈ (19.2 × 28.3)
Signed, l.r. of plate: *Dix*
Numbered, l.l. of plate: *10/70*
Watermark: *BSB* encircled
Karsch 114
1986.274

9tt
Die Schlafenden von Fort Vaux (Gas-Tote) (The
   Sleepers of Fort Vaux [Death by Gas])
Etching and aquatint
Sheet: 14¹/₁₆ × 18¹³/₁₆ (35.7 × 47.7)
Plate: 9⁹/₁₆ × 11¹/₂ (24.3 × 29.2)
Signed, l.r. of plate: *Dix*
Numbered, l.l. of plate: *10/70*
Karsch 115
1984.69

9uu
Verwundetentransport im Houthulster Wald
   (Transport of the Wounded in the Houthulster
   Wood)
Etching and aquatint
Sheet: 14¹/₁₆ × 18¹³/₁₆ (35.7 × 47.8)
Plate: 7⁹/₁₆ × 9¹⁵/₁₆ (19.2 × 25.1)
Signed, l.r. of plate: *Dix*
Numbered, l.l. of plate: *10/70*
Watermark: *BSB* encircled
Karsh 116
1984.70

9vv
*Die Sappenposten haben nachts das Feuer zu
   unterhalten* (The Trench Sentries Must Maintain
   the Fire during the Night)
Etching, aquatint, and drypoint
Sheet: 14 × 18³/₄ (35.6 × 47.6)
Plate: 9¹/₂ × 11¹/₂ (24.1 × 29.2)
Signed, l.r. of plate: *Dix*
Numbered, l.l. of plate: *10/70*
Karsch 117
1986.275

9ww
Appell der Zurückgekehrten (Roll Call of the
   Survivors)
Etching and aquatint on wove paper
Sheet: 14¹/₈ × 18¹³/₁₆ (35.9 × 47.8)
Plate: 7¹/₂ × 11¹/₈ (19.1 × 28.3)
Signed, l.r. of plate: *Dix*
Numbered, l.l. of plate: *10/70*
Karsch 118
1984.71

9xx
Tote vor der Stellung bei Tahure (Corpses Before the
   Position near Tahure)
Etching, aquatint, and drypoint
Sheet: 14 × 18⁷/₈ (35.6 × 47.9)
Plate: 7¹/₂ × 10 (19.1 × 25.4)
Signed, l.r. of plate: *Dix*
Numbered, l.l. of plate: *10/70*
Karsch 119
1986.276

Schiller, An die Freude
Schiller, Ode to Joy

1927

With the exception of four woodcuts made in 1910, Ernst Barlach did not regularly work in this print medium until 1918.[1] His return to the woodcut coincided with the relief print's contemporaneous widespread recognition by art dealers, art historians, and critics as a uniquely, historically German art form. As early as 1903 Max Osborn traced in his article "Die Wiedergeburt des Holzschnittes" (The Rebirth of the Woodcut) the modern German woodblock print back to its medieval origins, in which he called the woodcut a "pure and noble folk art."[2] Two years later, he explicitly stressed its specific German character in the introduction to his book *Der Holzschnitt* (The Woodcut):

> There is no art practice that is so closely tied [fused] with the innermost ways of our people as the woodcut; the German soul is mirrored by none other so truly as it. With the powerful simplicity, the rough naïveté, and the often angular awkwardness that its technique brings with it and with its equally frugal and eloquent writing, it has furnished the most vivid testimony of Germany's incomparable national culture that she has since lost and not yet regained . . . For us the word "woodcut-like" has become a designation for artistic expression of a precise type, from which we feel it is rooted with all of its fibers deep in the ground of our fatherland. The peculiar mixture of roughness and tenderness, of energy and dreaminess, which for the German essence is characteristic, has nowhere found clearer expression than in the production of the

woodcut, so long that it has remained on its natural course.[3]

But it was not until the end of the First World War and the rise in Germany of widespread disillusionment brought on by military defeat that publications emphasizing the specific national association of the woodcut appeared in increasing numbers. The Munich art dealer Hans Goltz, for example, mounted a large woodcut exhibition, *Der expressionistische Holzschnitt* (The Expressionist Woodcut) in 1918, and in the introduction to the exhibition catalogue he noted the cultural affinities between the Expres-

1. "Vier Holzschnittproben zum Michael Kohlhaas," in Friedrich Schult, ed., *Werkverzeichnis Ernst Barlach: Das graphische Werk*, vol. II (Hamburg: Dr. Ernst Hauswedell & Co., 1957), 23–24.

2. Max Osborn, "Die Wiedergeburt des Holzschnitts," *Zeitschrift für Bücherfreund: Monatshefte für Bibliophile und verwandte Interessen* 7 (1903/1904): 366.

3. "Keine Kunstübung ist von Hause aus so eng mit dem innersten Wesen unseres Volkes verwachsen wie der Holzschnitt, keine hat so treu wie er die deutsche Seele abgespiegelt. Mit der kraftvollen Schlichtheit, der derben Naivität und der oft eckigen Schwerfälligkeit, die seine Technik mit sich bringt, hat er in der zugleich sparsamen und vielsagenden Schrift seiner Linien von den Zeiten, da Deutschland eine unvergleichliche, später verloren gegangene und noch nicht wieder errungene nationale Kultur besaß, den eindringlichsten Bericht geliefert . . . das Wort 'holzschnittartig' eine Bezeichnung für künstlerische Äusserungen bestimmter Art geworden, von denen wir fühlen, daß sie mit allen Fasern tief im Boden unseres Vaterlandes wurzeln. Die seltsame Mischung von Derbheit und Innigkeit, von Energie und Verträumtheit, die für deutsches Wesen charakteristisch ist, hat nirgends klareren Ausdruck gefunden als in den Erzeugnissen der Holzschneidekunst, solange diese auf dem Wege blieb, der ihr natürlich war." Cited in Max Osborn, *Der Holzschnitt* (Bielefeld: Velhagen & Klasing, 1905), I.

10a

10b

sionist woodcut and its medieval prototype.[4] Reinhard Piper—collector, publisher, and friend of the Expressionist artist Max Beckmann—reprinted Wilhelm Worringer's *Die altdeutsche Buchillustration* (Old German Book Illustration), originally published in 1912. Similarly, the 1914 book by Max Bucherer and Fritz Ehlotzky entitled *Der original Holzschnitt* (The Original Woodcut) appeared in a second, expanded edition in 1922. Max Friedlaender's *Der Holzschnitt* (The Woodcut) was published in 1917; Paul Westheim followed a series of articles on the woodcut in his periodical *Das Kunstblatt* with the publication of *Das Holzschnittbuch* (The Woodcut Book) in 1921. Kurt Pfister's *Die primitiven Holzschnitte* (Primitive Woodcuts) appeared in 1922. All these stressed the woodcut's directness, simplicity, strong planar emphases, and linearity, as well as its capacity to visualize the German national identity.[5]

The reasons contributing to the emerging importance of the woodcut in German art at this time are not hard to find. The First World War had cut German artists off from the international art currents that had been so vital in shaping a modern aesthetic.[6] Artists such as Wassily Kandinsky, Franz Marc, and Ludwig Meidner had couched their prewar premonitions of an apocalypse (giving rise to a new age and new man)

in Nietzschean terms that did not admit to a higher religious order.[7] However, as the war dragged on, these artists increasingly lost faith in man's ability to effect change. With the end of the war, they returned to the notion of a new spiritual order rising now from the cataclysmic destruction. Increasingly, however, they relied on Christian symbolism and biblical

4. Hans Goltz, *46. Ausstellung der expressionistische Holzschnitt* (exh. cat.) (Munich: Hans Goltz, 1918). Also noted in Ida K. Rigby, "The Revival of Printmaking in Germany," in *German Expressionist Prints and Drawings: The Robert Gore Rifkind Center for German Expressionist Studies* (Los Angeles and Munich: Los Angeles County Museum of Art and Prestel Verlag, 1989), 57.

5. For the woodcut's significance in forming German national identity, see Robin Reisenfeld, "The Revival of the Woodcut in Germany, 1890–1920," (forthcoming Ph.D. dissertation, Chicago, Department of Art, The University of Chicago).

6. Otto Dix, for example, depended upon a Futurist-derived formal vocabulary in his early paintings of war such as *Der Krieg (Das Geschütz)* (The War [The Cannon], 1914, Düsseldorf, Kunstmuseum) and *Selbstbildnis als Mars* (Self-Portrait as Mars, 1915, Freital, Haus der Heimat). Later Dix developed a style derived from early Northern Renaissance painting in his examination of the dehumanization of war (see the essay for cat. no. 9).

7. Ludwig's Meidner's prewar series of apocalyptic landscapes, Wassily Kandinsky's *Hinterglasmalerei* (behind-glass painting) *The Apocalyptic Horsemen* (1911), and Franz Marc's *The Fate of the Beasts* are a few of the examples that invoke Friedrich Nietzsche's concept of a new order shaped by the new man; see Carol S. Eliel, *The Apocalyptic Landscapes of Ludwig Meidner* (Los Angeles and Munich: Los Angeles County Museum of Art and Prestel Verlag, 1989).

10c

10d

metaphor to convey this notion of rebirth.[8] For Karl Schmidt-Rottluff, who served in the German army, his daily proximity to death heightened the artist's spiritual awareness.[9]

Isolated from—and indeed the enemy of—their former European colleagues, German artists began to emphasize an indigenous vernacular formal vocabulary with its attendant ideological associations as one way of connecting themselves to their cultural past. They linked the woodcut to the spirituality and extreme piety of the late Gothic and Renaissance periods, when this print medium had witnessed its first fluorescence in the German-speaking states of Northern Europe. Expressionist artists such as Max Pechstein and Schmidt-Rottluff used Christain imagery of a traditional nature. The print *Christus* (Christ) from Schmidt-Rottluff's 1918–19 portfolio *Neun Holzschnitte* (Nine Woodcuts), for example, borrows from Early Christian as well as tribal African stylistic sources and uses quasi-historic references,[10] but the date 1918 branded on Christ's forehead and the caption beneath, "Christ did not appear to you", addresses a German audience.[11] Similarly, Max Pechstein's 1921 graphic cycle *Das Vater Unser* (The Lord's Prayer, Krüger 256–268) emphasizes Germanic culture in its use of the German-language translation by

Martin Luther instead of the universal Latin (and Roman Catholic) text. In addition, Pechstein looked to nineteenth-century religious iconography of peasants in the manner of German Realist artists including Wilhelm Leibl, Hans Thoma, and Fritz von Uhde for his visualization of the prayer.[12]

It is within this context that Ernst Barlach's *Schil-*

8. Rigby, "The Revival of Printmaking in Germany," 46–48.

9. Ibid., 46.

10. Karl Schmidt-Rottluff's *Nine Woodcuts* is loosely based on the story of Christ. For more about Schmidt-Rottluff's religious woodcuts, see Marilyn J. Derwinkus and Robin Reisenfeld's entries for *The Three Kings, Christ Cursing the Fig Tree,* and *Christ and the Woman Taken in Adultery* in Reinhold Heller et al., *Brücke: German Expressionist Prints from the Granvil and Marcia Specks Collection* (exh. cat.) (Evanston, Ill.: Mary & Leigh Block Gallery, Northwestern University, 1988), 294–95, 298–99, 300–301, respectively.

11. The German art historian William R. Valentiner described the image as ". . . a frightful vision on which is distinctly marked the stifling terror of the German people, who dragged themselves through four war years . . . The forehead, however, is branded with the number 1918 as a reminder to humanity, which in these times has gone astray, as an eternal sign that, as the caption reads, in this year, 'Christ did not appear to you.' The tragedy of a people on whom it suddenly dawns that it gave its best for iron instead of for the spirit trembles convulsively through these sheets." Quoted in Rigby, "The Revival of Printmaking in Germany," 45.

12. Discussed by Reinhold Heller in the entry for *The Lord's Prayer* in Heller, *Brücke: German Expressionist Prints,* 226–28.

10e

10f

ler, An die Freude (Schiller, Ode to Joy) should be placed. One can trace in Barlach's work a shift from overt, patriotic references during the early years of the war—as exemplified by his sculpture *Der Rächer* (The Avenger, 1914) and the lithographs *Der heilige Krieg* (The Holy War, Schult 65), *Erst Sieg, dann Frieden* (First Victory, then Freedom, Schult 66), and *Die Betlehem Steel-Company* (The Bethlehem Steel Company, Schult 70) for Paul Cassirer's journal *Die Kriegszeit*—to a more meditative mood in the drawings of 1916 for *Der Bildermann*.[13] Barlach became disillusioned with the war and the aggressiveness in his work disappeared; it was replaced by an identification with a decidedly German spiritual heritage. Writing to his cousin in 1919, Barlach related the woodcut specifically to his despair brought about by the war: "As the misfortune befell in November (1918), I threw myself into the woodcut . . . It is a technique that provokes one to confession, to the unmistakable statement of what one finally means. It, or far more she, enforces a certain general validity of expression . . . I have finished a number of large woodcuts that deal with all the distress of the times."[14]

At the same time he perceived the woodcut as a link to his visual German patrimony. In *Schiller, Ode to Joy* Barlach's previous flat, caricature-like Jugendstil manner gives way to more volumetric

forms reminiscent of German Gothic wood sculptures. The mythical landscape scene with its horsemen and single sailboat in *Die Jakobsleiter* (Jacob's Ladder, cat. no. 10e) from *Schiller, Ode to Joy* makes iconographical reference to the sixteenth-century woodcut tradition of Albrecht Dürer and Hans Holbein. With its biblical allusions and incorporation of German medieval and Renaissance motifs, Barlach's series reads as a modern, secular version of the *Flugblatt*, a pictorial religious pamphlet that was first introduced in fifteenth-century Germany with the invention of the woodcut. By revitalizing the artistic heritage of the fifteenth and sixteenth centuries, Barlach seeks to invoke the spirituality and piety of that age.

A prolific author of plays, poems, and novels as well as a renowned sculptor and graphic artist, Barlach turned to literary sources as inspiration for his graphic works throughout his career. Whatever the chosen medium, all of Barlach's works address the duality of emotions—joy and suffering, love and hate—and humanity's vulnerable place within the cosmic

13. Ernst Barlach's shifting attitude is touched upon by Peter Guenter, "An Introduction to the Expressionist Movement," in *German Expressionist Prints and Drawings*, 9–11.

14. Barlach, quoted in Rigby, "The Revival of German Printmaking in Germany," 46.

10g

10h

order. In his selection of the subject of Friedrich von Schiller's poem *Ode to Joy* Barlach deploys the woodcut to connect his visual patrimony with a German literary and musical heritage. He recognized in Schiller's hymn, conceived in celebration of the indomitable human spirit, an expression of his own world view. Describing his contemplation of a series devoted to the poem, Barlach wrote in 1924: "While I was in the woods today the idea took hold of me to make illustrations to the Hymn, *Ode to Joy* (woodcuts possibly). Joy as content, purpose, and meaning of the world, an idea which has long occupied me beyond time and space."[15] The final series consists of nine woodcuts; eight illustrate individual stanzas, and one, the final chorus. Comprising a visual rhythm, that builds to a crescendo with *Jacob's Ladder* (cat. no. 10e) and ends with a coda in the *Der Sternenrichter* (The Guide of the Stars, cat. no. 10i), Barlach utilized the sequential order of the print portfolio to create a pictorial counterpart to Ludwig von Beethoven's use of Schiller's ode in his *Ninth Symphony*.

While paying tribute to Germany's great literary and musical tradition, Barlach also reinvents the hymn's meaning through visual representation. Barlach expands on Schiller's poem to encompass a higher spiritual order. Schiller's work supposedly stems from an incident that occurred while the writer

was in Leipzig.[16] After preventing a destitute theology student from drowning himself in a river, Schiller gave him the money he had and elicited the student's promise to give up the idea of suicide. A few days later while at a marriage party, Schiller recounted the story to the guests. A subscription was made which enabled the student to complete his studies and enter an official work position. Elated with his success, Schiller commemorated humanity in his poem. In Barlach's version, the artist retains Schiller's theme of salvation but gives it universal implications. In his assertion that joy derives from God, Barlach reinterprets Schiller's pantheistic celebration of the universal order in religious terms.

Printed with Schiller's text in two signed editions of ten (?) and forty impressions (and a large, unsigned *Volksedition* printed from zinc plates),[17] the woodcut

15. Barlach, letter dated 24 September 1924, cited in Schult, *Werkverzeichnis Ernst Barlach*, 161.

16. Recounted by Sir Edward B. Lytton, ed., *The Poems and Ballads of Schiller* (New York: Harper & Bros., 1851), 332.

17. The set of woodcuts in the permanent collection of the Smart Museum is not from either signed edition. Each unsigned impression is blind-stamped "Ernst Barlach Nachlass," which indicates that this example was assembled from sheets in the artist's estate as one of the recorded *Nachlaß* impressions; see *Ernst Barlach: Das druckgraphische Werk: Dore und Kurt Reutti-Stiftung* (exh. cat.) (Bremen: Kunsthalle, 1968), 69.

10i

cycle *Schiller, Ode to Joy* was published and distributed by Paul Cassirer, one of the first Berlin dealers
to support French Impressionism and Post-Impres-
sionism and an early leader in the promotion of the
print as a fine art. Barlach's dealer, who also published the work of other Expressionists, considered
this portfolio an innovative means by which to make
the artist's graphics more widely known. Barlach's
cycle progresses from a timeless order to an historical
moment and then ascends again to the eternal realm
of the Divine. The first woodcut, *Freude, Schöner Götterfunken* (Joy, Fairest Spark Divine, cat. no. 10a),
refers to the opening line of Schiller's hymn. Barlach
depicts a robed man standing against a barren landscape. A hill, a rocky coastline, and a calm sea recede
into the far ground. Highlighted against an empty
sky, the figure's outstretched arms hold a goblet. As a
liturgical utensil, the cup establishes a mystical link
between man and God. As in the other woodcuts
in the series, Barlach rejects here decorative detail
for simple, straightforward representation, and by
describing only the essence of the form he seeks to
convey human inner feelings and desires on a universal level.

In the next two images Barlach presents the saints
and angels who act as God's messengers and bring joy
to mankind. The title *Seid umschlungen, Millionen*
(Be Embraced, All You Millions, cat. no. 10b) alludes
to the hymn's first chorus. Barlach depicts a saint
emerging from flames, who stands in an orant pose
between two fluted columns. His outstretched arms
signify piety, as he welcomes humanity into God's
holy temple. Barlach makes explicit the saint's integral place in God's sanctuary by portraying the folds
of his robe in the same manner as the fluted columns

that flank him. The massive columns and granite
floor, in turn, convey the strength and durability of
God's kingdom.

In *Engelreigen* (The Dance of Angels, cat. no. 10c)
the viewer looks up into a semi-circle of female
angels and towards the source of streaming light.
The central angel's gown opens to reveal calves and
feet. Resembling a bell and clapper, this configuration makes an allusion both to Beethoven's composition and the musical references contained within Schiller's text. By conflating the third and
seventh choruses, Barlach unites the emotion of joy
with musical sounds: "Look upward—search the
starry sky: Beyond the stars must He reside! . . .
Praised by the ever-whirling ring of stars, and the
seraphims' hymn . . ."[18] Barlach illustrates the lines
from the third stanza in *Der Cherub* (The Cherub, cat.
no. 10d): "Joy drinks from Nature's holy bosom; And
vice and worth alike follow Her blossomed foot-
prints, Joy in each link, to us . . . Sensual pleasure is
given to the worm, And the cherub stands before
God!"[19] A cherub looks heavenward towards the
streaming light while below and behind are three
humans: a couple engaged in love-making and the
third in prayer. Cherub and humans are divided by
four beams of light; as Schiller's emphatic "us"
implies, joy comes in varying amounts to those most

18. "Suchen ihn überm Sternenzelt! Über Sternen muß er wohnen . . . Den der
Sterne Wirbel loben, Den des Seraphs Hymne prießt." Friedrich Schiller, "An die
Freude," in *Schillers Gedichte und Dramen* (Stuttgart: Verlag des Schwäbischen
Schillervereins, 1905), 15–16.

19. "Freude trinken alle Wesen, An den Brüsten der Natur; Alles Guten, alle
Bösen Folgen ihrer Rosenspur . . . Wollust ward dem Wurm gegeben, Und der
Cherub steht vor Gott!" Schiller, ibid., 16.

deserving, the celestial servants of God, therefore, receiving the fullest share of light.[20]

Jacob's Ladder (cat. no. 10e) connects heavenly and earthly realms to form a pictorial whole. Among the nine illustrations, *Jacob's Ladder* is singular in that, departing from Schiller's text, it depicts a biblical parable. Its uniqueness and central position in the portfolio underscore its importance within the series. Conflating aspects of Schiller's ode with his own interpretation, Barlach emphasizes the primordial nature and universality of joy. Sharing the poet's sentiment that joy "propels the mainspring of eternal nature",[21] Barlach attaches his own religious explication to this pantheistic notion: by portraying Jacob's dream of a ladder descending from heaven (Gen. 28:12), the artist implies that joy originates from God.

The next woodcut in the portfolio, *Das Liebespaar* (The Lovers, cat. no. 10f), focuses solely on the earthly realm. As each print unfolds in the sequential reading of the cycle, Barlach sets up a chain of images that leads the viewer from a universal condition towards a specific manifestation of joy. Thus, while the artist makes explicit in *Jacob's Ladder* the joy that emanates from God, here he intimates that the human capacity for love itself derives from joy. The composition revolves around a tenderly embracing couple set in front of a banner of joy waving atop a distant mountain. Flanking the couple is a benevolent angel and two travelers. In the left foreground coffins of the dead open in a revelatory burst of joy.

Barlach depicts an avenging angel who wields an axe in the seventh woodcut, *Unser Schuldbuch sei Vernichtet* (Let All Old Scores Be Wiped Out, cat. no. 10g), an illustration of Schiller's seventh chorus: "Let our account book be eradicated! Reconcile the entire world! Brother-God judges us from above, as we judge ourselves."[22] In this composition Barlach interprets the verse by means of a fiendish creature busily recording a man's sins in God's account book while the angel prepares to slay the human. The angel is loosely derived from Barlach's lithograph *The Holy War* (Schult 65) that appeared in Paul Cassirer's jour-

nal *Die Kriegszeit* on 16 December 1914. Behind, another man on a staircase reaches out to save a woman, and from above, God descends to embrace a kneeling figure. In this image Barlach has recast the specific events of the Christian Last Judgement into a nonsectarian vision of damnation and salvation.

In the penultimate image, *Dieses Glas dem guten Geist* (This Glass, to the Good Spirit, cat. no. 10h), a man on a mountain top raises his goblet to heaven. Once again the viewer is transported to a celestial realm, and this visual ascent culminates like a thunderous chord in the final scene, where he (or she) comes face to face with the power and glory of God in *The Guide of the Stars* (cat. no. 10i). Circumscribed by an aura that illuminates the cosmos, the immobile and frontal deity is centrally placed in the heavens, a compositional scheme that echoes scenes of the eternal God in majesty (*majestas domini*) encountered in Early Christian apse mosaics and ivory carvings. Recognizing its ability to evoke extremes of emotion through black and white planar contrasts and a rugged quality of line, Barlach chose the woodcut for this cycle to convey the ecstasy and majesty of joy as distilled in this potent summation of the visual hymn presented in *Schiller, Ode to Joy*. Describing the medium's eminent suitability for the depiction of mythical themes, he stated: "The woodcut demands a complete avowal, an unambiguous explanation of what one really means. It dictates a certain universal expression and rejects the unimportant details or easy solution."[23]

20. The "us" is emphatic. Schiller discriminates between the measure of bliss assigned to "us", the "worm", and to the "cherub". See Lytton, *The Poems and Ballads of Schiller*, 332.

21. "Freude heißt die starke Feder In der ewigen Natur." Schiller, in *Schillers Gedichte und Dramen*, 16.

22. "Unser Schuldbuch sei vernichtet! Ausgesöhnt die ganze Welt! Brüder überm Sternenzelt Richtet Gott, wie wir gerichtet." Ibid.

23. Barlach, letter dated 1918, cited in Erhard Göpel, ed., *Deutsche Holzschnitte des XX. Jahrhunderts* (Weisbaden: Insel-Verlag, 1955), 44–45.

Ernst Barlach
German, 1870–1938

Schiller, An die Freude (Schiller, Ode to Joy)
Series of nine prints, an estate set from the 1927 portfolio assembled from the regular edition

Medium: woodcut

Ink: black

Paper: Galvanos

Publisher and Publication Date: Paul Cassirer, 1927

Reference: Schult 271–279
The David and Alfred Smart Museum of Art, Gift of Perry Goldberg
Acc. nos. 1983.123–1983.124 and 1983.161–1983.167

10a
Freude, schöner Götterfunken (Joy, Fairest Spark Divine)
Sheet: 14⁵/₁₆ × 18⁹/₁₆ (36.4 × 47.2)
Image: 9⁷/₈ × 14¹/₈ (25.1 × 35.9)
Embossed in blind stamp, l.l. of image: *ERNST BARLACH NACHLASS*
Schult 271
1983.123

10b
Seid umschlungen, Millionen (Be Embraced, All You Millions)
Sheet: 13³/₄ × 18¹/₈ (34.9 × 46)
Image: 10¹/₈ × 14¹/₄ (25.7 × 36.2)
Embossed in blind stamp, l.l. of image: *ERNST BARLACH NACHLASS*
Schult 272
1983.161

10c
Engelreigen (The Dance of Angels)
Sheet: 13³/₈ × 17³/₄ (34 × 45.1)
Image: 10¹/₄ × 14¹/₄ (26 × 36.2)
Embossed in blind stamp, l.l. of image: *ERNST BARLACH NACHLASS*
Schult 273
1983.162

10d
Der Cherub (The Cherub)
Sheet: 14³/₄ × 18⁷/₈ (37.5 × 48)
Image: 10¹/₄ × 14¹/₈ (26 × 35.9)
Embossed in blind stamp, l.l. of image: *ERNST BARLACH NACHLASS*
Schult 274
1983.163

10e
Die Jakobsleiter (Jacob's Ladder)
Sheet: 14⁵/₈ × 18⁵/₁₆ (37.2 × 46.5)
Image: 10⁵/₁₆ × 14¹/₈ (26.2 × 35.9)
Embossed in blind stamp, l.l. of image: *ERNST BARLACH NACHLASS*
Schult 275
1983.164

10f
Das Liebespaar (The Lovers)
Sheet: 13 × 17⁵/₁₆ (33 × 44)
Image: 10¹/₄ × 14³/₁₆ (26 × 36.1)
Embossed in blind stamp, l.l. of image: *ERNST BARLACH NACHLASS*
Schult 276
1983.165

10g
Unser Schuldbuch sei vernichtet (Let All Old Scores Be Wiped Out)
Sheet: 13¹/₄ × 17¹/₂ (33.7 × 44.5)
Image: 10³/₈ × 14¹/₄ (26.4 × 36.2)
Embossed in blind stamp, l.l. of image: *ERNST BARLACH NACHLASS*
Schult 277
1983.166

10h
Dieses Glas dem guten Geist (This Glass, to the Good Spirit)
Sheet: 15 × 18³/₈ (38.1 × 46.7)
Image: 10¹/₄ × 14³/₁₆ (26 × 36)
Embossed in blind stamp, l.l. of image: *ERNST BARLACH NACHLASS*
Schult 278
1983.167

10i
Der Sternenrichter (The Guide of the Stars)
Sheet: 12⁷/₈ × 16³/₄ (32.7 × 42.5)
Image: 10⁵/₁₆ × 14³/₁₆ (26.2 × 36)
Embossed in blind stamp, l.l. of image: *ERNST BARLACH NACHLASS*
Schult 279
1983.124

Select bibliography

Books

Allen, Ann Taylor. *Satire and Society in Wilhelmine Germany* Kladderadatsch & Simplicissimus *1890–1914*. Lexington: The University of Kentucky, 1984.

Appelbaum, Stanley, ed. *Simplicissimus: 180 Satirical Drawings from the Famous German Weekly*. New York: Dover Publications, Inc., 1975.

Bauer, Jens-Heiner. *Daniel Nikolaus Chodowiecki: Das druckgraphische Werk*. Hannover: Verlag Galerie J.H. Bauer, 1982.

Beckmann, Max. *Tagebücher, 1940–50*. Munich: A. Langon-G. Müller, 1955.

Belting, Hans. *Max Beckmann: Die Tradition als Problem in der Kunst der Moderne*. Berlin: Deutscher Kunstverlag, 1984.

——. *Bild und Kult: Eine Geschichte des Bild für dem Zeitalter der Kunst*. Munich: C.H. Beck, 1990.

Bernhard, Marianne, ed. *Hans Baldung Grien: Handzeichnungen Druckgraphik*. Munich: Südwest Verlag, 1978.

Blackbourn, David, and Richard J. Evans, eds. *The German Bourgeoisie: Essays on the Social History of the German Middle Class from the Late Eighteenth to the Early Twentieth Century*. London: Routledge, 1991.

Bohn's Standard Library. *Schiller's Early Dramas and Romances*. London: George Bell and Sons, 1907.

Broude, Norma, and Mary D. Garrard, eds. *Feminism and Art History: Questioning the Litany*. New York: Harper & Row, 1982.

Carey, Frances, and Antony Griffiths. *The Print in Germany 1880–1933: The Age of Expressionism*. New York: Harper & Row, 1984.

Conzelmann, Otto. *Der andere Dix: Sein Bild vom Menschen und vom Krieg*. Stuttgart: Klett-Cotta, 1983.

Corinth, Lovis. *Gesammelte Schriften*. Berlin: Fritz Gurlitt Verlag, 1920.

——. *Selbstbiographie*. Leipzig: Verlag S. Hirzel, 1926.

Corinth, Thomas. *Martin Luther*. Springfield, Ohio: Chantry Music Press at Wittenberg University, 1968.

Craig, Gordon C. *Germany: 1866–1945*. New York: Oxford University Press, 1978.

Dalphin, Marcia, Bertha M. Miller, and Ruth H. Viguers, comps. *Illustrators of Children's Books*. Boston: The Horn Book Inc., 1958.

Donath, Adolph. *Psychologie des Kunstsammelns*. 3rd ed. Berlin: Richard Carl Schmidt & Co., 1920.

Dube, Annemarie, and Wolf-Dieter Dube. *E.L. Kirchner: Das graphische Werk*. 2 vols. Munich: Prestel Verlag, 1967.

——. *Erich Heckel: Das graphische Werk*. 3 vols. New York: Ernest Rathenau and Berlin: Euphorion Verlag, 1964–74.

Dückers, Alexander. *Max Klinger*. Berlin: Rembrandt Verlag, 1976.

——. *George Grosz: Das druckgraphische Werk*. Frankfurt: Propyläen Verlag, 1979.

Eisenstein, Elizabeth. *The Printing Press as an Agent of Change*. 2 vols. Cambridge: Cambridge University Press, 1979.

——. *The Printing Revolution in Early Modern Europe*. Cambridge: Cambridge University Press, 1983.

Eliel, Carol S. *The Apocalyptic Landscapes of Ludwig Meidner*. Los Angeles and Munich: Los Angeles County Museum of Art and Prestel Verlag, 1989.

Evans, Richard J., see David Blackbourn.

Fechter, Paul. *Das graphische Werk Max Pechsteins*. Berlin: F. Gurlitt, 1920.

Fischer, Friedrich Wilhelm. *Max Beckmann: Symbol und Weltbild*. Munich: Wilhelm Fink Verlag, 1972.

Folmsbee, Beulah, Louise P. Latimer, and Bertha M. Miller, comps. *Illustrators of Children's Books, 1744–1945*. Boston: The Horn Book Inc., 1947.

Gallwitz, Klaus, ed. *Max Beckmann: Die Druckgraphik*. Karlsruhe: Badischer Kunstverein Karlsruhe, 1962.

Garrard, Mary D., see Norma Broude.

German Expressionist Prints and Drawings: The Robert Gore Rifkind Center for German Expressionist Studies. Los Angeles and Munich: Los Angeles County Museum of Art and Prestel Verlag, 1989.

Glaser, Curt. *Die Graphik der Neuzeit vom Anfang des XIX. Jahrhunderts bis zur Gegenwart*. Berlin: Bruno Cassirer, 1923.

Goethe, Johann Wolfgang von. *Faust*. Hundertjahrsausgabe im Askanischen Verlag. Berlin: Albert Kindle, 1938.

Göpel, Erhard, ed. *Deutsche Holzschnitte des XX. Jahrhunderts*. Wiesbaden: Insel-Verlag, 1955.

Griffiths, Antony, see Frances Carey.

Grosz, George. *George Grosz: An Autobiography*. Translated by Nora Hodges. New York: Macmillan Publishing Co., 1983.

Habermas, Jürgen. *The Structural Transformation of the Public Sphere: An Inquiry into a Category of Bourgeois Society*. Translated by Thomas Burger. Cambridge, Mass.: MIT Press, 1989.

Hall, James. *Dictionary of Subjects and Symbols in Art*. London: John Murray, 1974.

Haycraft, Howard, and Stanley Kunitz, eds. *The Junior Book of Authors*. New York: H.W. Wilson Company, 1951.

Heller, Reinhold. *Edvard Munch: The Scream*. Art in Context. New York: Viking Press, Inc., 1973.

Hind, Arthur M. *An Introduction to the History of Woodcut, with a Detailed Survey of Work Done in the Fifteenth Century*. New York: Houghton Mifflin, 1935; New York: Dover, 1963.

Hofmaier, James. *Max Beckmann: Catalogue Raisonné of His Prints*. 2 vols. Bern: Gallery Kornfeld, 1990.

Holborn, Hajo. *A History of Modern Germany: 1840–1945*. Princeton, N.J.: Princeton University Press, 1969.

Karsch, Florian, ed. *Otto Dix: Das graphische Werk*. Hannover: Fackelträger-Verlag Schmidt-Küster, 1970.

Klipstein, August. *Käthe Kollwitz: Verzeichnis das graphischen Werkes*. Bern: Klipstein & Cie., 1955.

Kleinbauer, W. Eugene, ed. *The Art of Byzantium and the Medieval West: Selected Studies by Ernst Kitzinger*. Bloomington: Indiana University Press, 1976.

Klinger, Max. *Malerei und Zeichnung: Tagebuchaufzeichnungen und Briefe*. Edited by Anneliese Hübscher. Leipzig: Verlag Philipp Reclam, 1985.

Kracauer, Siegfried. *From Caligari to Hitler: A Psychological History of the German Film*. Princeton, N.J.: Princeton University Press, 1947.

Kunitz, Stanley, see Howard Haycraft.

Latimer, Louise P., see Beulah Folmsbee.

Lewis, Beth Irwin. *George Grosz: Art and Politics in the Weimar Republic*. Rev. ed. Princeton, N.J.: Princeton University Press, 1991.

Lichtenberg, Georg Christoph. *Handlkungen des Lebens: Erklärungen zu 72 Monatskupfern von Daniel Chodowiecki*. Stuttgart: Deutsche Verlags-Anstalt, 1971.

Lloyd, Jill. *German Expressionism: Primitivism and Modernity*. New Haven, Conn.: Yale University Press, 1991.

Löffler, Fritz. *Otto Dix und der Krieg*. Leipzig: Philipp Reclam, 1986.

Lytton, Sir Edward B., ed. *The Poems and Ballads of Schiller*. New York: Harper & Bros., 1851.

McGreevy, Linda F. *The Life and Works of Otto Dix: German Critical Realist*. Ann Arbor: UMI Research Press, 1981.

Michael, Erika. *The Drawings of Hans Holbein the Younger for Erasmus' [sic] "Praise of Folly"*. New York: Garland Books, 1986.

Miesel, Victor H., ed. *Voices of German Expressionism*. Englewood Cliffs, N.J.: Prentice-Hall, 1970.

Miller, Bertha M., see Marcia Dalphin and Beulah Folmsbee.

Moeller, Magdalena M., ed. *Die Jahresmappen der "Brücke" — 1906–1912*. Berlin: Brücke-Archiv Heft 17, 1989.

Mosel, Christel, see Gustav Schiefler.

Müller, Heinrich. *Die späte Graphik von Lovis Corinth*. Hamburg: Lichtwarkstiftung, 1960.

Nagel, Otto. *Käthe Kollwitz*. Greenwich, Conn.: New York Graphic Society Ltd., 1963.

Neuerburg, Waltraut. "Der graphische Zyklus im Deutschen Expressionismus und seine Typen, 1905–1925." Ph.D. diss., Bonn, Rheinischen Friederich-Wilhelms-Universität, 1976.

Osborn, Max. *Der Holzschnitt*. Bielefeld: Velhagen & Klasing, 1905.

———. ed. *Berlins Aufstieg zur Weltstadt*. Berlin: Reimar Hobbing, 1929.

Pachter, Henry M. *Modern Germany: A Social, Cultural and Political History*. Boulder, Col.: Westview Press, 1978.

Paret, Peter. *The Berlin Secession: Modernism and its Enemies in Imperial Germany*. Cambridge, Mass.: Harvard University Press, 1980.

———. *Art as History: Episodes in the Culture and Politics of Nineteenth-Century Germany*. Princeton: Princeton University Press, 1988.

Reidemeister, Leopold. *Künstlergruppe Brücke: Fragment eines Stammbuches mit Beiträgen von Ernst Ludwig Kirchner, Fritz Bleyl und Erich Heckel*. Berlin: Mann, 1975.

Riegl, Hermann. *Peter Cornelius: Festschrift zu des großen Künstlers hundertstem Geburtstag*. Berlin: R.v. Decker, 1883.

Reisenfeld, Robin. "The Revival of the Woodcut in Germany, 1890–1920." Forthcoming Ph.D. dissertation, Chicago, Department of Art, The University of Chicago.

Rogoff, Irit, ed. *The Divided Heritage: Themes and Problems in German Modernism*. Cambridge: Cambridge University Press, 1991.

Runge, Philipp Otto. *Hinterlassene Schriften*. 2 vols. Hamburg: Fredrich Perthes, 1841; Gottingen: Vandenhoeck & Ruprecht, 1965.

Schiefler, Gustav. *Meine Graphik-Sammlung*. Edited by Gerhard Schack. Hamburg: Gesellschaft der Bücherfreunde, 1927; Hamburg: Christian Verlag, 1974.

———, and Christel Mosel. *Emil Nolde. Das graphische Werk. Neu bearbeitete und ergänzte Ausgabe*. 2 vols. Cologne: M. DuMont Schauberg, 1966–67.

Schiller, Friedrich. *Schillers Gedichte und Dramen*. Stuttgart: Verlag des Schwäbischen Schillervereins, 1905.

Schneede, Uwe M. *George Grosz: The Artist in His Society*. Translated by Robert and Rita Kimber. Woodbury, N.Y.: Barron's Educational Series, 1985.

Schult, Friedrich, ed. *Werkverzeichnis Ernst Barlach: Das graphische Werk*. Hamburg: Dr. Ernst Hauswedell & Co., 1972.

Schvey, Henry I. *Oskar Kokoschka: The Painter as Playwright*. Detroit: Wayne State University Press, 1982.

Schwarz, Karl. *Das graphische Werk von Lovis Corinth*. Berlin: Fritz Gurlitt Verlag, 1922.

Shapire, Rosa. *Karl Schmidt-Rottluff graphisches Werk bis 1923*. Berlin: Euphorion Verlag, 1924.

Singer, Hans W. *Klingers Radierungen: Stiche und Steindrucke*. New York: Martin Gordon, Inc., 1978.

Spielmann, Heinz, ed. *Oskar Kokoschka: Dichtungen und Dramen*. Hamburg: Hans Christians Verlag, 1973.

Strauss, Walter L., ed. *Albrecht Dürer Woodcuts and Woodblocks*. New York: Abraris Books, 1980.

Streichner, Elizabeth, see J. Kirk Varnedoe.

Stuffmann, Margret, see Klaus Gallwitz.

Teeuwisse, Nicolaas. *Vom Salon zur Secession*. Berlin: Deutsche Verlag für Kunstwissenschaft, 1986.

Traeger, Jörg. *Philipp Otto Runge und sein Werk: Monographie und kritischer Katalog*. Munich: Prestel Verlag, 1975.

Uhr, Horst. *Lovis Corinth*. Berkeley: University of California Press, 1990.

Varnedoe, J. Kirk, and Elizabeth Streichner. *Graphic Works of Max Klinger*. New York: Dover Publications, Inc., 1977.

Viguers, Ruth H., see Marcia Dalphin.

Waldmann, Emil. *Sammler und ihresgleichen.* Berlin: Bruno Cassirer Verlag, 1920.

Wegner, Wolfgang. *Die Faustdarstellung vom 16. Jahrhundert bis zur Gegenwart.* Amsterdam: Verlag der Erasmus Buchhandlung, 1962.

Weiss, Judith C., see Carla Schulz-Hoffmann.

Weiss, Peg. *Kandinsky in Munich: The Formative Jugendstil Years.* Princeton, N.J.: Princeton University Press, 1979.

Wingler, H.M., and F. Welz. *Oskar Kokoschka: Das druckgraphische Werk.* Salzburg: Galerie Welz, 1975.

Exhibition catalogues

Arts Council of Great Britain. *Kokoschka Lithographs.* London: Arts Council of Great Britain, 1966.

Barron, Stephanie, ed. *Degenerate Art: The Fate of the Avant-Garde in Nazi Germany.* Los Angeles and Munich: Los Angeles County Museum of Art and Prestel Verlag, 1991.

Diehl, Gustav Eugen, ed. *Austellung Otto Dix: Katalog mit Verzeichnis der gesamten Graphik bis 1925.* Berlin: Kunstarchiv Verlag, 1926.

Gallwitz, Klaus, and Margret Stuffmann. *Bürgerlisches Leben im 18. Jahrhundert: Daniel Chodowiecki 1726–1801 Zeichnungen und Druckgraphik.* Frankfurt a.M.: Städtelsches Kunstinstitut und Städtische Galerie, 1978.

Goltz, Hans, *46. Ausstellung der expressionistische Holzschnitt.* Munich: Hans Goltz, 1918.

Hagenlocher, Alfred, ed. *Otto Dix: Bestandskatalog.* Albstadt: Städtischen Galerie Albstadt, 1985.

Heller, Reinhold, et al. *The Earthly Chimera and the Femme Fatale: Fear of Women in Nineteenth-Century Art.* Chicago: The David and Alfred Smart Gallery, The University of Chicago, 1981.

———. *Art in Germany 1909–1936: From Expressionism to Resistance: The Marvin and Janet Fishman Collection.* Munich: Prestel Verlag in association with the Milwaukee Art Museum, 1990.

———. *Brücke: German Expressionist Prints from the Granvil and Marcia Specks Collection.* Evanston, Ill.: Mary & Leigh Block Gallery, Northwestern University, 1988.

Kunsthalle. *Ernst Barlach: Das druckgraphische Werk: Dore und Kurt Reutti-Stiftung.* Bremen: Kunsthalle, 1968.

Kunsthalle Bielefeld. *Max Klinger.* Bielefeld: Kunsthalle Bielefeld, 1976.

Martin-Gropius-Bau. *Der unverbrauchte Blick.* Berlin: Martin-Gropius-Bau, 1987.

Rigby, Ida K. *An alle Künstler: War—Revolution—Weimar.* San Diego: San Diego State University Press, 1983.

Schulz-Hoffmann, Carla, and Judith C. Weiss, eds. *Max Beckmann: Retrospektive.* Munich: Prestel Verlag, 1984.

Stuffmann, Margret, see Klaus Gallwitz.

Vienna Secession. *XIV. Ausstellung der Vereinigung Bilden der Künstler Österreichs Secession Wien, 1902 April–Juni.* Vienna: Ver Sacrum, [1902].

Wallraf-Richartz-Museum. *Maler suchen Freunde: Jahresmappen, Plakate und andere werbende Graphik der Künstlergruppe Brücke.* Cologne: Wallraf-Richartz-Museum, 1971.

Weiss, Judith C., see Carla Schulz-Hoffmann.

Articles

Glaser, Curt. "Vom Graphik-Sammeln." *Das Kunstblatt* 3, no. 11 (1919).

Heller, Reinhold. *"Die Brücke* at Cornell." *Art Forum* 8 (May 1970).

Haitt, Charles. "Joseph Sattler." *The International Studio* 4 (1894).

Kitzinger, Ernst. "World Map and Fortune's Wheel: A Medieval Mosaic Floor in Turin." *Proceedings of the American Philosophical Society* 117, no. 5 (1973).

Knorr, Theodor. "Josef Sattler: Sein Leben und seine Kunst." *Elsaß-Lothringisches Jahrbuch* 11 (1932).

Kuhn, Alfred. "Corinth als Graphiker." *Kunst und Künstler* 22 (1924).

Lenman, Robin. "A Community in Transition: Painters in Munich, 1886–1924." *Central European History* 15 (March 1982).

———. "Painters, Patronage and the Art Market in Germany 1850–1914." *Past and Present: A Journal of Historical Studies,* no. 123 (May 1989).

Ley, Walter. "Graphische Neuerscheinungen." *Das Kunstblatt* 3, no. 11 (1919).

Makela, Maria. "A Late Self-Portrait." *The Art Institute of Chicago Museum Studies* 16 (1990).

Osborn, Max. "Die Wiedergeburt des Holzschnitts." *Zeitschrift für Bücherfreund: Monatshefte für Bibliophile und verwandte Interessen* 7 (1903/1904).

Shapiro, Maurice L. "Klee's *Twittering Machine,*" *Art Bulletin* 50 (March 1968).

Stutzer, Beat. "Das Stammbuch 'Odi Profanum' der Künstlergruppe 'Brücke'." *Zeitschrift des Deutschen Vereins für Kunstwissenschaft* 36 (1982).

Wentzel, Hans. "Zu den frühen Werken der 'Brücke'-Künstler." *Brücke-Archiv* 1 (1967).

Index